Just Results:
Ethical Foundations for Policy Analysis

Just Results:
Ethical Foundations for Policy Analysis

Ralph D. Ellis

GEORGETOWN UNIVERSITY PRESS / WASHINGTON, D.C.

H
97
.E56
1998

Georgetown University Press, Washington, D.C.
© 1998 by Georgetown University Press. All rights reserved.
Printed in the United States of America

10 9 8 7 6 5 4 3 2 1   1998

Library of Congress Cataloging-in-Publication Data

Ellis, Ralph D.
    Just results—ethical foundations for policy analysis / Ralph D.
Ellis.
        p. cm.
    Includes bibliographical references and index.
    1. Policy sciences—Moral and ethical aspects. 2. Political
ethics. I. Title.
H97.E56 1998
170—dc21
ISBN 0-87840-666-2 (cloth)
ISBN 0-87840-667-0 (paper)   97-37199

Contents

Acknowledgments

Friends and colleagues who contributed to this work by means of their helpful and patient criticisms are too numerous to thank them all. Special thanks, however, are due to John Samples, John Martin Gillroy, Gene Gendlin, Jim Sauer, and Tracie Ravita for challenging discussions. I would also like to thank the editors of *Policy Sciences* and *Philosophical Papers* for permission to reprint some materials from articles published there.

Introduction

One of the most distressing problems facing policy analysts and planners is the apparent incommensurability between the quantitative methods used to calculate beneficial outcomes on the one hand, and on the other hand, the reasoning of opponents who charge that the resulting policies are "unfair." For example, quantitative methods lead the State of California to conclude that the spraying of malathion to protect citrus crops is beneficial on the whole or in net terms, even though it may entail a relatively small risk of negative health effects. But opponents of the spraying argue not on quantitative but qualitative grounds that it is "unfair" to "trade off" a few cancer deaths for the sake of a slight (or even fairly substantial) increase in economic well-being for the state as a whole ("Californians Will Pay for Not Spraying" 1989; "Controversy over Malathion Continues" 1989).

To use a quite different illustration of the same problem, quantitative methods may suggest that the destruction of a poverty-stricken ghetto to make room for a badly needed downtown expressway system (for example, Buttermilk Bottom in Atlanta) is beneficial on the whole or in net terms, whereas the destruction of even a small strip of very well-to-do suburban properties to make room for a similarly needed expressway (for example, the proposed "Jimmy Carter Expressway" in Atlanta, which was to go through the neighborhood of Emory University) is *not* beneficial in net terms. But here again, opponents see this issue not in quantitative, but in qualitative terms—as an instance of requiring the poor to endure additional burdens whereas the well-to-do are spared the responsibility of an exactly analogous burden ("Proposed Jimmy Carter Expressway" 1987).

A similar incommensurability between the language of justice and the language of resource-optimization occurred when conservative U.S. congressional leaders recently supported an increase in investment tax credits for well-to-do citizens in an attempt to stimulate investment, thereby improving the economy as a whole, and in turn, benefiting the population in net terms (given their economic assumptions). Many Democratic congressmen opposed this proposal not on quantitative or empirical grounds, but on the grounds of "fairness."

Although philosophical discussions of this conflict between justice and the maximization of beneficial consequences are numerous and easy to find (for example, Bradie and Braybrooke 1982; Pojman and Westmoreland 1997; Gillroy and Wade 1992; Ellis 1992; Rawls 1971; Hearn 1971; Kaye 1980; and others to be cited later), these studies usually remain on such a purely abstract and qualitative plane that— even on those rare occasions when they produce fairly convincing results—no way is made apparent by which these abstract considerations can be translated into the precise, concrete, nuts-and-bolts terms needed for real-life applications. We are always left in the dark as to how the importance of specific instances of justice or injustice can be measured relative to the importance of specific instances of aggregate utility. No one proposes or defends a quantitative formula by which the comparative value of justice and utility could be made commensurable with each other in the concretely applicable terms needed by policy analysts and planners. Thus Rawls's *Theory of Justice* (1971), for example, argues for a concept of "justice as fairness" that seems somewhat convincing in the abstract, yet its concrete political implications are interpreted in diametrically opposite ways. James Sterba (1980; 1986) derives ultraconservative, laissez-faire, almost libertarian policy implications from Rawls's theory, whereas David Schweickart (1978) and Kai Nielson (1997) interpret the same theory as implying very socialistic, redistributive policies. Both Schweickart and Nielson go so far as to suggest that Rawls should have been a "socialist," given the basic premises of his arguments.

The purpose of this book, therefore, is very simple, but also very formidable. We shall attempt to develop a *concretely applicable* way of reasoning about the conflict between considerations of justice (which traditionally have been framed in qualitative terms) and considerations of aggregate utility (which have been framed in quantitative terms). In essence, we must develop *quantitative* methods of measuring justice, so that it can become commensurable with utility in a coherent and rationally defensible decision principle. Such a method is needed to empower policy analysts and planners not only with a way to defend the justice of their decisions, but in fact to *make* those decisions more just.

Policy analysts are increasingly inclined to believe that cost–benefit analysis, at least as developed so far, does not provide a method to incorporate a philosophically defensible concept of justice into aggregate decision contexts. According to Holtmann, "Apparently, theoretical welfare economics and the Pareto principles are not helpful in allowing policy analysts to determine the ideal distribution of well-being in society" (Holtmann 1991, 47). Gillroy states this problem still more strongly:

Welfare economics has no vocabulary for the problem that is basic to ethical and political discourse: conflicts of interest. . . . In many cases, the policy decision involves distribution of goods where inherent conflicts of interest exist involving the nonexistence of a baseline of equality for fair transactions. In such cases, some new principle must be found on which the pre-exchange situation can be rearranged through positive redistribution of endowments, freedom, and risk. . . . (Gillroy 1992b, 492–93)

Some approaches to policy analysis, especially in recent decades, might give the initial impression of a completely empirical and mathematical discipline whose purpose is to determine the most efficient means toward certain social goals which somehow already have been settled upon before the policy analyst comes on the scene. As MacIntyre characterizes such approaches:

The presupposed agreement on ends allows all disagreement within the organization to take place on questions of means. . . . If these arguments are to be settlable, then there must also be preestablished methods both for isolating all the relevant elements in each situation and for estimating the costs and benefits of proceeding by this route rather than that. . . . The norms of rationality, which on a Weberian or a neo-Weberian view of bureaucracies must govern public discourse within bureaucracies and between bureaucracies and their masters, clients, customers, or other external agents, are such that the cost–benefit analysis provides the essential normative form of argument. (MacIntyre 1992, 180)

Such a science supposedly would proceed as if philosophical problems either were not relevant at all, or else could be quickly disposed of through public opinion polls. All too little attention is paid to the effect of a "tyranny of the majority" arising from such majoritarian opinion polling; or to the problems produced by the extent of technological ignorance among the public; or to the possibility that the public may prefer to entrust some value-priority decisions to public officials to whom technical knowledge is more readily available; or to the fact that financial interests may have the power to sway the public's emotions at a politically crucial moment through expensive and sophisticated advertising; or to the fact that these same financial interests may unduly influence the election of legislators. Purely "empirical" approaches, by trying to avoid the philosophical problem of setting value priorities, also tend to ignore or minimize the problem of the legitimacy of consent, whether in an actual or hypothetical social contract. For example, did American teenagers of 1967 really "tacitly consent" to fight in Vietnam by virtue of being United States citizens? Do citizens of California "tacitly consent" to malathion exposure if a cost–benefit analysis establishes that overwhelming economic benefits and minimal risks result from the spraying?

Extremely quantitative approaches also often ignore the interrelations between the inherent uncertainties in scientific research and the differing standards of proof required for governments to take action under different interpretations of the social contract—and thus the ways in which science may lend itself to ideologically driven and value-driven interpretations which then pass themselves off to the public as "objective facts." The utterly contradictory findings on the relationship between Agent Orange and cancer among Vietnam veterans is a well-known example. This and other examples will be discussed in a later context.

Perhaps a still more frequent shortcoming in empirically based approaches to policy analysis is that they pay too little attention to the importance of philosophical value theory in guiding public officials toward the right choices in difficult cases in which opposing values conflict. Many government workers and elected officials initially choose the path of public service out of a sincere desire to do something socially beneficial with their lives, and are not mere cynical calculators of the best way to get reelected or to get a promotion; such public-spirited officials thus spend a good bit of their time trying to decide which alternative course of action *really is* the most beneficial, the fairest, and the most conducive to a good society. The same point could be made with regard to policy makers for religious and charitable organizations, and even for private business corporations—which, after all, do at least need to *appear* beneficent and public-spirited. Thomas

Nagel suggests that "[e]thics, and the ethical basis of political theory, have to be understood as arising from a division in each individual between two standpoints, the personal and the impersonal. It is because a human being does not occupy only his own point of view that each of us is susceptible to the claims of others through private and public morality" (Nagel 1991, 250–51).

It is true, of course, that the public is often confused in its philosophical thinking. Sometimes government workers have little alternative in such cases but to let popular opinion have its day. Other times, they must argue their case, helping people to see the issue in a more clear way, pointing out the fallacies in the opposing view. "Public discourse," much touted in recent European philosophy, does have its place in the shaping of public opinion. At still other times, the public servant, like Earl Warren in his desegregation decisions, must simply stand firm for what seems right, hoping that popular thinking will change when a calmer attitude prevails (as it did in the instance of desegregation, for example). In any of these possible scenarios, nothing is to be gained by ignoring the importance of value-priority systems in grounding public policy. A central argument of this book, in fact, is that without such value assumptions, no public policy would be possible—and that the less clearly these value issues are thought out, the more incoherent, nonbeneficial, or even destructive the resulting policies will be.

The purpose of this book is therefore to inform and stimulate the philosophical thinking of policy analysts, while at the same time urging a more practically applicable political philosophy—one that is relevant to the concern of addressing the concrete problems that real-life social and political policies must address. The goal, then, is to make utility, justice, and procedural legitimacy commensurable with each other in a coherent and practically accessible way. Chapters 1 through 4 will lay the basic philosophical groundwork needed to accomplish this task, developing, as we proceed, the broad outline of a proposed method for weighing conflicting values against each other, not by relying on cost–benefit analysis, but by giving both utility maximization *and* distributive justice their appropriate place within a comprehensive decision principle. Chapters 5 through 7 will then elaborate this unified theory for beneficial and just collective action in a more detailed way, and finally will more precisely formulate the overarching decision principle that I believe reasonably results from all these considerations. Ultimately, what must be done is to derive legal rights and obligations from a coherent concept of distributive justice, which in turn is conceivable as a type of social *outcome* and, therefore, is quantitatively commensurable with a consequentialist approach to maximizing beneficial social outcomes. I call this a "nonutilitarian consequentialist" approach to collective policy making.

1

The Value Component
of Policy Analysis

1. Policy Opinions and Value Opinions

Suppose we define a social or political policy belief as the belief that some social or political action (or type of action) ought to be taken or ought not to be taken, or that taking such an action would be desirable (good) or undesirable (bad). For example, "The government ought to execute convicted murderers" is a political policy belief. By contrast, the statement "Executing murderers would deter crime" is *not* a policy belief *unless* it is combined with the assumption that crime *ought* to be deterred, or that deterring crime is *desirable.*

Since all such policy beliefs include or imply the belief that something *ought* to be done or that something *ought not* to be done, or that something is desirable (good) or undesirable (bad), it would seem that no policy belief can be logically justified unless it is supported by (a) at least one *value belief* and (b) at least one *factual belief* concerning how the value in question can effectively be achieved. A value belief is the belief that certain kinds of things are desirable or that certain kinds of actions ought to be taken. For example, "Benefiting the majority is desirable" is a value belief.

A policy belief, then, is really a compound belief composed of both a factual and a value belief. Some people believe that policy beliefs do not need to be grounded in value assumptions, but rather that the value component of a policy belief can be resolved simply by allowing the people in a society to express their preferences. But we shall see increasingly that this assumption itself presupposes value beliefs, some of which are highly questionable. If the idea is that the moral beliefs of the majority ought to be accepted, then we would inevitably end up with the kind of "tyranny of the majority" that Alexis de Tocqueville

7

warned against—the very problem over which James Madison ago-
nized in *The Federalist Papers* and which led to the Bill of Rights in the
U.S. Constitution. The purpose of the Bill of Rights was essentially to
ensure that a majority—even a strong majority—would not unjustly
impose its will, or its value preferences, on individuals and small
groups whose interests or beliefs might conflict with those of the majority with regard to some political issue. In one way or another, any
proposed method of circumventing the philosophical consideration of
competing value assumptions will involve its own value assumptions
in ways that are easily debatable. It is thus inescapable that, as Gillroy
and Wade put it, "If [policy analysis] cannot sustain, protect, and
empower intrinsic value, then it must justify its exclusion from the
analysis. In either case, policy argument cannot ignore the existence
of such value or it will have ignored the most important aspect of its
nature as a normative pursuit: the creation of a 'better' environment
for human beings" (Gillroy and Wade 1992, 519).

Sometimes the value component of a political or social policy
belief is not explicitly stated by the person who asserts the policy belief,
but is tacitly assumed. For example, someone might attempt to justify
the statement "Murderers ought to be executed" by saying "Executing
murderers deters crime." If E stands for "executing murderers," D
stands for "deterring crime," and O stands for "ought to be done,"
then this person's argument can be diagrammed as follows:

E implies D.
Therefore, E implies O.

That is, "Executing murderers deters crime; therefore, executing murderers ought to be done." Clearly, this is not a valid argument until
we add the missing assumption, which the speaker obviously has
tacitly assumed without explicitly stating it. The tacit assumption is
that "D implies O," i.e., that "Anything that deters crime ought to be
done." The argument then reads this way: "Executing murderers deters
crime. Anything that deters crime ought to be done. Therefore, executing murderers ought to be done," or

E implies D.
D implies O.
Therefore, E implies O.

The pattern of this logic, of course, is the most familiar of all patterns:

> X implies Y.
> Y implies Z.
> Therefore, X implies Z.

Notice that this argument form would *not* be valid if it said:

> X implies Y.
> Some Y implies Z.
> Therefore, X implies Z.

This would be like saying, "All Republicans are conservatives; *some* conservatives are Democrats; therefore (all) Republicans are Democrats." Nor would the argument be valid if it said:

> X implies Y.
> Some Y implies Z.
> Therefore, some X implies Z.

This would be like saying, "All Republicans are conservatives; *some* conservatives are Democrats; therefore *some* Republicans are Democrats." Nor, finally, would the argument be valid if it said

> Some X implies Y.
> Some Y implies Z.
> Therefore, some X implies Z.

This would be like saying, "*Some* Republicans are conservatives; *some* conservatives are Democrats; therefore *some* Republicans are Democrats." In order for this kind of argument to be valid, the assumption "Y implies Z" *must* be *universally* true (not just some of the time or in some cases). Similarly, in our argument about deterring crime, "D implies O" (i.e., "Anything that deters crime ought to be done.") would have to be universally true in order for the logic to be valid.

Now it is easy to see that the argument

> E implies D.
> D implies O.
> Therefore, E implies O.

is a *valid* argument, in the sense that the assumptions do indeed imply the conclusion; but the problem remains that the argument is *unsound* because its second assumption is extremely questionable, and in fact is almost certainly false. It is very unlikely to be true that *all* actions that deter crime ought to be done. This would mean that executing petty thieves is something that ought to be done as well, since this also would deter crime. It would mean that executing marijuana users, depriving defendants of their right to a fair trial, and many other such practices ought to be done, since these actions also would deter crime. The problem, obviously, is that *not everything* that would deter crime ought to be done. Thus the assumption that "Anything that deters crime ought to be done" (i.e., "*D* implies *O*") *is not true*. And there certainly is no reason why anyone should accept the conclusion of an argument that has obviously untrue assumptions and is, therefore, unsound. (Since this chapter concerns value assumptions, we are ignoring for the moment the *empirical* question as to whether the death penalty *does* in fact deter crime. This type of assumption will be discussed in a later chapter.)

It might therefore initially appear that it is impossible to give a sound argument in which one of the premises is a value belief. If the value belief states that *all* actions that deter crime ought to be done, then the value belief, as we have seen, is false, so the argument is unsound. But if the value belief states that *some* actions that deter crime ought to be done, then the value belief may well be true. However, it is not generalizable enough to support the conclusion of a deductive logical argument (since it is true not *in all cases* but only *in some cases*); thus the argument is invalid, as the diagrams examined above clearly show. And it seems that the same problem will arise with any other argument containing a value assumption. Thus it might appear that no policy belief can ever be logically justifiable, since the justification of any policy belief requires the assumption of at least one value belief.

The next section will attempt to show, however, that there is a solution to this problem.

2. Prima Facie Values and Value Conflicts

To those who have not thought much about the logic of value beliefs, the problem just described may seem insurmountable. Many people who reach this point in their thinking are thus tempted to throw up their arms and say, "Then there is no truth!"—at least when it comes to value beliefs and policy beliefs. But, to any experienced moral philosopher the solution is quite elementary. It is only necessary to add a certain qualification to the value assumption, and then add this same qualification to the conclusion of the argument.

The qualification that must be added to these statements, in order to make the argument both valid and sound, involves the use of the term "prima facie." In the context of value theory, "prima facie" can be taken to mean "unless some more important value takes priority." The addition of this qualification to our argument thus changes it so that it reads as follows: "Executing murderers deters crime. Anything that deters crime ought prima facie to be done. Therefore, executing murderers is something which ought prima facie to be done." Bearing in mind the definition just stated for the term prima facie, this argument can be paraphrased as follows: "Executing murderers deters crime. Anything that deters crime ought to be done *unless some more important value takes priority*. Therefore, executing murderers ought to be done *unless some more important value takes priority*."

We now have an argument that is not only valid, it is also very likely that its value assumption is *true*, provided that the qualification "prima facie" is tacked onto it. We can, therefore, use value assumptions to logically justify policy beliefs, provided that the value assumptions are true. And if the initial opponents in a policy dispute agree in accepting a prima facie value assumption (for example, "Deterring crime has prima facie value" seems to be a very noncontroversial one), then they should also be able to reach agreement with regard to a prima facie policy conclusion that follows from it.

But this solution immediately raises another problem. Granted that you can prove to me that the execution of murderers ought to be done *unless some more important value takes priority*, how do we decide whether or not there *are* more important values that ought to take priority? I might argue, for example, as follows:

Abolishing the death penalty would prevent the execution of innocent men.
Preventing the execution of innocent men ought prima facie to be done.
Therefore, abolishing the death penalty ought prima facie to be done.

This also appears to be a sound argument, but its conclusion conflicts with the other one. Thus we have two conflicting prima facie policy opinions, both of which have been demonstrated to be true. Both, in fact, probably *are* true (if, that is, we assume that the *first* premise—the factual premise—is true in each case). The only question that remains to be resolved, as far as the value component of the arguments is concerned, is which of them should take priority over the other. And the only way to resolve this question is to decide which of the conflicting *values* should take priority. Which is more important—deterring crime or preventing the execution of innocent men?

Most disagreements about value issues—and, therefore, also about social and political policy—have nothing to do with the question as to what kinds of things *have value*. The disagreements usually have to do with the comparative *importance* of these agreed-upon values in those situations in which the values *conflict* with each other.

Here again, some readers may be tempted to throw up their arms and conclude that there is no way to discover the truth when it comes to such issues. If one person believes that preventing the execution of innocent men is more important (i.e., has more value, is more desirable) than deterring crime, whereas someone else believes the opposite, there still seems to be no logical way to establish that one belief is right and the other is wrong. And if this cannot be established, then there is no way to logically justify following one policy rather than the other in any given set of real-life circumstances.

There are, however, ways to solve this problem as well. In many instances, the solution is fairly easy. In those instances in which the easy solution is not available, a more difficult one can still be accomplished.

3. Intrinsic and Extrinsic Values

First, let's examine the easier type of solution. Many value conflicts are conflicts between *extrinsic* (or instrumental) values rather than between *intrinsic* values. An intrinsic value can be defined as something that is valuable *for its own sake*. An extrinsic value is valuable not for its own sake, but because it facilitates getting or accomplishing something that *is* valuable for its own sake. Nothing can be extrinsically valuable, then, unless it serves to help us get or accomplish some *intrinsic* value. Yet most values in life *are* merely extrinsic. In any given person's value system, there are literally thousands of extrinsic values. But all of these thousands of extrinsic values serve the sole purpose of promoting the small handful of intrinsic values which that person believes in. The reason for this, as we shall soon see, is that there are only a very few things that could possibly be construed as valuable for their own sake, even if they were to accomplish no purpose beyond themselves.

Take money, for example. Obviously, money has only extrinsic value, because it would have no value at all if it did not help us get something other than money—say, a car. The car, too, has only extrinsic value. Its purpose is to help us achieve something else, for example, getting to work.

Then what kinds of things *do* have intrinsic value? The most clear-cut example (and, thus, the one that is most universally agreed on) might be happiness. Most people consider happiness to be valuable for its own sake. It would seem odd, perhaps even nonsensical, if someone were to say, "I don't value happiness for its own sake, but only because experiencing happiness helps me to accomplish some other purpose." After all, what purpose *can* be accomplished by experiencing happiness, unless the happiness is valued for its own sake? Happiness, therefore, is usually considered to have intrinsic value. By contrast, things like money and cars have only extrinsic value, because they ultimately help us to achieve something that has intrinsic value—such as, for example, happiness.

Many value conflicts are automatically resolved as soon as this distinction is made. If two extrinsic values have as their only purpose to promote the same intrinsic value, yet conflict with each other, then the conflict between them can be resolved by determining which one will *most effectively* promote the intrinsic value at stake. For example, I might extrinsically value an ice cream cone because eating it would make me happy, and I might extrinsically value losing weight because doing so would make me happy. The conflict (I cannot both eat the ice cream and lose weight) can be resolved simply by determining which alternative would make me happier. The reason for this is that happiness is the intrinsic value that both of these extrinsic values are meant to promote. (This does not imply, of course, that happiness is the *only* intrinsic value, as we shall soon see.)

To consider a policy-related example, a government might have to choose between the extrinsic value of paving roads and the extrinsic value of keeping taxes low—both of which have value only because they promote an intrinsic value, the general happiness. If the general happiness is the only intrinsic value at stake in the situation, then the conflict can be resolved simply by choosing whichever of the two policies would *most effectively* promote the general happiness.

Notice that if two people disagree about whether the government should pave roads or keep taxes low, each believing that her preferred policy would promote the general happiness, then these people do not really disagree about *values*, but only about *facts*. Each of the two opponents in the dispute believes that her proposed policy will promote *the same* value—the general happiness. The disagreement has to do only with which *method* of accomplishing this purpose *is likely to be more effective*. And this is merely a factual issue, which can be resolved only in the same way as any other factual issue—by collecting empirical evidence and interpreting it as accurately as possible. Any good book on empirical methods for policy analysis (for example, Weimer 1991; Sinden and Worrell 1979) will explain the use of public opinion polls and other empirical ways to determine which of two courses of action is likely to make the public happier and to assess the comparative importance that people place on the effects of various policies on their general well-being. Of course, this assessment is not as simple as it may at first seem, because the astute policy analyst will want to determine the effect on the public welfare (or happiness) of the *real consequences* that are likely to follow from a policy decision, not the effects which an uninformed public may *erroneously believe* are likely to follow (as Sagoff, 1992, emphasizes with his distinction between "happiness" and "preferences"). But, in principle, the way in which these effects on the general happiness can be determined is by using essentially empirical methods; it requires no value assumptions. The proposed actions in this case are only *extrinsic* values, meant to promote the *same* intrinsic value—maximizing the general happiness.

Any disagreement that is genuinely a *value* dispute, on the other hand, must be one in which different and conflicting *intrinsic* values are meant to be promoted by the conflicting policies. For example, one politician may be in favor of eliminating the Legal Services Corporation, which provides legal services to people too poor to hire lawyers in civil cases, in order to save money for the government so that the general public can pay lower taxes and thus be happier. The opponent, on the other hand, may argue that, even though eliminating the Legal Services Corporation would probably promote a slight increase in the general happiness, it would not be *fair* to do so, because the poor would then have no defense against violations of their basic legal rights. If this politician believes that the intrinsic value of fairness should take priority over the intrinsic value of maximizing the general happiness (in this type of case), she may therefore conclude that, all things considered, the Legal Services Corporation ought *not* to be eliminated. In this case, we have a genuine value disagreement, because the two politicians at this point disagree about which intrinsic value is more important than the other. It is in these types of situations that we must resort to the more difficult mode of analysis, which will now be considered.

4. *Five Basic Types of Value Systems*

Although each person's value system contains thousands of extrinsic values, the justification of all these extrinsic value beliefs (if there is any such thing as "justification" in this domain—an issue to which we shall return shortly) depends in turn on the justification of the intrinsic values that the extrinsic values are meant to promote. It is, therefore, convenient to identify each person's value system by listing only the intrinsic values the person believes in. Fortunately, the number of things which can be reasonably construed as intrinsically valuable are very few in number. In fact, I shall suggest in what follows that there are really only four types of things that can arguably be considered intrinsically valuable. The various possible types of value systems therefore arise from the various possible combinations and priority rankings of these four possible basic values. If we add to this list the additional possibility that someone might not believe that *any* value statements are true (i.e., an extreme ethical relativist or a nonrelativistic type of nihilist), it then becomes possible to divide all the resulting value systems into five general types, as follows:

(a) *Egoistic hedonism.* An egoistic hedonist advocates the simplest of all value systems. It contains only one intrinsic value: one's own personal happiness. The egoistic hedonist may, of course, believe that other people's happiness has *extrinsic* value—but only when and if others' happiness indirectly leads to the egoistic hedonist's own happiness. For example, the egoistic hedonist may help other people so that they will help her later. Thus the only intrinsic value the person recognizes is her own happiness.

Within this general type of value system, it is also possible to distinguish a subdivision that is usually called '*universal* egoistic hedonism.' Universal egoistic hedonism would assert that *all* individuals should simply do whatever best promotes their own happiness. We should note, however, that if the reason someone believes in this is that everyone will be better off if we all look out for our own interests, then the *intrinsic* value that the speaker really believes in is the maximization of the *general* happiness—that is, the greatest possible happiness of the greatest possible number of people. But if this is the reasoning, then the view being advocated is not really a form of egoistic hedonism at all, but rather a form of *utilitarianism:* the belief that promoting the greatest possible happiness for the greatest possible number of people is the only intrinsic value. This reasoning is not really a form of egoistic hedonism because as soon as we posit that maximizing the *general* happiness has intrinsic value, then we are committed to the consequence that it would be beneficial for an individual to do something *other than* look out for her own well-being, if doing so would promote the maximization of the *general* happiness.

Logically consistent egoistic hedonists, therefore, do not believe in egoistic hedonism for this type of reason. Instead, their reasoning is more like the following:

1. Human psychology is such that people *cannot* do anything but seek their own happiness.
2. If people *cannot* do something, then it makes no sense to claim that they *ought* to do it (i.e., "ought implies can").

Therefore, people *ought* not to do anything other than seek their own happiness.

Although this argument at first seems convincing to many people, the problem is that it contains a hidden ambiguity. That is, it may be that human beings, if socialized in a certain way, are prone to value *not only* their own happiness, but *also* the happiness of others. In this case, to say that giving money to a charity is really an egoistic act because it "makes me happy" to do so becomes ambiguous. If it "makes me happy" to make other people happy, then it would seem illogical to conclude that I ought not to work to promote others' happiness on the basis of the assumption that I cannot do so. If what makes me happy *is* to make others happy, then obviously I can. Moreover, it seems logically possible that, if I have been socialized in a certain way, I may be the kind of person who prefers to sacrifice my own happiness in order to promote other values; and, if I understand the principles of psychological conditioning well enough, I may have chosen at some past time to condition *myself* in ways that would end up causing me to become that type of person. Also, it seems self-contradictory to claim that it makes people "happy" to *sacrifice* their own happiness for others; yet as an empirical fact sometimes people seem to do so. (For example, consider the white integrationist ministers in the southern United States in the 1960s who knowingly sacrificed their careers to work toward desegregation.)

This paradox of "altruistic egoism" is interestingly illustrated by Hobbes's remark that the reason he gave money to a beggar was that it relieved his own misery at the sight of him (Etzioni 1991, 323). It would seem that, if Hobbes *really* intrinsically valued only his own well-being, then the sight of the beggar's misery would not have made Hobbes miserable in the first place. More important, if alleged egoists like Hobbes have altruistic feelings toward others, for whatever reason, then the "ought implies can" thesis in the second premise above does not have the implications that egoistic hedonists want. The problem is that it is not *impossible* for Hobbes to value others' well-being, and, therefore, it is not false or meaningless to say that he ought to (or even that he ought to value them to a greater extent than he does, since this also would be *possible* for him [see Ellis 1992]). We shall consider this issue more carefully in a later context. For now, our purpose is only to establish an overview of the various arguable types of value systems, along with the main reasons people have for endorsing them.

(b) Utilitarianism. Utilitarians are traditionally taken as agreeing with egoistic hedonists that the only intrinsic value is happiness, but rather than believing that only one's own happiness matters, they believe that *the general* happiness should be maximized (i.e., the greatest possible amount of happiness for the greatest possible number of people should be achieved). They therefore believe that, in every situation, we should do whatever produces the greatest net total of happiness on the whole and in the long run, counting every person's happiness as having the same value. Notice that the value of *maximizing* the amount of happiness may sometimes conflict with fairness, as in the example cited earlier about the Legal Services Corporation, which is paid for by the majority of people (who pay taxes) but is needed to ensure fairness for a small number (the very poor). However, utilitarians do not believe that fairness has any *intrinsic* value at all; fairness has only *extrinsic* value, when and if fairness serves to increase the general happiness. In many cases, fairness *does* serve to increase the general happiness, because most people are happier if they feel confident that they will be treated fairly than if they must continually fear injustice. John Stuart Mill argued this point very persuasively in his famous pamphlet *On Liberty* (1859–1947). More recently, this view has been defended quite eloquently by Robert Goodin (1995) and by J. J. C. Smart (1956; 1984). Goodin states it this way: "Public officials cannot systematically violate people's rights, as a matter of *policy*, and expect that policy to continue yielding the same utility payoffs time and again. . . . Once news of such a policy gets out, people revise their expectations in the light of it . . ." (Goodin 1995, 70–71). Despite these attempts

to derive the (extrinsic) value of justice from the (intrinsic) value of maximizing human happiness, it seems obvious that there are *some* cases in which fairness does *not* promote the maximum possible general happiness, even when the utilitarian effects of the policy on future expectations are considered. In these cases utilitarians apparently must choose against fairness, since in their view fairness has no intrinsic value, whereas the general happiness does.

The essential argument for utilitarianism (which will be discussed in more detail in Chapter 3) runs as follows:

1. Each person values her own happiness, at least prima facie (this is an empirical fact).
2. Therefore, each person's happiness has prima facie value.
3. Therefore, everyone's happiness has prima facie value.
4. Therefore, maximizing the general happiness has prima facie value.
5. No one can demonstrate adequately that anything *other* than the general happiness (such as distributive justice, for example) has intrinsic value (although such things would, of course, have *extrinsic* value if they promote the general happiness).

Therefore, maximizing the general happiness is the only intrinsic value.

In case anyone questions the validity of the inference from step 1 to step 2 of this proof, utilitarians provide essentially the following defense of the inference: Either (a) there are objective values, such as the common good, which sometimes supersede what the individual subjectively values, or (b) there are not—in which case what the individual values is the only meaning of the term 'value', and thus the individual ought to get what she values. If (a) is the case, then there are a number of prima facie values which can conflict, and what the individual subjectively values is one of them. The common good might be another. On the other hand, if (b) is the case, then what the individual subjectively values *has* value in the only meaningful sense of "value." In both cases, it is *objectively true* that what the individual subjectively values (i.e., her own happiness) has at least prima facie value. So if Bill denies that John's getting the ice cream cone that John wants has prima facie value, then Bill is making a false statement. For Mill and other utilitarians, then, this proves that each person's happiness has value, at least prima facie.[1]

But, even though this part of the reasoning seems very convincing to many people, the overall argument for utilitarianism usually ceases to be so convincing when we begin to consider how questionable statement 5 in the above diagram is. What kind of demonstration is to be considered "adequate" here? Is empirical evidence the only way to demonstrate a statement? (The statement "237 + 2 = 239" is one that most people have never seen empirically verified, yet we are all quite certain that it is true.) There seem to be some statements whose truth is based on pure logic rather than (or perhaps in addition to) empirical evidence. For example, many philosophers (for instance, Rawls 1971) have given arguments to demonstrate that not only the maximization of human happiness has value but also *justice in the distribution* of human happiness. Also, it is unclear how strict a demand for certainty Mill and other utilitarians want to require for demonstrations of the value of things like justice before they would be willing to accept them as intrinsic values. Must something be demonstrated with absolute certainty before we decide to go ahead and act on the assumption that it is probably true? That is an issue which will recur throughout this book. One of the more convincing arguments for the demonstrability of a certain notion of justice will be considered in the following subsection.

(c) Value systems based on concepts of justice (often called "deontic" systems). There are many different types of systems based on the many types of concepts of justice (or fairness), but they all have two things in common: First, they intrinsically value *both* the general happiness (including one's own happiness) *and* fairness in the distribution of such intrinsic values as happiness. Second, they believe that, at least in some cases, the value of fairness should *take priority over* the value of the general happiness. Those whose value system is a justice system, for example, may believe that it is intrinsically valuable to respect certain "inalienable rights" even if doing so causes a decrease in the general happiness, or that goods should be distributed in a fair way, or that people should get what they "deserve" in some moral sense, or that there are certain duties that should be done regardless of the consequences. Duties and rights, of course, are correlative: If Bill has a duty toward John, this means that John has a right for Bill to behave in a certain way toward him. Rights, in turn, can be analyzed in terms of the most fair way for people to behave toward each other. Every right is ultimately the right to be treated fairly. There are, of course, many possible interpretations of what *is* "fair" that can be supported with rational arguments, and many of these interpretations

are diametrically opposed to each other. But fairness is ultimately the intrinsic value that is meant to be promoted by 'rights' and 'duties'.

It is often useful to divide value systems based on concepts of justice into two broad categories, based on two entirely different kinds of 'justice'. In many instances, the same person may believe in the intrinsic value of both kinds of justice, but it is still important to realize that they are different.

(i) **Distributive justice** refers to the belief that "distributing opportunities and/or benefits equitably" (in one sense or another) has intrinsic value, even if doing so conflicts with the value of *maximizing* the amount of such opportunities and benefits. For example, a distributive justice thinker might well be opposed to increasing tax breaks for corporations or wealthy investors in order to spur economic investment (thus improving the economy in order to maximize the general happiness); distributive justice would demand that tax burdens be distributed equitably, even if doing so conflicted with the value of maximizing the general welfare by stimulating the economy. As another example, a distributive justice thinker would favor adequate legal representation for defendants in criminal cases—even if this required the state to pay for the attorney, and even if this made it more difficult to convict criminals and ultimately led to a net decrease in *retributive* justice by causing many guilty individuals to go without punishment because their guilt could not be proven satisfactorily. This last example also shows how the purposes of retributive and distributive justice may often conflict with *each other*, as well as conflicting with the value of maximizing utility for the society as a whole. John Rawls (1971, 1993), perhaps the most currently influential distributive justice theorist, explicitly rejects the intrinsic value of retribution, maintaining that it has only extrinsic value.

Within the broad categories of retributive and distributive justice, there are, of course, many different notions of what such 'justice' would consist of, and many arguments can be given pro and con regarding these various notions. For the present, our purpose is only to outline the main types of value systems by showing that each emphasizes one or a few particular intrinsic values and advocates numerous extrinsic value beliefs based on the assumption that these extrinsic values are effective ways to promote the particular intrinsic values that the person believes in or wants to promote.

One of the strongest arguments for a particular concept of distributive justice is the one John Rawls proposed in *A Theory of Justice*. Because of criticisms of this argument, Rawls later (especially in *Political*

Liberalism 1993) dressed it up with a few additional complexities (which will be discussed in a later chapter), but the basic idea is as follows:

1. 'Fairness' means the best way to distribute opportunities and benefits (as opposed to the best way to maximize them).
2. Objectively speaking, the best way to distribute opportunities and benefits can be decided only by a completely unbiased observer whose self-interest is not affected by the decision.
3. A person in the "original position" (i.e., who would not know any facts about herself that might prejudice her judgment) would make an objective decision as to what is fair (i.e., how opportunities and benefits should be distributed).
4. In such a position, this person would realize that a given amount of *very necessary* goods are more valuable than an equal amount of *less necessary* goods (defining the 'degree of necessity' as the extent to which the goods in question affect the person's total sense of well-being). The person judging from this neutral standpoint would not be willing to risk deprivation of extremely necessary goods for the chance of gaining less necessary goods.
5. If this person were to favor an extremely unequal distribution of goods, in which some must go without extremely necessary goods in order that others may enjoy less necessary (or luxury) goods, this would be taking an illogical risk, since the person in the original position knows that she is going to have to occupy one of the resulting social positions, but does not know which one. Thus she would not want to risk ending up in a very deprived position. On the other hand, it would also be illogical to favor exactly equal distribution, since this would lead to lack of incentive to work hard and, thus, a completely unproductive economy.
6. The person in this "original position" would, therefore, favor a decision principle that would distribute goods with the minimum amount of inequality necessary to give people incentive to work hard, and would give priority to extremely necessary benefits and opportunities, as compared with equal amounts of less necessary benefits and opportunities.

Therefore, the decision principle described in step 6 is the one that defines fairness, according to the definitions given in steps 1, 3, and 4, along with the assumption in step 2.

Because the kind of reasoning used in this argument is a relatively recent development in contemporary philosophy, those who champion it have not been able to propose modifications of the argument rapidly enough to counter all the many criticisms that other philosophers have raised (see Ellis 1991, 1992). It takes more time to develop a better version of a theory than it does to attack the logic in an existing version. The most serious problem with the argument as Rawls originally proposed it is that there is no way to determine how safe or daring the person in the original position would want to be in her risk-taking behavior. As Kaye (1980) and other critics to be discussed later have shown, a very daring risk taker in the original position might be willing to risk the loss of some very necessary kinds of goods for the chance of gaining a very large amount of less necessary goods. For example, a musician might live a life of abject poverty for a long-shot chance of making a big success. If Rawls is asserting that to be this daring a risk taker is "irrational" or "illogical," on what basis does he assert this? But if not, then why should we not suppose that a person in the original position would never take such a risk? We, therefore, cannot determine how much equality or inequality would be tolerated in a society from the standpoint of the original position. It may be, however, that a modified version of the argument could get around this kind of problem. In fact, this is essentially what we shall attempt to do later in this book: to ground a concept of distributive justice suitable to be used for purposes of everyday policy decisions.

Many theories are often classified as theories of "distributive" justice (as opposed to retributive justice) simply because they advocate some criterion for the distribution not of goods, resources, or happiness, but rather of such things as 'rights' (for example, Gewirth), 'freedom' (Nozick), or the material and other conditions needed for "moral autonomy" (Kant). Typically, the criterion advocated in such theories is one of "formal" equality, that is, rights, freedom, and conditions needed for moral autonomy should be distributed equally. Some authors regard the equal distribution of rights, freedom, and conditions for moral autonomy as "*merely* formal" equality (Pojman and Westmoreland 1997, 2ff), in the sense that having an equal right to sleep elsewhere than under a bridge does not mean that one has an equal *ability* to sleep elsewhere, unless one also has access to certain tangible resources. On the other hand, such theorists of equality often respond that the instrumental value of the needed resources—since they are needed to facilitate the exercise of equal rights, freedom, or moral autonomy—ought, therefore, to be distributed in some equitable way as well, so that such theories are *not* merely theories of formal equality, but also substantive equity (Gillroy 1992a, 1992b). For our purposes, such theories can be classified as theories of distributive rather than retributive justice.

Some value systems *seem* to be based on a notion of retributive justice, when in reality they are theories of distributive justice instead, because their most basic premises have to do with distributive equity rather than with judgments of moral desert. For example, Nozick (1974) is sometimes mistakenly thought of as a retributive thinker because he believes that the most important right people have is the right to keep whatever property they have acquired, as long as the goods were not acquired "unjustly." It might seem that Nozick assumes here that people ought not to be deprived of the legitimate rewards of their honest labor, and thus that they morally "deserve" to keep what they have "earned." But, in fact, this is not Nozick's reasoning. Rather, Nozick argues that all social intervention must be justified by the *consent* (real or hypothetical) of those who would be affected, and that no one would consent to giving up property unless compensated in some way; thus *"redistributive"* notions of justice would become untenable (Goodin 1995). Yet notice that the first premise of this argument is that *freedom* should be *equally* distributed, unless the parties involved consent to give it up. So Nozick's approach is a distributive rather than retributive theory.

Similarly, Kant's theory should not be regarded as retributive in its basic foundation, even though Kant took a retributive approach to criminal justice; the retributive principle was grounded in a more fundamental principle of *distributive* equity, with 'moral autonomy' rather than material goods or happiness constituting that which was to be distributed equitably (and, in fact, equally). Thus, Kant may sound retributive when making such remarks as this:

> When someone who delights in annoying and vexing peace-loving folk receives at last a right good beating ... everyone approves of it and considers it good in itself even if nothing further results from it; nay, even he who gets the beating must acknowledge in his reason that justice has been done to him, because he sees the proportion between welfare and well-doing. (Kant 1956, 40)

But the *reason* for such judgments was grounded in the more fundamental assumption that each person should be respected as an autonomous moral agent, and that this respect should be distributed *equally*. Punishment was considered a means toward the end of facilitating moral agency, including the ability to take responsibility for one's own actions.

(ii) **Retributive justice** refers to the belief that giving people what they "morally deserve" has intrinsic (and not merely extrinsic) value. In other words, there should be a proportion between the rewards and punishments people receive on the one hand, and on the other hand, the moral worth of their actions, intended actions, personality dispositions, etc. For example, a retributive justice thinker would believe that people should be paid according to how well or how hard they work, even if doing so eventually led to such unequal economic conditions that some children would be forced to grow up in poverty and, thus, with unequal opportunities in life. As another example, retributive justice would demand that criminals be punished in proportion to their moral desert, even if doing so required an extremely painful tax increase to pay for the additional prison space, or even if it conflicted with the ability of prosecutors to make deals with petty criminals in order to procure information to track down more serious ones. In both these instances, retributive justice conflicts with the utilitarian value of maximizing the general happiness, and in the former instance it seems to conflict with distributive equity as well. Retributive justice can, therefore, conflict with utility maximization and with considerations of distributive justice; retributive thinkers thus believe that retributive justice in principle can override these other intrinsic values.

Many proponents of the retributive view argue that people have a moral right to keep any goods they have acquired as long as the goods were not acquired unjustly. George Sher (1987), for example, assumes that people ought not to be deprived of the legitimate rewards of their honest labor, and this implies that they ought to be rewarded or punished according to their actions—a retributive assumption.[2] This basic assumption has also been defended by Wallace Matson (1997), by James Sterba (1980), and by Herbert Morris (1976). I shall argue in Chapter 4 that the most intractable problem typically encountered by such approaches is that, in order to show that the proportion between people's behavior and their rewards and punishments *has value*, they usually must show that such a proportionality produces some beneficial or desirable result—for example, that it tends to promote some other intrinsic value such as the moral autonomy of people or distributive equity of some sort, or to have utilitarian value. But, by arguing that the proportionality produces some *result*, they make it into an *extrinsic* rather than intrinsic value. On the other hand, if they wish it to remain an intrinsic value, they are at a loss to say *why* we should believe that it has intrinsic value.

Sher (1987) provides the following argument for the intrinsic value of retributive justice (i.e., that people should get what they "deserve"), adapting it from Morris (1976):

1. Autonomous moral agency has intrinsic value.
2. Rewarding or punishing people in proportion to the rightness or wrongness of their actions facilitates moral agency.

Therefore, we ought to reward or punish people in proportion to the rightness or wrongness of their actions.

One problem with this argument is that it is not logically valid, for the same reason that the above arguments about the death penalty were not valid. To be valid, it would need to assume that rewarding and punishing in proportion to the rightness or wrongness of actions is *always* the *best* way to facilitate moral agency, and that the only effective way to promote moral agency is to *always* reward and punish people on this basis, rather than merely doing so *in a substantial number of instances.* But the more serious point that these objections really lead to is that Sher's argument makes the desert criterion into an *extrinsic* value whose purpose is to promote something else: autonomous moral agency. But to promote autonomous moral agency for all people, other methods besides retribution may sometimes be more effective—for example, rehabilitation, deterrence, or even the showing of mercy; whether these other methods are more or less effective than retribution, and in which kinds of instances, is an empirical question. Retributive justice (getting what we "morally deserve") is thus being valued extrinsically rather than intrinsically in this kind of argument. For similar reasons, it seems to be a difficult and fundamental problem with retributive concepts of justice that, on the one hand, if we justify them by showing that their results are good or desirable, then we reduce them to merely instrumental or extrinsic values; on the other hand, if we do not wish to justify them on the grounds that their general adoption would produce desirable results, then it is very difficult to think of any convincing reason why anyone should agree that they ought to be adopted, let alone that they should take priority over other values. An appeal to intuition will not suffice as a justification because, as Hare says in discussing Rawls and Nozick, "How are we to decide between them? Not by intuition, because there seems to be a deadlock between their intuitions" (Hare 1997, 222).

Moreover, now that so much evidence has accumulated to suggest that what happens to people in life results largely from their circumstances—genetic predispositions combined with environmental factors such as poverty, gang-ridden neighborhoods, child abuse, broken homes, unequal educational opportunities, etc.—it becomes less and less credible to attribute much, if any, *intrinsic* value to people's getting what they "morally deserve" for behavior that can be traced in such large part to these kinds of factors. The more such empirical correlations accumulate to explain what causes young people to become involved in crime, for example, the more sense it seems to make that punishing criminals has *extrinsic* value (because it deters crime and protects future victims), but not *intrinsic* value (Ellis 1989). Charles Taylor (1985) has eloquently pressed this type of concern. We shall return to this issue in a later chapter.

(d) Personalism   (sometimes called 'self-actualizationism'). The most complex of all value systems is the one that intrinsically values not only the general happiness, and/or one's own happiness, and/or fairness, but also *self-actualization,* that is, the opportunity to actualize one's potential as a human being in a full sense. Utilitarians, of course, might very well *extrinsically* value self-actualization, but only when doing so promotes the intrinsic value of happiness. By contrast, personalists *intrinsically* value self-actualization (i.e., facilitating opportunities for people to actualize their potential as human beings) *even if doing so does not lead to an increase in happiness,* and sometimes even if it *decreases* one's happiness. For example, they believe that we should strive to increase our consciousness by developing our intellects, even if remaining ignorant would keep us happier, by protecting us from the pain of acknowledging unpleasant realities. In simple terms, if given the choice whether to be a very happy dog or a less happy human being, the personalist would choose to be the less happy human being. Personalism is thus based on the assumption that the purpose of human life is not merely to be happy, contented, or in an enjoyable frame of mind, but also to exercise certain capacities of the human mind (or 'soul'), which cannot be understood in terms of a happiness-maximizing motivational theory. For example, Martin Luther King Jr. often defined himself as a personalist. He believed that creating opportunities for people to actualize their potential as conscious beings

was more important than either the general happiness or justice, although he recognized the importance of these other intrinsic values as well. In fact, King chose to do graduate work in philosophy at Boston University in order to study with an important personalist philosopher who taught there, Edgar Brightman, who in turn was influenced by B. P. Bowne, a personalist of the previous generation whose ideas had impressed King.

For our purposes here, it is important to notice that if self-actualization as a human or moral agent is believed to have intrinsic value, then the same questions of *distributive justice* can be raised with regard to this value as with regard to such values as happiness: How should opportunities and resources that facilitate a person's capacity to realize her potential as a human being or moral agent be *distributed?* And what is the appropriate balance between *maximizing* such opportunities and resources on the one hand, and on the other hand, *distributing them in a fair way?* The same conflicts arise between these two goals as we saw earlier arise between the values of maximizing and of fairly distributing the opportunities and resources that facilitate happiness. So the central problem with which this book is concerned—finding a coherent decision principle to resolve conflict between fairness and utility maximization—is just as pressing a problem for personalists as it is for utilitarians or justice theorists.

(e) Ethical relativism.   Ethical relativists believe simply that *there is no objectively true answer* to the question as to which things have intrinsic value. Instead, value "beliefs" are not really beliefs at all, but only expressions of emotion or cultural traditions. They therefore believe that no one person's value system is any more or less correct than anyone else's. Hitler's value system was no more or less correct than Martin Luther King Jr.'s. Things can "have value," in the opinion of ethical relativists, only if and because someone values them; the values are, therefore, only subjective emotions and have no objective validity or invalidity. One person's emotions are no more valid than another's, and one culture's preferred customs are no more valid than another's. This philosophy was advocated by the Ancient Greek sophists such as Lycophron, who was criticized in Aristotle's *Politics.* Essentially the same view as Lycophron's has been urged by many influential sociologists and anthropologists of the twentieth century—notably Edward Westermarck and Ruth Benedict—as well as by such noted contemporary philosophers as Alasdair MacIntyre and Richard Rorty.

The appeal of ethical relativism seems to derive largely from the following inference:

1. If rational, well-informed people cannot reach agreement on some given issue, then there can be no objective truth on that particular issue.
2. But when it comes to value issues, rational and well-informed people can argue until doomsday and never reach agreement. Therefore, when it comes to value issues, there is no objective truth.

Most philosophers are aware that there are several glaring fallacies in this argument. In the first place, it is not true that if rational, well-informed people cannot reach agreement on an issue, then there is no objective truth on that issue. Consider, for example, the issue of whether the Earth goes around the sun. Until the late 1600s, rational and well-informed people could not reach agreement on that issue, even though there was enough evidence available to enable them to reach the correct conclusion, and this evidence had been available to them for over a century. People simply were unwilling to give up views to which they were emotionally committed for religious reasons. (The Catholic Church at that time insisted on the theological importance of the idea that the Earth should be the center of the universe; as Kuhn shows in *The Copernican Revolution,* this led many people to hotly disagree with each other even though the evidence was incontrovertible.) So, although there *was* an objective truth on the issue (after all, the Earth *was* busily going around the sun the entire time the scientists were arguing about it), rational and well-informed people could not reach agreement on the issue. This proves that the first premise of the relativists' argument is *not true.* Certainly, it is not universally true, which it would have to be in order to make the logic in the argument valid.

Another fallacy in the relativists' argument is that the second premise is not universally true. Although it is true that there are *some* value issues on which rational, well-informed people cannot reach agreement, there are also many value issues on which different cultures throughout the world *have* reached nearly universal agreement. For example, any rational, well-informed person can be fairly easily convinced (if, indeed, she does not already believe it) that the general happiness has prima facie, intrinsic value. It is only necessary to point out that each person values her own happiness, and that, therefore, each person's happiness has value *unless some more important value takes priority* over it. If no other value were to take priority over my own happiness, then it would be absurd for me to deny that my happiness has value; it would be the only value that would exist in this case, and I could not deny that I value it. Moreover, the same thing can be said about every other person. Therefore, every person's happiness has prima facie value. Here, then, is an example of a value statement on which all rational and well-informed people can reach agreement. They *disagree*, of course, on the question as to whether other values, such as fairness, should take priority over the prima facie value of the general happiness. But this means that there are *some* value issues on which people *do* agree, and *some* on which they *do not* agree. Premise 2 of the ethical relativist argument, however, must assert that *all* value issues are issues on which rational, well-informed people cannot reach agreement. Premise 2, then, is false.

Since both premise 1 and premise 2 are false, there is no reason why we should believe that the conclusion of the argument is true. That is, there is no reason why we should believe that all value statements are devoid of objective truth and are only subjective emotions.

Another argument for ethical relativism is the argument given by A. J. Ayer (1936) and other logical positivists in favor of the now popular theory of 'emotivism' in ethics—the version of relativism that says that ethical beliefs are not the sorts of claims that are capable of being true or false, but are merely expressions of emotion or "pro-feeling," and that these emotions and pro-feelings may be either individual preferences or culturally transmitted dogmas. Either way, the emotivists defend a relativistic account by means of the following reasoning:

1. Any statement that cannot possibly be verified is literally meaningless (i.e., has no meaning as a descriptive statement about reality).
2. Empirical evidence and logical proof are the only ways to verify statements.
3. Value judgments cannot be verified by empirical evidence or logical proof.
   Therefore, value judgments lack literal meaning and thus are only expressions of emotion.

The conclusion of this argument seems to follow logically from its assumptions, but there are several objections against the assumptions themselves. Statement 1 is questionable, because some philosophers

have strongly argued that there is another method of verification besides either empirical evidence or logical proof. Consider the argument
for personalism, for example. It holds that it is better to be a less happy
human being than a more happy dog, and this fact is revealed through
a careful kind of subjective introspection, which also reveals that the
reason for preferring the condition of the less happy human has to do
with the fact that humans are capable of a form of consciousness of
which dogs are not capable. This information comes from neither empirical verification nor logical proof, yet it seems to constitute a type
of reason for believing something. Perhaps more important, just as in
the argument for utilitarianism presented earlier, it is not clear how
strict a criterion for proof the emotivists want to insist on. If they are
demanding absolute certainty, then they are setting a standard that
would be too rigid for even natural science to meet. And we have seen
that there *are* very reasonable arguments that can be presented in
favor of certain value statements. For example, consider the utilitarians'
demonstration that everyone's happiness has prima facie intrinsic value
(although they fail to demonstrate that this is the *only* intrinsic value).
Or consider Rawls's demonstration that a certain kind of distributive
justice has value; even though the argument may fail to nail down
precisely *how much* distributive inequality would constitute injustice,
it still seems to show that there is *some* amount that is unjust.

In fact, we could construct an argument to refute *all* theories that
assert that there are no objectively true value statements (i.e., all forms
of ethical relativism in the true sense), as follows:

Either

(1) there are things that have value for reasons other than the fact
that people value them,

or

(2) to say that something has value is merely to say that someone
values it.

If (1) is true, then it is *objectively true* that these things have value.
If (2) is true, and if we assume that each person values her own
happiness, at least prima facie, then it follows that each
person's happiness *has* prima facie value.

Therefore, (2) implies that anyone who denies that each person's happiness has prima facie value is wrong.

Therefore, (2) also implies that the statement that each person's happiness has prima facie value is *objectively true*.

Since *either (1) or (2) must be true*, and both (1) and (2) imply that there are objectively true value statements, then there are objectively true value statements.

Discovering what the truth *is* in the realm of value issues, of course, is much more difficult than merely demonstrating that there is some truth. But we have already seen some arguments—pretty closely resembling commonsense reasoning as used by many people—that make some modest headway in this direction. This is particularly true of the demonstration that everyone's happiness or well-being has prima facie intrinsic value and the general type of reasoning that Rawls and his followers have been using to show that distributive justice has prima facie intrinsic value, although we have seen that the latter is less successful in demonstrating *how much* distributive inequality is unjust than it is at showing simply that *there is some amount* of distributive inequality that is unjust. Making this determination more precise, then, is part of what must be done if we are to apply the concept to concrete policy decisions.

In scrutinizing any value-issue argument, one must ask: What are the prima facie, *intrinsic* values in the value system being advocated or presupposed by the argument in question? What *conflict-resolution principles* does the system use to decide on the order of priority of these prima facie values when they conflict with each other? What is the structure of the logic in the arguments that are supposed to justify these intrinsic values and conflict-resolution principles? Are its assumptions compelling, or are they merely arbitrary? Finally, how do these arguments stack up when compared with the arguments in favor of different value systems?[3]

The problem of establishing the possibility of value consensus through rational argument is an entirely separate problem from whether ethical relativism is true or whether there is any moral truth. The next chapter will be devoted to the former problem, which is really more difficult than merely refuting relativism. Does the fact that different people within a society hold different values imply that there can be no consensus or demonstrable truth about the formula according to which such valuable "goods" (not just economic goods, but all types of valued goods) are to be *quantitatively maximized* on the one hand, yet *fairly distributed* on the other? Although we may not be able to establish such a formula with absolute precision, our goal here is to show that we can come close enough to doing so to provide a sound basis for sensible policy decisions. That is, in principle, it is possible to show on what kind of basis the conflict between quantitative maximization of valued outcomes and just distribution of these valued outcomes is to be resolved. The next chapter, therefore, will begin to lay a foundation for this solution by showing that, in the final analysis, there is not really an 'incommensurable pluralism' of values and value systems. There may be a pluralism—certainly in urban-industrial cultures there will be—but this pluralism is not an incommensurable one.

NOTES

1. For further discussion of this point, see Ellis (1992), Chapter 2.
2. For discussion, see Ellis (1990).
3. These issues are discussed with more detail and precision in my book *Coherence and Verification in Ethics*, in which I consider some further objections that might be raised by theoretical ethicists against some of the arguments outlined in this chapter. Our purpose here is not to consider every possible objection against every possible theoretical statement. It is rather to provide solid enough reasoning to show that some positions on some value disputes are considerably more justifiable than competing positions, so that we can then be safe in making the basic value assumptions needed in the realm of aggregate policy decisions.

2

Why There Is No 'Incommensurable Pluralism' of Value Systems

Many nonphilosophers—often including social scientists—are only vaguely aware of the intrinsic–extrinsic value distinction and normally do not draw the distinction in any formal and self-conscious way. For philosophers, by contrast, the distinction is rudimentary and is hammered home repeatedly at the undergraduate level, although in recent years one has heard less and less of it at the graduate and professional levels. In many of the more "pluralistic" schools of recent philosophy—notably poststructuralism, communitarianism, deconstructionism, 'multiculturalism' in its more relativistic versions, and many emotivisms of both the positivistic and existential varieties—authors give the impression that they have either lost sight of or rejected this elementary distinction. If they have rejected it, then their reasons for doing so ought to be submitted to critical scrutiny. If they have forgotten it, perhaps a reminder will help to clarify some of the confusion in current moral and social philosophy. I shall suggest that much of this confusion results from the psychological difficulty of distinguishing between intrinsic and extrinsic values in one's own valuational consciousness. In traditional philosophical usage, intrinsic values are supposed to be valuable for their own sake, whereas extrinsic (or instrumental) values are valued only because they facilitate the attainment of intrinsic values; yet it is sometimes psychologically difficult to decide whether we attribute value to something intrinsically or only extrinsically, because value feelings are hard to interpret.

If by 'pluralism of values' is meant a pluralism of *extrinsic* values, then, of course, such a pluralism is a truism. But I shall argue that people everywhere generally tend to be able to reach agreement, upon reflection, as to the *intrinsic* values that these many extrinsic values are meant to promote. Disagreement pertains primarily to (a) factual questions regarding the most effective ways to achieve the intrinsic values, and (b) ethical questions as to what conflict-resolution principles should be used to compare the importance of the intrinsic values in various contexts. If the pluralism of values is only a pluralism of extrinsic values, then it cannot be argued that values are "incommensurable" in the sense that there is no independent basis for a resolution of the conflict between them and for a judgment as to their validity, because the basis of the judgment of extrinsic values is their effectiveness in promoting intrinsic values. And people, regardless of culture, are capable of a kind of rational reflection that, within certain limits, can help to resolve conflicts between intrinsic values, the latter being very few in number. (See DePaul 1986 on ordinary people's use of 'reflective equilibrium'.)

Section 1 of this chapter will examine the consequences of the intrinsic–extrinsic value distinction for philosophies, that emphasize an 'incommensurable pluralism' of values. Section 2 will argue that "social traditions and practices," which include "community values" and "cultural values," are valued only *extrinsically*, but that the extrinsicness of such values is sometimes obscured by the *psychological* difficulty of relating the distinction to everyday valuational consciousness, which normally occurs at a less than fully reflective level.

1. Is the Value of Cultural Traditions Intrinsic or Extrinsic?

Ethical relativisms of all kinds—even the benign pluralisms of discourse ethics and communitarianism—lose much of their persuasive power when we remember, as Ralph Linton pointed out many years ago, that the values that are supposed to result from social conventions (or, in current jargon, "social practices, traditions, and institutions") are only extrinsic values, and that the intrinsic values that constitute the raison d'être of these various and sundry extrinsic values may well be the same or very similar for all cultures (and for all "practices," "traditions," and "institutions"). For example, the Hottentots do not put their parents to death in order mindlessly to follow some cultural tradition just for the sake of doing so, but rather, in their own words, *"as a means"* to relieve their "suffering and misery" (Duncker 1939, 40). Thus, even in the worst case scenario, there may be only a small handful of fundamental intrinsic values whose relative importances compete with each other, rather than the supposedly hundreds or even infinite numbers of possible conflicting values envisioned in radically pluralistic value theories.

The importance of this complex of issues in contemporary philosophy corresponds to the importance attributed to the supposed pluralism of values by communitarians, discourse ethicists, deconstructionists, emotivists, many multiculturalists, and people generally of late. Clarification of this problem is crucial for the contemporary debate about multiculturalism (see Kymlicka 1989, 1990; Lind 1995). 'Multiculturalism' can actually refer to at least two quite different positions: Its more modest version, as discussed by Kymlicka, holds that (1) the importance of cultural traditions ought to be recognized, promoted, and reflected in legal institutions, even when these traditions sometimes conflict with universalistic values such as equal rights, freedom, and maximization or equitable distribution of benefits or resources. The more radical version, discussed by Lind, posits that (2) a political entity is composed of cultural groups, and the values that determine political decisions (a) inevitably reflect the values defined by some or all of these intermingling "cultures," whose value beliefs are rationally incommensurable with each other and cannot be subsumed by a universal, rational set of value beliefs that would apply equally to all people; and/or (b) such a political entity ought to reflect the values of all the cultures of which the entity is composed.

Kymlicka shows effectively that multiculturalism in sense 1 is not a relativistic viewpoint at all, and does not assert or depend on an incommensurable pluralism of values, but instead is based on universalizable and rationally defensible (or in some cases defeasible) philosophical arguments. Similarly, thesis b of the *second* type of multiculturalism is based on philosophical reasoning that stands or falls independently of which specific cultural traditions are to be subsumed within such a claim for just representation. As for those multiculturalists in sense 2 who would endorse thesis a, my suggestion is that thesis a is simply false, because what it really amounts to is either a complete ethical relativism or a belief that, although there may be rationally arguable philosophical truths about what justice consists of, practical impediments such as conflicting interests and inflamed passions will always prevent people from incorporating such philosophical truths into collective decisionmaking. We should note, however, as Lind points out, that if these impediments prevent the implementation of rationally demonstrable truths regarding good and bad political policies, then these same impediments will *even more* drastically prevent the implementation of the multiculturalist value posited by thesis b above—that is, the multiculturalists' cherished ideal of representing the beliefs and interests of all cultural groups on some "equitable" basis. Lind argues that such multiculturalism is the perfect recipe for a "divide and conquer" strategy on the part of an elite power group hoping to prevent the less powerful from being able to reach enough consensus to curb that power through common political action. So the real point of contention between multiculturalists and others is not whether their proposals are more *practically feasible,* but rather whether they are more *philosophically appropriate*—in other words, whether it is possible for people from different cultural traditions to reach agreement on philosophical questions about justice in the *distribution* of the various things valued by various people (rights, opportunities, freedoms, and collective material resources that various people need or want for various reasons, such as transportation systems, social security, and educational resources). My contention is that rational conclusions can be reached on such questions of distributive justice, using modes of reasoning that in principle are accessible to all rational beings regardless of cultural background. The first step in grounding such a consensus is to understand why so many have assumed or argued that the values represented by different cultural traditions *cannot* be rationally commensurable, and to show that in fact they can be.

Since multiculturalist theses 1 and 2b are both amenable to rational and even liberal theories of justice, thesis 2a is at the heart of the real controversy over multiculturalism—that is, the debate over whether there is an incommensurable pluralism of intrinsic values.

As an example of the importance of such a pluralism in communitarian approaches (or at least some types of communitarianism[1]), consider Alasdair MacIntyre's (1981) view that "tradition" must form our "moral starting point" (205). As Roger Paden (1987) well summarizes MacIntyre on this point,

> Not only does tradition provide the moral standpoint from which various practices and possible lives can be criticized, but, MacIntyre claims, it also shapes our existence. It is through participation in our tradition that our lives gain content. . . . Tradition gives our lives meaning and purpose. . . . MacIntyre also wants to avoid the foundationalism of humanistic ethical theories. . . . Ethical

arguments will involve appeals to reasonable interpretations of our tradition. An action or project which cannot be justified on any reasonable interpretation of our tradition can be rejected as unethical. (Paden 1987, 135–36)

Similarly, as a particularly clear example of the relevance of this point to "discourse ethics," consider the recent work of Agnes Heller:

To each way of life must go its own distributive justice. What form of distribution is just or unjust is something that only members of each community—each way of life—are qualified to decide. . . . The plurality of such social ideals can be nothing but the happy anticipation of a pluralistic universe, where each culture is tied to every other by the bonds of symmetric reciprocity. (Heller 1987, 205, 234)

Heller explicitly rejects the notion that such values can be regarded as accomplishing anything beyond themselves:

Moral norms are related to values and not to problems or objectives. They cannot be established (or seen) as *means* to achieve something. . . . The maxim "keep your human dignity" is, for example, not valid (and can never be rationally validated) with respect to a problem it "solves" or a non-evaluated objective it achieves. . . . I have made a case for a pluralistic moral universe, one in which different sets of moral norms and rules coexist, and in which people are free to choose one or another of these sets. (Heller 1987, 244, 294)

As for the pluralism of values in poststructuralist thought, Foucault seems to be a straightforward case in point. In the first place, Foucault delights in relativizing not just moral truth, but all truth. As Dreyfus and Rabinow (1983) summarize, "Foucault holds that what counts as truth is determined by the conceptual system or, more accurately, the discursive practices of a particular discipline" (31), whereas these discursive practices themselves are determined historically in terms of power relations and conspiracies of domination. In the second place, by emphasizing "the genealogy of the modern individual as subject," Foucault deprives moral philosophy of the possibility of a firm reference point in relation to which things could be said to be valuable or not valuable. Nothing can be valuable for man per se—merely valued by men "as produced" in utterly different ways at different times and places (Foucault 1980).

If possible, Richard Rorty is still more relativistic. Rorty's version of pragmatism does not think

> that there is anything isolable as "the purpose which we construct vocabularies and cultures to fulfill" against which to test vocabularies and cultures. But . . . in the process of playing vocabularies and cultures off against each other, we produce new and better ways of talking and acting—not better by reference to a previously known standard, but just better in the sense that they come to *seem* clearly better than their predecessors. (Rorty 1979, xxxvii)

It is sufficient to mention briefly, however, that there is no need to step outside the mainstream of analytic philosophy to find instances of relativism. Recent examples are David Wong (1984) and Philippa Foot (1978). As for the increasing relativism in the thinking of nonacademic philosophers, Allan Bloom seems to have made a solid case in *The Closing of the American Mind* (1987) that there has been such an increase, whether one agrees with his other points or not.

Obviously, much of the wind would leave the sails of these relativistic viewpoints if it were granted that, in fact, there is not a pluralism of values, where by values we mean *intrinsic* values; and, therefore, that value systems, once they become reflective, are not "incommensurable" with each other.

Emphasizing the intrinsic–extrinsic value distinction in relation to social traditions and practices has three important consequences for contemporary philosophy. First, it provides a non-culturally relative foundation from which to compare the adequacy of different traditions and practices. The traditions and practices themselves may have only extrinsic value (though a very important type of extrinsic value), because they may serve only to facilitate such basic intrinsic values as a sense of well-being, security, or meaningful existence. The nonrelative foundation for comparison and criticism would then be that some traditions and practices are more effective than others at giving people (given their historical and personal situations) a sense of meaningful existence. As G. J. Warnock points out, such a sense of meaningful existence need not necessarily be conceived in utilitarian terms in order to be conceived essentially as an intrinsic value.

There are ways for people to be and to feel . . . circumstances for them to be in, which—because of what people are and what their situation is—are good. Not morally good, just good; better than . . . alternative predicaments which people might quite easily be in. . . . I would submit, then, that what is good in the moral virtues . . . is that their cultivation and exercise to a rather large extent actually does—and to a far greater extent would, if their cultivation and exercise were more effective and general—tend to promote [these situations]. (Warnock 1980, 86)

The second important consequence would then follow from the first: If it could be shown that the traditions and practices have only extrinsic value, then it would be possible to provide good reasons to reject or change a certain tradition or practice if it does not accomplish its purpose as well as some other seriously-thought-out-but-as-yet-only-dreamt-of organization of society might accomplish that same purpose. Sweeping social changes thus sometimes become not only justifiable from a vantagepoint outside the value assumptions of the tradition to be changed, but also overwhelmingly desirable.

The third important consequence is that the "anti-humanist" strain in pluralistic theories would lose its foundation. If it can be shown (as I propose to show here) that traditions and practices are meant to promote more basic goods (such as happiness, social stability, a sense that life has meaning, etc.), then it will no longer be convincing to argue that the value of practices within traditions must be understood at the social or cultural level rather than at the level of the individual subject of experience, since practices and traditions at the social and cultural level in this case have only extrinsic value, and this value is contingent on the purposes they serve for individual subjects. The importance of this point is stressed by G. B. Madison in criticizing the trend in hermeneutic philosophy toward substituting "traditions" in place of individual subjects:

While, in order to counteract [epistemological] subjectivism, it is necessary to maintain that the Tradition, Being, or What-not has *ontological primacy* and that "in the last analysis" it is this which "expresses itself" or "comes to expression" in the understanding of the individual, it is nevertheless necessary to recognize that it is the subjectivity of the interpreter himself which has *methodological primacy*. This is necessary because only the individual, human, conscious, reflecting subject can be held *responsible* for what she says or does. . . . To be responsible means to be able to respond, i.e., to be able to make an attempt at defending or justifying one's own words and deeds, which is to say, at providing arguments for them. (Madison 1990, 27)

In fairness to the radical pluralists, however, we must recognize that a pluralism of extrinsic values has some important consequences, even if the intrinsic values that these extrinsic values are meant to promote are essentially shared by people generally. These differing extrinsic values arise from differences of factual belief, historical and personal situation, and personality constitution. Such a pluralism of extrinsic values may have some of the same social and political implications as a pluralism of intrinsic values would have. It is very difficult for anyone other then the individual involved (and it is often difficult even for that individual) to understand exactly which intrinsic values are served by the extrinsic values to which she is committed, or to explain why the intrinsic value in question is best served, under the circumstances, by just this particular extrinsic value and no other. For example, a visual artist will have difficulty understanding why she values visual art, and why the purposes served by it could not be served equally well by music or football. Thus it would be very dangerous for any society to set up some ethical decision principle as a formula by which various extrinsic values should be encouraged or discouraged.

However, the consequences of this point can be accounted for within the traditional "liberal" theories of justice, such as those of Rawls and Dworkin, which insist that the decision as to which "goods" to pursue (i.e., which extrinsic values to value) can be left up to individuals, and that government can be concerned primarily with maximizing opportunities for people to achieve those ends and with distributing the opportunities as fairly as possible (see Ellis 1991). The reason for this point is that two intrinsic values that people generally, upon reflection, accept as extremely important ones, and that at the same time do not conflict per se with the variety of tenable extrinsic values interpreted as such, are (a) maximizing the general welfare (i.e., opportunities for people to realize whatever they value) and (b) distributive justice (i.e., distributing these opportunities fairly).[2] Liberals and other traditional philosophers do, of course, face serious problems in dealing with such issues as how the community is to constitute itself as a community and to what extent undesirable personality characteristics (such as widespread criminal attitudes, overly selfish value systems, etc.) *result* from the practices and traditions of the community.[3] However, these problems can be addressed without abandoning the basic idea that there are objectively true and universally binding principles of justice that should govern collective action, and that the truth of these principles in no way depends on cultural traditions and practices, nor on any discursive resolution of a supposedly incommensurable plurality of values. The reason is that the principles of justice require for their epistemological justification only a knowledge of *intrinsic* values, and, as I shall try to show, an 'incommensurable pluralism' becomes much less plausible as soon as we realize that the values at issue in this pluralism are extrinsic ones and then trace them to their corresponding intrinsic ones.

Although it is beyond the scope of this early chapter to prove systematically that there are objectively groundable intrinsic values that are subject to universal agreement through reason (whereas disagreement pertains only to extrinsic values and to minor discrepancies with regard to conflict-resolution principles), it is necessary, in order to establish my essential thesis, to show that there are at least *rational procedures* that everyone agrees are proper ways to resolve such disputes and to ground such intrinsic values. If everyone agrees that there are rational methods toward this end, then values are not "incommensurable." To take a very simple example, suppose a government must decide whether to feed its people fish or chicken. And suppose there are different preferences within the population, derived from differences in cultural heritage. Those from the South, for example, prefer chicken, whereas those who grew up in the North prefer fish. The "incommensurable pluralist" viewpoint, as we have been defining it, might lead us to believe that there is no rational way to resolve this disagreement, since there is no objective way to determine whose cultural tradition is the "correct" one. Such a relativism might be tenable *if* the value that the two groups attributed to fish or chicken were *intrinsic*. But no one would seriously hold that whether one eats fish or chicken is an issue whose resolution would entail an intrinsic value to be associated with one or the other type of food. Everyone knows that fish and chicken are valued because they promote certain values beyond themselves. They contribute to the values of survival, pleasure, happiness, and also to the sense of the "fullness" and "meaningfulness" of life, in some sense, which people experience when they are able to participate in cultural traditions by eating traditional foods.

Because fish and chicken are extrinsic rather than intrinsic values, it is possible to resolve the conflict between them through reference to the intrinsic values they are supposed to facilitate. Suppose that the intrinsic values of survival, pleasure, happiness, and sense-of-fullness-and-meaningfulness-of-life are served exactly as well by fish for the Northerners as they are by chicken for the Southerners. For brevity's sake, we can summarize by saying simply that the 'well-being' of the Southerners is served as well by the chicken as the well-being of the Northerners is served by the fish. The conflict can then be framed as follows: How should the government decide whose well-being to serve and under what circumstances and in what proportion? When the question is posed in these terms, the rational methods people will use to resolve it (provided that they are honest with themselves in asking what is really right, as opposed to what is best for them individually) do not depend on whether one is a Northerner or a Southerner. On the contrary, each person will be able to see that the well-being of each other person has prima facie, intrinsic value, and each will be able to see that fairness in the distribution of well-being among people also has prima facie, intrinsic value. Each will then ask herself, first of all, how the fairest possible distribution system can be determined and, second, how the value of *maximizing* the well-being of people is to be balanced against the value of *distributing* this well-being fairly. Although there may never be perfect agreement on these intrinsic-value questions, there is agreement within certain limits.

For example, no one would say that, given 100 people and 100 pieces of fish, the fairest way to distribute the fish, prima facie, is to give it all to one person. Everyone can agree, with a certain margin for error, that the principle of diminishing marginal utility entails that the more goods one has, the less difference it makes whether one acquires additional goods (broadly speaking and all else being equal), and, therefore, that value tends to be optimized (again, all else being equal) if goods are distributed to those for whom they are most needed, thus increasing their use value without adding to or subtracting from the total amount of exchange value in existence. Rawls's original position argument is merely an elaboration of this simple, commonsense principle—which accounts for the widespread intuitive appeal of Rawls's theory. Now, of course, there will be minor disagreements—pertaining, for example, to whether the person in the original position will have a "thick" or "thin" conception of the good, or to which decision principle the person in the original position would choose, or to how ignorant this person should be assumed to be with regard to his own psychology. But there is still a fairly narrow range of choices within which everyone would agree the person in the original position would end up. No one would say that the person in the original position would choose a decision principle that would lead him to risk, say, $1,000 for an equal chance of winning $100; or that the veil of ignorance should be defined so liberally that the person in the original position is allowed to know that he is a drooling child molester and therefore would oppose any laws against child molesting. There is a range of options within which rational people may still disagree, but outside of which no rational person would stray. Certainly, whether the person would stray outside this range of options has nothing to do with whether he is a Northerner or a Southerner. Thus the original value dispute—whether the government should feed people fish or chicken— is not an "incommensurable" one; the methods used to determine what should be done have nothing to do with whether one initially preferred fish or chicken, but rather are ones that, within certain limits, are rationally definable. That rational methods can never allow a quantita- tively exact solution to questions of justice or beneficence, or the correct balance between the two, no more shows that intrinsic values are incommensurable, than the fact that physical measurements can never be absolutely exact shows that opinions as to the length of an object are incommensurable.

But if a rational commensurability of values *can* be established, then we should be able to move in the general type of direction sug- gested by Dworkin on this issue: Although there is a plurality of differ- ent values, and although there are different theories about what it means for the opportunities or for different people's realizing what they value to be distributed equitably, still, the basic point of agreement among all political viewpoints is that these means and opportunities for people's realizing whatever they value ought to be distributed in a fair or equitable way, and the question that all competing viewpoints are trying to answer is the question as to *what* the fairest or most equitable distribution consists of. Even though the things to be distrib- uted may include rights protections, or the material conditions to exer- cise rights, or autonomous moral agency, or the opportunity to actualize one's potential as a conscious being or moral agent, and are not limited to mere material resources or to "happiness" and "preference satisfac- tion"—still, the fundamental question at stake is how the various goods, granted people's different views of the good, are to be distributed among them (Dworkin 1986, 296-301; 1987, 7–8). Kymlicka picks up on this point: "If each theory shares the same 'egalitarian plateau'— that is, if each theory is attempting to define the social, economic, and political conditions under which the members of the community are treated as equals—then we might be able to show that one of the theories does a better job living up to the standard that they all recognize" (Kymlicka 1990, 5).

Again, I do not pretend to have established in this brief discussion the ultimate truth with regard to universally valid intrinsic values, nor do I mean to suggest that the procedures for resolving such issues are easy, simple, or absolutely exact. The remainder of this book will attempt to show compelling reasons why there are limits to the amount of distributive inequality that any rational person could have reason to accept. What I have shown at this point is only that *if* the divergent values which vary and conflict because of their relativity to cultural tradition, individual emotional differences, etc., are merely *extrinsic* values (as the next section will try to establish), *then* such conflicts can be resolved in ways that are not relative to these cultural traditions, individual emotional differences, etc., by being traced to their corresponding intrinsic values, which tend to be accessible to rational discourse between the conflicting groups and frequently are found to be already shared by both groups. The reason for this is essentially that a great diversity of cultural values, once analyzed, turn out to promote identical or very similar ends. It is just that, under different circumstances and for different people, different extrinsic values must be chosen in order to promote similar intrinsic values. The following section will attempt to develop and justify this last point.

2. The Psychological Difficulty of Introspectively Distinguishing Intrinsic from Extrinsic Values

We can see from the above discussion that the really determinative question to answer in resolving the 'pluralism of values' issue is how the intrinsic–extrinsic value distinction is psychologically relevant to the valuational consciousness of people in the course of their lives. If ordinary people do not normally make the distinction, then they may indeed be committed to an incommensurable pluralism of values. The pluralism would be incommensurable in this case, because any philosophical attempt to convince people that the various apparently conflicting values can be reduced to a few intrinsic values could very well fail. It is not necessary, of course, that people be aware in a formal way of the intrinsic values on which their extrinsic values depend—only that, upon reflection (if they were to reflect), they *would* agree that, if value *A* would no longer be valued unless expected to promote value *B*, then *A* is valued extrinsically because and only because *B* is valued intrinsically. But this is precisely where it becomes difficult to determine just what people *would* say upon reflection. The difficulty of applying the intrinsic–extrinsic distinction to the supposed pluralism of values thus stems from the difficulty that people ordinarily have in relating the distinction to their own experience of their own values. That is what we must now consider.

Although I mentioned at the outset that nonphilosophers are not usually *formally* aware of the intrinsic–extrinsic value distinction, they do often seem to make informal use of it. Indeed, for many people, these instances probably rank among their most thoughtful moral moments. Consider, for example, the thinking that a good part of the draftable-age generation did concerning the Vietnam War. The following thought pattern might be typical: "I had always believed that loyalty to my country was an important value. But now I see that there are contravening considerations against this value. First, I also value staying alive. Perhaps more morally significant, there are good reasons for considering the war both imprudent and morally wrong. Aha! Now I see that what I really feel is that loyalty to one's country is a valuable thing if the course upon which the country is embarked is the right one, or if there are other reasons or justifications for the value of the loyalty (for example, it may produce better consequences on the whole if people are loyal, even in some cases in which the country's course of action is slightly wrong-headed). But when the consequences of loyalty are grotesquely evil, then not only does that loyalty lack positive value, but it has negative value. I therefore understand now that loyalty has positive value only to the extent that it tends to accomplish some worthwhile purpose, and negative value to the extent that it tends to accomplish an evil purpose. Thus its value is contingent on the value it promotes, whereas I had earlier thought and behaved as if it were valuable for its own sake." In technical terms, it has only extrinsic value.

MacIntyre, of course, would be quick to object here that, to the extent that some young man undergoes such a thought process, he is not merely clarifying to himself what he *already* believed but in fact is *changing* it. In fact, he is well on his way toward stepping hopelessly outside of the tradition that previously had given his life meaning, and into an empty functional rationalism whose values ultimately feed into a misguided utilitarianism. MacIntyre would further point out that this young man forgets or fails to understand that traditions are not only valuable because they accomplish specific purposes but also, and more importantly, because life without a tradition would be meaningless.

It is true, of course, that as Eugene Gendlin (1962, 1981, 1992) has effectively argued, when we focus on our emotional life, it does change as a result of the focusing. But this does not mean that the old feeling was more "authentic" than the new one. The new feeling may be a truer interpretation of how I "really" feel than the old interpretation was. All else being equal (i.e., if the process of reflection is not usurped by outside forces such as propaganda specialists), and if the reflection is done in an honest way, the change tends to be toward a truer interpretation rather than a less true one. Suppose, for example, that I am furious with my son because he forgot to take out the garbage. After a moment's honest reflection, I realize that I was not really furious with my son at all but merely frustrated with the day I had at work, which I took too seriously because I had mistakenly invested too much of the meaning of life in the performance of my students, etc. It is the nature of reflection—especially reflection on the emotional life—that the reflective process, if done in an honest way, makes more clear what was previously vague and confused and thus brings us closer to the truth about the contents of our own consciousness. Many elements that previously were implicit now become explicit (Ellis 1986). The same thing generally happens when we begin with a confused notion and use a reflective process to clarify it, or as Gendlin puts it (borrowing a term from Merleau-Ponty), to "explicate" it. The same thing happened to Meno's slave boy when Socrates put the appropriate questions to him.

Foucault would object at this point that the reflective process is always usurped, in a sense, by propaganda specialists—that is, by the "conspiratorless conspiracy of domination." But concrete examples such as the one just described show that, in many instances, there is a way that I really feel, as opposed to an inauthentic misinterpretation of the feeling. Even if Foucault is correct in assuming that the way I feel is determined by my cultural milieu or a conspiracy of domination, this would not imply that I do not really feel the way I feel—only that the way I feel has been predetermined by the combination of factors that caused me to be the kind of person I am (see Ellis 1987a, 1992). It is possible to know how I feel even if the way I feel has been predetermined. Thus it is not the reflective process that is necessarily usurped by the conspiracy of domination, but rather the process of producing subjects who (really) feel one way instead of another. But that is a different issue.

Of course, MacIntyre could still insist that the young draft evader may be deceiving himself into thinking that his earlier valuing of loyalty was merely extrinsic in nature, whereas in reality he only lacks the courage of his commitments or bends to peer pressure. It is true that there is always the possibility of self-deception. However, as I have argued in more detail elsewhere (1986), the probability of self-deception is usually greater, at least for most mature adults, with unconsidered and unreflective beliefs and feelings than with considered and reflective ones. An adult has learned through experience to watch for the earmarks of self-deception in herself (such as, for example, a tendency to multiply ad hoc hypotheses or irrelevant objections in order to hide self-contradictory implications) and makes this watchfulness a natural part of the ground rules for any reflection (DePaul 1986; Ellis 1986). The reason it is possible to learn to recognize these earmarks is that there were times in our youth when some strong motivation to deceive ourselves eventually dropped away simply because of extraneous circumstances. For example, a teenage trackman fancies that he may someday become a world-class runner. Later, having quit the track team, he can freely admit to himself the objective truth (based on consistent running times)—that he was only a mediocre runner—since he now no longer has the need to believe that he can become a great runner. At this point, he can also cheerfully admit that the former belief was a self-deception, though perhaps not a harmful one. After many such experiences of admitting that we have deceived ourselves on earlier occasions (which we are better able to do after the motivation for the self-deception has disappeared), we learn to recognize the kinds of situations in which we are prone to self-deception, even when the motivation to self-deception *is* present.

The changed interpretation of a feeling that results from reflection cannot be explained simply as the movement from one emotion to another; it often involves the movement from a confused and vague emotion to one that is at least likely to be somewhat less confused and vague. The important point for our purposes here is that we cannot simply assume, when the draft evader changes his interpretation of a value belief (realizing that he values loyalty extrinsically rather than intrinsically), that this change constitutes a rejection of what he genuinely valued; it often constitutes a clarification of it.

MacIntyre is right to point out that the virtues practiced within social traditions give our lives meaning. But the feeling that life has meaning is for this very reason the *intrinsic* value at stake in these traditions; the practices themselves are merely extrinsic values whose purpose is to give people a sense that life has meaning. Some may insist on phenomenological grounds that, when I value an objective state of affairs in the world (such as "the glory of my country"), this is not the same thing as valuing my *consciousness of* that state of affairs. Thus the intrinsic value at stake is external to my consciousness, not internal to it (Ellis 1982). Suppose we were to grant this point. It would still remain true that, if the criterion for the extrinsicness of a value is that it would not be valued if it did not promote some further value, then, clearly, to say that the value of the practices that take place within traditions is that these practices give life meaning is to say that such practices and traditions have extrinsic value only if, and to the extent to which, they are the most effective way to give life meaning under the circumstances. Therefore, other practices or traditions might serve the same purpose equally well. Practices and traditions thus have only extrinsic value, although it is difficult to describe the intrinsic value they promote because it is difficult to say what it is for life to have meaning.

As Kymlicka points out, people do not mindlessly take over value beliefs from their culture; they form them through reflection, thought, experience, and deliberation, using cultural traditions as a starting point. What the cultural traditions provide in this context is a set of options that people can use to fuel this thought process. Thus there are good reasons for even a liberal state to protect and enhance the conditions needed for cultural traditions to thrive, except where the traditions themselves depend on an unjust exploitation (for example, if a traditional culture's male supremacy depends on the illegitimate exploitation of women, which would not have been consented to under conditions of real choice). With this qualification, Kymlicka points out, the protection and enhancement of traditional cultures should have a certain priority, even in a society based on universal notions of distributive justice, rights, and autonomy. Without a tradition to start from, people would be at a loss to develop their convictions through rational reflection. But this does not mean that people do not change their thinking on value issues as they reflect. Reflection shows that the value of cultural traditions is contingent on their ability to provide a sense that human existence has meaning; this, then, is the main intrinsic value served by cultural traditions (given that in contemporary settings they are not necessarily the best means to promote survival, economic well-being, individual rights, just distribution, etc.).

We have seen that the primary reason for the difficulty of applying the intrinsic–extrinsic value distinction to the 'pluralism of values' issue hinges on the extreme subtlety of the psychological questions surrounding the way people distinguish, in their everyday lives, between intrinsic and extrinsic value feelings. It is perhaps no coincidence that many of those who posit an incommensurable pluralism of values have been influenced by behavioristic or strongly operationalized approaches to the social sciences.[4] The intrinsic–extrinsic value distinction is difficult to observe and measure within a behavioristic or strongly operationalized approach, especially in the field of psychology. If a behaviorist observes that a person is willing to die for his country, this behavior might be described as loyalty and the inference made that the person values loyalty in some sense. But whether the person attributes intrinsic or extrinsic value to the loyalty would be exceedingly difficult to infer from objectively observable behaviors. To really understand which values are intrinsic and which are extrinsic requires a more comprehensive kind of psychology that is willing to consider introspective processes (for example, by taking account of phenomenological data; see Ellis 1986) and that can hope to have access to the delicate nuances of subjective feelings. At the least, we must make inferences to determine how people *would* interpret the structural interdependencies of their value beliefs (with the extrinsic ones depending on the intrinsic ones) *if* they were to become more reflective about these structures than people often are (especially when emotionally aroused, as is typical with controversial issues).

The way we know which values are intrinsic and which are extrinsic is by asking ourselves certain kinds of questions about our value feelings. The essential question we must put to ourselves is: What purpose does the value in question accomplish, and would it still have value if it failed to accomplish its purpose or even defeated the purpose? This question is experienced phenomenologically as being different from the question as to whether the value under consideration is a merely prima facie value, whose value might at times be superseded by other prima facie values. The value of the extrinsic value is completely *dependent* on some other value, though that other value may be difficult to describe or pinpoint.

At a certain stage in the reflective process, one might be tempted to think that participating in certain social practices, such as writing music, has no purpose beyond itself and, therefore, that such activities cannot be interpreted as having merely extrinsic value. But if I ask myself, "*Why* do I write music?" I can give a more concrete answer than simply that "I find the activity meaningful." Sometimes the activity is *not* meaningful. For example, I may find that it is not meaningful when I remain "stuck" or "blocked" in my attempt to break through to a new, deeper level of emotional, intellectual, and/or aesthetic consciousness than I would have experienced had I never written (or appreciated as a listener) any music. In these cases, the composition is considered a failure, and the experience has negative rather than positive value—not because I fail to win the rewards granted by the institution of music to outstanding composers, but because I have failed to achieve the purpose that was my reason to become (or remain) a composer and to participate in the musical tradition in the first place. This purpose can be characterized, though in a very rough and approximate way, as some sort of emotional, intellectual, and artistic experience that is valued and *for the sake* of which I value the practice of writing music. Thus the practice, the tradition, and the institutions that facilitate the practice all have merely *extrinsic* value. It is highly conceivable, in fact, that the purpose of the practice—that is, the particular kind of experience of meaningfulness that it facilitates—could have been approximately and for the most part accomplished in other ways had I cultivated the necessary abilities; for example, I could have used poetry or visual art for the same purpose, in which case I would not need to write music. A similar argument could be constructed with respect to the value of *listening* to music. Thus, although a person who is greatly immersed in the appreciation of music may intellectually acknowledge the value of, say, visual art, he will not *need* to avail himself of visual art experiences in the same intense way that he needs to avail himself of musical experiences, since he has now learned to use the musical experiences for the same emotional purposes for which (he realizes intellectually) he *could* have used visual art if music had not seemed more accessible for one reason or another. It is thus easy to see that the practice of creating or consuming any given art form—granted that each is unique and not precisely replaceable—has extrinsic value whose purpose is some experiential event, though perhaps a more complex and less "end-state"-oriented one than many utilitarians and functional rationalists would admit. Because the kind of experiencing process facilitated by artistic expression is much more complex than the somewhat static notions of 'happiness' and 'pleasure', one can say that poetry is better than push-pin, even if the amounts of pleasure involved are equal, without thereby elevating poetry to the status of an intrinsic value.

Let us return now to the psychological difficulties people often have in trying to distinguish between intrinsic and extrinsic values in their own valuational consciousness. People often try to mask this difficulty by pretending that "cultural" or "community" values are intrinsic rather than extrinsic. I have argued on the contrary that patterns of social behavior are normally valued not for their own sake but because it is believed that a particular pattern of behavior leads to the accomplishment of some value or values beyond the existence of the pattern itself. This thesis is consistent with the fact that, in many cases, if we ask a member of a group committed to a certain behavior pattern why she is committed to that pattern, the response may be expressed as a claim that the pattern in question promotes some value of a more general nature. The above-quoted response of the Hottentots that the purpose of putting their parents to death is "as a means" to relieve their "suffering" and "misery" is a straightforward admission that the value of the practice is merely extrinsic.

However, in some cases, the champion of a particular cultural practice might be hard put to provide any justification for the practice other than something to the effect that "It's just our tradition, and we value our traditions." This inability to justify a value, however, can hardly suffice to establish that the practice is valued intrinsically rather than extrinsically. It may instead result from the questioned person's inability to sort out and articulate the structure of his value system. Segregationists of the southern United States seem to have fallen (or in some cases still do fall) within this category. The Civil Rights Movement, by emphasizing the self-contradictoriness of the total value systems of such people, prompted many of them to realize that the value of segregation was only extrinsic and would have to be abandoned and replaced by other traditions and practices if more important intrinsic values were to be promoted. To realize that this was essentially the structure of a reflective process that actually occurred, it is only necessary to talk to a few former segregationists.

One common reason for valuing a tradition without being able to specify reasons for that valuation has been well pointed out by Whitehead (1967). People tend to feel threatened by social change per se (not just particular kinds of social change), because any change may lead to drastically unforeseen consequences. Thus, if the unforeseen consequences are bad, the very survival or minimal well-being of the people in the group may be endangered. And it would be foolish to risk perishing—even though that risk may be small—in order to introduce a change whose benefits are minimal, when the traditional way of doing things has been proven to be at least conducive to survival and a minimal amount of well-being. The more traditional the society, the more prominent this fear of change is. Thus in completely traditional societies—those whose main strategy for survival is to do things in just the way they have always been done—people resist even slight changes in the design of a simple tool.

Cultures cease being completely traditional and become historical to the extent that knowledge of their own history and observation of the histories of other cultures teaches them that social change is not necessarily a threat to survival. Quite the contrary, an extremely stubborn resistance to social change in the face of changing circumstances (for example, changing technology, changing environment, or changes in intercultural relationships) may then become a real threat to survival. In such societies, *questioning* the wisdom of earlier generations becomes as firmly entrenched a "tradition" as the veneration of them.

Psychologically, then, the unquestioned commitment of traditional peoples to their traditions is often an extrinsic value of a negative kind. It is not so much that people think that the tradition is likely to accomplish a specific desirable purpose as that they are afraid that if the tradition is abandoned something bad might happen. And in this case, what counts as "bad" will usually be definable in terms that are separable from the specific tradition in question—for example, that people will find themselves unable to attain survival, pleasure, meaningful existence, or the actualization and exercise of their potential as fully conscious, fully functional human beings. Notice that the values just mentioned are widely shared as intrinsic values by people generally and are not linked to any particular culture or tradition.

I mentioned above that historical societies cannot rely on the traditional method of ensuring at least a minimal amount of intrinsic value—that is, cannot simply do things exactly as they have always been done in that culture so as to always enjoy the security of the tried-and-true. One reason for this distinguishing feature of historical societies is that they are characterized by changing circumstances. Indeed, they become historical largely *because* of changing circumstances. And the preservation of intrinsic values in changing circumstances requires that extrinsic values be correspondingly changed. But this continual readaptation of extrinsic values requires that people become reflective in their moral consciousness. It requires that they distinguish between extrinsic and intrinsic values and then create ways to change the extrinsic ones in order to preserve the intrinsic ones. As we have seen, among the extrinsic values that must be changed in the process are the practices and traditions that in the past have characterized a culture or society. Also, we should not fail to notice that, if such a reflective examination and continual change of practices and traditions was necessary for "modern" societies because of the ever-changing circumstances of modern times, then the same thing becomes even more necessary in "postmodern" times, in which circumstances are ever more rapidly changing.

MacIntyre is correct in pointing out that positive intrinsic values are frequently facilitated by having cultural traditions of some sort (even if they must be ever-more-rapidly changing ones) as opposed to not having any traditions. Having cultural traditions often does something for people in the absence of which their lives would be comparatively empty or would lack as much of a sense of meaningful existence. But as soon as this is stated, it becomes inescapable that the traditions in question are extrinsic values whose purpose is to realize an intrinsic value; people's having a sense of meaningful existence. It would then follow that if some *other* practice or tradition than the one in question were to achieve the same purpose, it would be valued just as much. It would even follow that if something altogether different from a cultural tradition were to achieve this purpose, it would become just as fruitful a strategy as the tradition in question; in this case, it would be a matter of both moral and psychological indifference whether people chose the tradition or the alternative method of achieving the same intrinsic value, except that the threat of insecurity or instability associated with social upheaval gives us some reason to fear too-rapid or poorly-thought-out social changes. Thus changing circumstances require that different "practices and traditions" replace the old ones.

Once this basic point is admitted, it would be illogical for any member of any culture to deny that the value of cultural traditions consists only of extrinsic value, though a very important kind of extrinsic value. But if the person *would upon reflection* admit that the value of something is only an extrinsic value, then, by the definition of extrinsic value, he values the thing in question only extrinsically. Thus the apparent plurality of culture-specific or tradition-specific values turns out to be only a plurality of extrinsic values whose purpose is to realize certain intrinsic values that are not culture-specific or tradition-specific but that are common to people generally. And the values in question are therefore humanistically grounded, in the sense that they are valued for what they accomplish at the level of social traditions and practices, which have only extrinsic value. Nor, therefore, is the pluralism of extrinsic values "incommensurable."

It is true that people with different cultural traditions will tend to value somewhat different things. But this fact in itself does not mean that disagreements over the question as to how the various things that various people value should be equitably *distributed* are incommensurable disagreements. Such disagreements would become incommensurable only if opinions with regard to the most equitable distribution depended, in turn, on whether or not someone values the specific things that are to be distributed. And this could be the case only if principles of just distribution were merely arbitrary and culturally relative presuppositions.

It is also true that liberal notions of universal rights are sometimes in prima facie conflict with the requirements for preserving cultural values and traditions. For example, if a subculture is strongly committed to a patriarchal tradition in which the eldest male owns all property in a family, this tradition will conflict prima facie with the idea of sexual equality implied by universal rights. But, as Kymlicka points out, cultural traditions involving sexual oppression have maintained themselves only because the oppressed were denied a real voice. In this case, the cultural tradition is genuinely valuable not to all members of the cultural group but only to the dominant members. This point is well illustrated by the quickness of women in sexually oppressive Muslim countries (and in Christian ones within the past century) to try to throw off their shackles once the opportunity seems to present itself. They may appear compliant when there is no viable alternative, but the increasing demand of such oppressed subgroups for fair treatment suggests that they would have chosen fair treatment earlier if given a viable choice. The more basic problem here is that cultural relativists speak as though all members of a given "culture" or "community" share the same interests and values, when in fact crucial questions of intracultural conflict are being swept under the rug.

There are, of course, plenty of cultural practices and traditions that do *not* fundamentally conflict with a universalistic assessment of equitable distribution of values. In those cases, the cultural practices and traditions become valuable things to be maximized and equitably distributed in some appropriate balance. And as Kymlicka argues, there may well be rational reasons for treating some such cultural values as enjoying a certain amount of priority over other prima facie values, especially in cases in which special benefits or considerations to a cultural subgroup would be required to compensate for an initially disadvantaged bargaining position. For example, many liberals in the United States argue for a racial quota system in affirmative action policies, as opposed to "color-blind" policies (which in a formal sense would seem more egalitarian), because blacks have already been discriminated against in their access to the educational and other prerequisites to acquiring the "qualifications" for a given position (such as letters of recommendation from influential people and degrees from expensive universities or prep schools). Other liberals argue that discrimination would proceed in subtle ways without quotas, or that "color-blindness" cannot efficiently be monitored in the absence of quotas, or that quotas are a temporary means to eventually elevate the oppressed minority's access to material and social conditions needed to compete on a fair playing field. Regardless of whether these arguments are valid, the point is that they are all *liberal* arguments (not communitarian and certainly not relativistic ones) in favor of according special treatment to a cultural group. The mere existence of such arguments shows that the prima facie value of universalistic rights and privileges is not incommensurable with culturally specific claims to special treatment. Disagreements over such issues, thus, are not incommensurable standoffs in which the only grounds for taking a given position would be arbitrary and culturally relative.

NOTES

1. There is, of course, a type of "communitarian" perspective, represented by neo-Marxists of the 1960s and '70s, followers of the "Frankfurt school," such Muslim social thinkers as ibn Khaldun and extreme determinists as J. J. C. Smart, who would not argue for an incommensurable pluralism or emphasize cultural norms as a reference point for defining values. These less relativized kinds of theories are "communitarian" in that they emphasize that the community produces its individuals and/or should take responsibility to produce individuals well—to produce virtuous individuals. Those communitarians who do define values relative to community norms are predominantly more recent and would seem to include MacIntyre (1981) and Sandel (1982),

although later Sandel (1984) seems to reject a complete relativization of moral truth to community norms.

2. The traditional principle of diminishing marginal utility in economics shows that, all else being equal, it would maximize the amount of value that there is if we distribute "goods" as evenly as possible among people, since a given amount of exchange value has greater use value when used to obtain more necessary goods (i.e., those that contribute more importantly to the well-being of their users). At the same time, of course, no one would want distribution to be completely equal, because it is necessary that people have incentives to be productive, and, therefore, that there will be something to distribute. But it is possible through rational reflection to find a good balance between these two demands, though perhaps not in a very precise way. The relevant point for our purposes is that anyone can see that distributive fairness has prima facie value, and the "goods" to be distributed by this fairness principle may be as diverse as one wishes. (See Pareto 1971; Jaffe 1972; Kohler 1979.)

3. Problems pertaining to the community's roles in producing its individuals are discussed in Ellis (1989, 1987b). See also Sandel (1984) and Gutman (1986).

4. Rorty is particularly a case in point, having wanted in his earlier work on the mind–body problem to eliminate all talk of "consciousness" altogether. Such anthropologists as Westermarck and Sumner are also products of a strongly operationalized approach to social research. And of course the great-grand-father of emotivism, A. J. Ayer, advocated strict behaviorism in the social sciences.

3

Crucial Problems with Utilitarian Decision Principles

Although apparently divergent value systems may be commensurable in that the various extrinsic values they contain are meant to promote similar intrinsic values, methods of verifying and prioritizing the intrinsic values themselves remain controversial. In the hope of establishing consensus for collective action, many empirically minded policy analysts are attracted to utility-maximizing approaches such as cost–benefit analysis, because the ultimate value assumption of utilitarianism—that human happiness (or "want-satisfaction") has intrinsic value—is *empirically verifiable*. It is an empirical fact that people value happiness, and there are even tangible ways to *measure* this value, even if only approximately and indirectly (for example, see Sinden and Worrell 1979; Kniesner and Leeth 1995; Viscusi 1983, 1993; Zeckhauser 1975; Kneese and Schultze 1975). But the more we examine the philosophical basis of a purely utilitarian value system, the more obviously we see that it involves assumptions that are not empirical at all and that, furthermore, are quite questionable.

Ethics textbooks used to be able to say without oversimplification that utilitarianism was a philosophy of nonegoistic hedonism that championed the ideal of the "greatest happiness of the greatest number" and regarded an act as right if it tended toward this goal, wrong if it did not (for example, Frankena 1963; Sahakian 1974). This straightforward characterization might have been true of the earliest utilitarians—Smith, Bentham, Mill, and Sidgwick (although recent scholars deny that even these early versions of utilitarianism were so simplistic as all that—for example, see Hearn 1971). However, partly in response to various criticisms of the early versions of utilitarianism, new varieties of utilitarian theory have now been devised that are quite different and are not always subject to the same criticisms. Moreover, these new theories do not always recommend the same kinds of choices in similar situations as the older versions.

It will be convenient for our purposes here to divide the types of utilitarianism into two main classes: (1) Extreme utilitarianism is represented by the three early, classic exponents of the theory, Bentham, Mill, and Sidgwick, and recently claims the more sophisticated adherents, J. J. C. Smart and many cost–benefit-oriented economists such as Richard Zeckhauser and W. K. Viscusi; (2) rule utilitarianism (sometimes known as 'restricted utilitarianism', is represented by Robert Goodin, Patrick Nowell-Smith, Richard Brandt, J. L. Austin, and John Rawls in his earlier period (before he rejected the label 'utilitarianism' altogether).

1. Extreme Utilitarianism

(a) The principle of utility. It can hardly be coincidental that one of the first important utilitarian philosophers was also an economist. Adam Smith was a professor of philosophy and a friend and colleague of David Hume. Smith (1776) saw utilitarianism as a necessary response to the rapid changes taking place in the moral thinking of Western Europeans as a result of the dramatic political, social, and economic changes of the times. In essence, traditional moral codes had been accepted based on authority or tradition, and without the need for much philosophical foundation or criticism. But, as happens in every historical culture in which change is necessary, it became important to rethink older value assumptions. For example, usury had been considered a terribly immoral act, until it became evident that enterprises begun with borrowed money could dramatically increase the well-being of large numbers of people—enterprises that would have been impossible without the practice of usury. In rethinking the increasingly outmoded moral codes of the times, philosophers like Smith and Hume proposed that the real criterion for the appropriateness of any rule of conduct was ultimately whether or not it tended to promote human happiness or well-being. This implied that the moral rules themselves were only extrinsic values, and that the real intrinsic value for the sake of which moral codes should be followed or rejected was human happiness.

A major advantage of Smith's version of utilitarianism was that his economic theory made it unnecessary to *measure* happiness or well-being. The free-market system advocated in *The Wealth of Nations* made such measurement unnecessary, because it was possible to assume that everyone could judge for themselves what kinds of goods or services were or were not conducive to the maximization of their happiness. In Smith's view, if each person simply chooses which goods to trade for on the open market, we can assume that everyone is obtaining the goods needed to maximize well being, insofar as possible given the total amount of goods being produced. Moreover, the ultimate effect of this free-trade system would be to enhance the productivity of the society as a whole, so that not only would there be more goods to go around than in a controlled economy, but also the *types* of goods produced would be determined by the demands of individuals, all choosing for themselves. Such a system would therefore maximize human well-being on the whole by enabling more people to obtain more of whatever it is that they happen to want than in any other possible social system. Thus there would be no need for some omniscient social scientist to figure out what everyone wanted and how best to obtain it. Since demand would determine supply, the "invisible hand" of the marketplace would see to it that the things people most want would be produced. As Rakowski states in more contemporary terms,

> Because the market ensures that traders will be made as well off as they could be consistent with some initial distribution of resources . . . the market is efficiency's handmaid. Although trades among people whose initial shares are equal might enhance their happiness to different degrees, and although they might allow some people to increase their holdings faster than if trades were prohibited and thus to bring about greater disparities in wealth or income than would otherwise arise, no one can possibly be made worse off absolutely by market exchanges, so long as the market remains competitive. (Rakowski 1991, 70)

The problem with this kind of utilitarianism, however, was evident even to Smith himself. It was an obvious empirical fact about the economic conditions of Smith's time (as well as our own) that the free market would not be likely to benefit everyone. As Marx clearly showed in his *1844 Manuscripts,* tenant farming and many kinds of industrial work were little better than slavery as far as the worker's freedom to bargain or choose alternatives was concerned. One out of twelve

women in London could find no other means of survival than prostitu-
tion (Foucault 1978). The problem, in Hume's (1752) view, was that
such a system might dramatically increase the *total amount* of well-
being, but it provided each individual little feeling of *security* in the
expectation of sharing in this well-being. In Hume's view, the insecurity
of a world in which everyone pursues personal well-being without
regard for others was worse than any amount of economic well-being
enjoyed without security as to its future status. As a result of this
problem, both Hume and Smith had to assume that charitable senti-
ments would motivate people to take care of the many casualties of
the free-market system, and Hume tried to develop a theory of 'fellow-
feeling,' which was supposed to motivate people to act according to
altruistic moral principles. This theory, however, moved Hume farther
and farther away from what can be unequivocally construed as a
utilitarian value system (Laird 1932; Kydd 1946; Ross 1942).

Both Hume and Smith shied away from allowing a strong role
for *government* in seeing to the maximization of human well being.
Like the earliest 'social contract' political theorists, Hobbes and Locke,
they thought that the government's role was merely to guarantee that
people's most basic rights would not be infringed, either by each other
or by their government, and these rights were conceived exclusively
as negative ones—as rights not to be interfered with by having one's
freedom, life, or property taken away. But this minimalist notion of
government also conflicted with the basic principle of utilitarianism,
since this principle would seem to imply that the government simply
ought to do *anything* within its power to facilitate human happiness
or well-being.

The first philosopher to take a really thoroughgoing utilitarian
approach was Jeremy Bentham, who published his major work *An
Introduction to the Principles of Morals and Legislation* in 1789. As the
name implies, this treatise placed great emphasis on the legislative
implications of Bentham's ethical doctrine. This practical application
may have had a certain influence on the direction of Bentham's thinking; it is arguable that certain aspects of Bentham's approach are somewhat more persuasive when we think of the issues in terms of legislation than in other contexts.

Until the time of Bentham, thinking about value issues had been
dominated by essentially retributive notions of justice, as documented
by Durkheim (1947), Foucault (1979), and many others. The revolution-
ary idea that Bentham introduced into this retributive moral climate—

the notion that *all* valuational problems can be solved by reference to the principle of utility—shook the foundations of ethical theory and had quite liberal political implications for its time. The proposed principle of utility (sometimes called the 'principle of beneficence') stated, quite simply, that the rightness of any action can be determined in an objective way, or even in a mathematical way, by computing the amount of benefit that would result from the action, as compared with the amount that would result from all alternative actions available in the same circumstances. This principle might not perhaps have struck eighteenth-century thinkers as being quite so outrageous had not Bentham very quickly declared that by 'benefit', he meant simply "human happiness." The formula expressed in terms of 'happiness' would then become: Always act in such a way as to produce the greatest possible happiness for the greatest possible number of people.

Because of the straightforward hedonism of this doctrine, it became known by more conservative thinkers as "the pig philosophy"; it appeared to imply that the purpose of human life was no different from that of lower animals—to get pleasure. Indeed, Bentham did not hesitate to admit that he saw no distinction between the terms 'happiness' and 'pleasure', except that 'happiness' connotes a longer lasting and more general state of pleasure. Thus Bentham made the famous irreverent statement that "[t]he quantity of pleasure being equal, push-pin is as good as poetry" (Bentham 1789–1962, 20).

Bentham combined his principle of utility with a second postulate, which he sometimes seemed to think followed from the principle of utility. It was expressed in the dictum, "Each to count for one, none for more than one" (18). At first glance, this principle seems to imply a more or less straightforward equity in the distribution of the benefits of the society and, judging from Bentham's own political views, he apparently thought of utilitarianism as a very egalitarian viewpoint. But the real test of its egalitarian emphasis arises when we consider a case in which the maximization of the vast *majority's* happiness *conflicts* with the welfare of a small minority of people. Then we might wonder whether the principle of utility, in combination with the axiom that "each [should] count for one," would recommend sacrificing some of the happiness of the majority for the sake of a more just distribution of that happiness among the disadvantaged. It turns out that this is not what Bentham means by his dictum. Rather, what he means is that when we set about to "compute" the amount of happiness that will result from each of the alternative actions, we should simply count each person's happiness as a single unit. Thus, if action A would produce 100 units of happiness, to be distributed among 100 people, this is to be preferred over action B, which, let us say, would produce 99 units of happiness to be distributed among 1,000 people. In this case, the happiness of 100 people would be preferred over the happiness of 1,000, even after taking into consideration that "each [should] count for one, none for more than one." Of course, we have computed the happiness in such a way that perfect happiness for one person counts no more than perfect happiness for another person, but we have not thereby ensured that the happiness will be equitably distributed, or even necessarily that it will *tend* toward equity of distribution. According to the principle of utility, we must do that which causes the greatest absolute *quantity* of happiness, regardless of the relative *distribution* of this happiness among the population. This has been one of the most severe criticisms of utilitarianism over the years, and it is one of the criticisms that have played a major role in prompting more recent utilitarians to modify the doctrine considerably. Many of the modifications of utilitarianism have been concerned with getting around this apparent unfairness of the doctrine by claiming that some sort of rigid *rules* that are equally applicable to everyone (and thus are fair) *follow from* the principle of utility. Others prefer simply to introduce a new principle, alongside the principle of utility, that recommends fairness in the distribution of benefits. This is no small point, however, because the conflict between the majority interest and the interests of small minorities—such as the unemployed and those who live below the poverty level—is always one of the prominent sources of moral conflict.

Bentham apparently thought, however, that if the principle of utility were applied in legislative decision making, it would imply some tendency toward distributive justice, because the legislator would be concerned with winning as many *votes* as possible. The legislator would thus "count each as one" in a very literal and pragmatic sense. If the vote of the poor hinged almost exclusively on those policies that most affected them, then the legislator would take this fact into account when writing legislation. The vote of the middle class would not hinge on the particular issues affecting the poor, so one would gain more votes than one would lose by supporting policies that help the poor.

But this vote-getting notion raises a fundamental ambiguity. Is Bentham recommending that the legislator make decisions according to the principle of utility, or according to what will win the most votes? These alternatives do not necessarily amount to the same thing. Also,

whichever criterion the legislator chooses, the interests of a small minority are likely to be left out of consideration, and others will have
unequal weight.

A similar criticism of extreme utilitarianism in its application to
justice is that it does not always recommend punishment in proportion
to desert (Kelman 1992). Utilitarianism, in Bentham's original, uncom-
promising conception of it, errs both in recommending punishment of
the innocent in certain kinds of situations and in not recommending
punishment of the guilty in certain other kinds of situations. An example of the former is the case in which an innocent black man has been
accused of raping a white woman in the midst of a race riot, and the
white people think that the black man is guilty although the sheriff
knows that the man is probably innocent. Should the sheriff turn over
the black man to a lynch mob in order to quell still more widespread
violence to come, or should he protect the man's rights, even if it means
risking his own life in the process? It seems contrary to most people's
normal intuition, to say the least, to grant that if more happiness would
result from the punishment of the innocent man, then that is what
should be done. On the other hand, consider a case in which there is
no way the punishment of a *guilty* man can make anyone the happier.
Suppose he has killed his wife in a fit of provoked rage but is obviously
not likely to kill again (as most "sudden murderers" of this type do
not—see McCaghy 1980, 97–99). Suppose further that his wife has no
surviving relatives to be upset by his being set free. Should he not be
sentenced nonetheless? Would it not be unfair to set him free, whereas
other equally guilty criminals must serve their time? Would this be
"counting each as one and none as more than one?"

A more recent utilitarian response to this type of criticism, again,
is rule utilitarianism, which will be discussed in the next section. Rule
utilitarianism will say that, *for utilitarian reasons,* one should punish
the guilty and not the innocent, because this policy will do the most
good in the long run by preserving the institution of justice, which in
general is a beneficial institution to have (that is, it is conducive to the
greatest happiness of the greatest number on the whole and in the
long run). Robert Goodin (1995), for example, defends such a position,
holding that rule utilitarianism is better suited as a system of collective
than of individual decision making. Goodin thus blunts a major type
of criticism of extreme utilitarianism summarized by Pojman: "Suppose
that I could create more utility by letting my children starve or go
without books and sending my income to the starving people in

Ethiopia or Bangladesh or West Virginia. I do not see any reason to follow utilitarian prescriptions here" (Pojman 1997, 289). Goodin's response to this type of problem is that "[s]uch embarrassments for the utilitarian arise, at root, from addressing moral injunctions to individuals alone" (Goodin 1995, 66). Rule utilitarianism would prescribe that people assume more responsibility for people with whom they have certain kinds of relations, such as for family members, because of the general utility of maintaining such rules. Moreover, according to rule utilitarianism, utility is maximized not by requiring *individuals* to take unilateral action to maximize utility, which would create a hopeless matrix of prisoners' dilemmas (Singer 1979, Chapter 8), but rather by setting up contexts of *collective* action through institutions (for example, governments) whose structure of rules is most beneficial on the whole and in the long run. This position, however, is also vulnerable to attack from several directions, as we shall see in the next section.

Another answer to the objection that utilitarianism is "counter-intuitive" (i.e., contradicts our commonsense intuition that fairness is worthwhile for its own sake) has been given by the contemporary extreme utilitarian, J. J. C. Smart (1956, 1984). Smart simply says that our commonsense intuition is no viable source for the verification of ethical beliefs and that, quite bluntly, intuitions are frequently wrong.

We have only to read the newspaper correspondence about capital punishment or about what should be done with Formosa to realize that the common moral consciousness is in part made up of superstitious elements, of morally bad elements, and of logically confused elements. . . . "The obligation to obey a rule," says No-well-Smith (*Ethics,* p. 239), "does not, *in the opinion of ordinary men,*" (my italics), "rest on the beneficial consequences of obeying it in a particular case." What does this prove? Surely it is more than likely that ordinary men are confused here. Philosophers should be able to examine the question more rationally. (Smart 1956, 346)

The only way to check the intuitions in order to find out whether they are correct or not, Smart says, is to ask whether the action in question produces the greatest happiness of the greatest number of people. Smart's response reiterates, in somewhat "smarter" language perhaps, one of the original appeals of utilitarianism. The only alternative to the principle of utility appeared to be intuitionism. And it is obvious that intuition is not a very trustworthy method of supporting ethical beliefs. Given that different people's "intuitions" utterly contradict each other where values are concerned, even when they have studied the issues very carefully, there is no way to know whose intuitions to believe; thus, in the absence of a more rational criterion, no intuition can claim to be a good reason for holding a belief. This is why defenders of nonutilitarian notions of fairness—for example, regarding the distribution of income and property—eventually begin supplying us with *utilitarian* reasons why their view of "fairness" in this instance is the correct one. The reason is that, when it comes to "fairness," the "intuitions" of the rich and the poor will never agree (Hare 1997, 222). So the only arguments that cannot be rejected by anyone are those that appeal to the principle of utility. And the reason such an appeal to utility is tempting even for nonutilitarians is that no one can deny the obvious fact that maximizing human happiness is a good thing, at least prima facie.

Mill therefore declares in his justification of utilitarianism that all moral intuitions are really confused intuitions of the validity of the principle of utility.

> To all those *a priori* moralists who deem it necessary to argue at all, utilitarian arguments are indispensable. For example, Kant says, "So act that the rule on which thou actest would admit of being adopted as a law by all rational beings." But when he begins to deduce from this precept any of the actual duties of morality, he fails, almost grotesquely, to show that there would be any contradiction, any logical (not to say physical) impossibility, in the adoption by all rational beings of the most outrageously immoral rules of conduct. All he shows is that the *consequences* of their universal adoption would be such as no one would choose to incur. (Mill 1859, 3–4)

According to Mill, intuitionists make the mistake of believing that some noble or self-sacrificing action is *intrinsically* valuable, whereas if they would further clarify their thinking, they would realize that really they regard such an action as *extrinsically* valuable. If the agent did not intend to produce some good consequence, then the action would be simply an exercise in futility. Mill therefore maintains that when we search for the intrinsic value for the sake of which all other values are considered valuable, the only thing that can qualify for this role is human happiness. The following subsection will examine the utilitarians' (and especially Mill's) reasons for believing that this is the case, so as to pinpoint some very serious difficulties with this kind of reasoning.

(b) The "proof" of utilitarianism. What, then, is the rational basis for adopting the principle of utility? The demonstration of the principle seems to rest on a doctrine of psychological hedonism. Human beings, by a law of human nature, cannot conceive of anything as being desirable in itself except happiness; therefore, it would be meaningless to require of us that we act by any principle except the maximization of happiness. "Ought implies can"—that is, it is meaningless and absurd to prescribe that people *should* do what they *cannot* do by virtue of the constitution of their essential psychology. The only thing that can be desirable, then, is happiness, which is essentially a form of pleasure—in other words, a positive, gratifying or enjoyable quality of experiencing. Thus psychological hedonism, according to Mill, is the "proof" of the principle of utility.

The only proof capable of being given that an object is visible is that people actually see it. The only proof that a sound is audible is that people hear it; and so of the other sources of our experience. In like manner I apprehend that the sole evidence it is possible to produce that anything is desirable is that people actually desire it. If the end which the utilitarian doctrine proposes to itself were not, in theory and in practice, acknowledged to be an end, nothing could convince any person that it was so. No reason can be given why the general happiness is desirable, except that each person, so far as he believes it to be attainable, desires his own happiness. This, however, being a fact, we have not only all the proof which the case admits of, but all which it is possible to require, that happiness is a good, that each person's happiness is a good to that person, and the general happiness, therefore, a good to the aggregate of all persons. (Mill 1857, 32–33)

Several serious criticisms have been levelled against this demonstration that happiness is the only value. In the first place, G. E. Moore (1903) holds that if "desirable" according to Mill means "what people actually desire," then the word simply means a different thing to Mill from what it means to other ethical theorists. In Moore's view, if a person *desires* to benefit from an unjust arrangement of society, then the person desires something that, from the moral point of view, one *should* not desire; thus the person desires something that is not desirable in the moral sense. Mill's equation between "desirable" and "actually desired" is thus sometimes referred to as a "figure of speech fallacy." By the same reasoning, no one could ever eat anything that was not *edible*, yet we know that people sometimes do. Moreover, as to the impact of the "ought implies can" thesis, we have already seen that it is entirely *possible* for people to value justice, honesty, courage, etc., so Mill has shown no reason why these things should not be counted as morally "desirable."

Another objection is that Mill's reasoning at best shows only that happiness is *a* value; it does not show that it is the *only* value. This is a common criticism of purely hedonistic psychological theories as well. The fact that we frequently choose to do what is in our own self-interest does not show that this is the *only* motivation we have. People sometimes do appear to act for reasons other than their own happiness—sometimes in order to promote the happiness of others and sometimes to promote their own 'self-actualization', which, as emphasized by the personalists, is not always conducive to happiness in any clear sense of the word.

A related objection is that if the epistemological basis of utilitarianism is a complete psychological hedonism in combination with the "ought implies can" dictum, then the premises of the doctrine contradict its conclusion. The contradiction arises from the fact that the ethical hedonism with which Bentham and Mill end up is a *nonegoistic* hedonism. According to Mill, "As between our own happiness and that of others, utilitarianism requires us to be as strictly impartial as a disinterested and benevolent spectator" (16). But the form of *psychological* hedonism relevant to the "ought implies can" principle is *egoistic* hedonism. If it is meaningless to ask that anyone value anything other than happiness because no one *can* value anything other than happiness according to a law of nature (i.e., *one's own* happiness), then it should be as meaningless for utilitarianism to ask that I sacrifice my own happiness for others as it is for any other moral philosophy to ask me to value something that I do not, in fact, already value. A similar criticism that focuses essentially on the same point is that if no one *can* desire anything except that which we already desire (i.e., our own happiness), then there should be no need of an ethical system at all.

Why not just allow each person to do what will fulfill our desires most adequately, since that is all we *can* do anyway?

Perhaps one response to these criticisms, at least in terms of Bentham's thinking, is that Bentham was addressing himself primarily to legislators, and that if a legislator acts in the interest of *the general* happiness, then he is doing his job as adequately as he possibly can and, therefore, presumably will be made personally happy either by the realization that he is doing a good job or by the likelihood that he will be reelected as the result of his good work. But, as we have already seen, this represents a somewhat naive conception of the relationship between the legislator and the various elements of her constituency. Less powerful interests are likely to be shortchanged in the process because their few votes (and small campaign contributions) count for little, either in terms of getting the legislator reelected or in terms of a mathematical computation of the total happiness produced by a given political policy.

Bentham also seems to assume that the happiness of each individual will tend to be promoted more if we all try to promote the welfare of the society. But this empirical claim would entail that there is never any real conflict between the interests of the individual and the interests of fellow citizens, which seems absurd. Besides being contradicted by most people's experience, which suggests that there is such a conflict, Bentham's facile assumption here would seem to ignore precisely those very cases of conflict that necessitate decision principles in policy analysis to begin with.

But there are also other possible responses to the charge that the *egoistic* psychological hedonism in the "proof" contradicts the *nonegoistic* ethical hedonism of the principle of utility. The best utilitarian response to this charge seems to be a denial that utilitarianism is based on psychological egoistic hedonism in the first place. While such a defense cannot possibly work in Bentham's case (because he straightforwardly affirms psychological hedonism on too many occasions and specifically interprets it as an ironclad law of human nature—see his *Principles*, p. 20, for example), it may be a viable defense in Mill's case. Mill says, "The utilitarian morality does recognize in human beings the power of sacrificing their own greatest good for the good of others" (15). If we reexamine Mill's "proof" from this perspective, we notice that rather than wording his hedonistic premise so as to imply that no one can desire anything but *one's own* happiness, Mill seems also to leave open the possible interpretation that he means simply that people desire *both* their own happiness and the happiness of others. Perhaps, as Everett Hall (1949) has suggested, Mill is only pointing out that *people have a commonsense intuition* that the happiness of others is important, rather than trying to provide independent evidence that it is important (Hall, 1–18).

In point of fact, Mill explicitly points out that this "proof" is no real proof in the ordinary sense, and that he does not believe the first principles of any discipline can be proven. This raises the general question as to what kind of verification procedure is used by the utilitarians. They originally derided the intuitionist theories, proposing utilitarianism as the only possible alternative to intuitionism. Yet, now it seems that utilitarianism is just another variety of intuitionism—or is it? Mill points out that the first principles of ethics cannot be demonstrated through deductive logic, and he seems now to agree that such principles cannot be demonstrated empirically either. What alternatives does this leave?

That value judgments cannot be demonstrated either through logic or through empirical experience does not mean that they cannot be demonstrated in any way at all, at least with some degree of probability. Nor does the want of empirical or logical demonstrability entitle us simply to adopt any old first principle we want. No reasonable value theory can begin its line of reasoning by saying, "No ethical first principles can be demonstrated, so I arbitrarily select as my first principle that such-and-such is the case." There must be some reason for preferring one first principle over another.

Mill's first principle seems to be based primarily on a coherence theory of truth. Since the initial assumption that happiness is the only intrinsic value leads to a general theory that hangs together in such a way as to involve us in no self-contradictions or statements that contradict other things we strongly believe are true, then the theory is better than other theories that do not pass this test of coherence. Thus Hall, in defense of Mill, makes the following statement:

A good way of going about gaining acceptance of a philosophic system is to show that, though clearer and more consistent, it yet squares in some over-all large fashion with common sense, with those ways of organizing experience that we all adopt when not in the closet of philosophic speculation. (Hall 1949, 8)

This is clearly a coherentist defense, but a certain kind of coherentism that verges on intuitionism. It affirms that people's commonsense assumptions about morality must be correct—something that the earlier quotation from Smart strongly denies. This type of coherence procedure would simply take people's commonsense thinking, clarify its terminology, and make it self-consistent. Since we all know that we value our own happiness, and it is fairly obvious that others do as well, it makes sense to assume that the sum total of human happiness has intrinsic value unless some more important value takes priority. But, whereas there is good reason to believe that human happiness has value, no one can offer any comparably compelling reason to believe that anything else has intrinsic value (although it is reasonable to believe that other things do have *extrinsic* value if they tend to promote the general happiness). Thus it makes sense to believe that the general happiness is the only intrinsic value and that it alone ought to serve as the criterion for establishing other things as extrinsically valuable.

Yet there are several reasons not to regard this as a good defense of extreme utilitarianism. In the first place, the principle of utility contradicts common sense on several key points, as mentioned earlier. It seems intuitively obvious that, as Moore puts it, a world containing a given amount of economic goods distributed fairly is preferable to one containing that same amount of goods distributed unfairly—yet extreme utilitarianism denies the intrinsic value of this distributive fairness. In the second place, there are other moral theories besides utilitarianism that clearly contradict its basic thrust as well as its practical applications, but that also claim to be based on commonsense beliefs made more coherent—for example, the theory of Kant, which Mill ridicules for its intuitionist assumptions. In the third place, utilitarianism does not seem to be free of internal contradictions on certain points discussed above—such as its stance on the issue of psychological hedonism and on the acceptability of intuitionism as a verification procedure. And finally, a criticism of any 'coherence' theory that bases its first principles on the commonsense beliefs of ordinary people, made consistent with themselves, is that such a theory tends to be impotent to recommend much moral *progress*. In the context of Old Testament morality, it seemed perfectly consistent with the commonsense morality of the Israelites, when they discovered that the Promised Land was already inhabited by "a peaceful people," that they should "utterly destroy all in the city, both men and women, young and old, oxen, sheep, and asses, with the edge of the sword . . . . But all silver and gold . . . are sacred to the Lord; they shall go into the treasury of the Lord" (Josh. 7:21). Similarly, infanticide seemed perfectly consistent with commonsense morality in the time of the Ancient Greeks, just as the burning of heretics in Europe and the lynching of blacks in the southern United States seemed consistent with commonsense morality to those who participated in such activities. The divine right of kings seemed an item of common sense to many people during a certain period of history, and so on.

In the final analysis, the main argument in favor of utilitarianism as an intuitively obvious principle, in contrast to other principles that claim to be intuitively obvious, is Mill's contention that all other moral intuitions *presuppose* the principle of utility, whether they realize it or not. For example, in praising a self-sacrificing action, we unconsciously assume that the purpose of the self-sacrifice is to bring happiness to others; otherwise, Mill maintains, we would regard the self-sacrifice as folly rather than nobility.

This claim, however, can still be questioned. One of the main contentions of anti-utilitarians is precisely that justice should be done *even if it does not increase the sum total of happiness*. While it is true that nonutilitarian systems do endorse the intrinsic value of human happiness, the problem is that it is not the *only* intrinsic value they endorse, nor are the other values completely derived from the value of happiness. Nonutilitarians do want to maximize the sum of human happiness when doing so does not conflict with other prima facie values that, to them, seem just as much based on common sense as is the utility principle. The two main values of this kind are: (1) If someone were to take a completely *objective* (rather than self-interested or biased) point of view on the distribution of goods, that person would prefer to see the goods distributed in a fair way—this is the argument John Rawls has developed in a very rigorous way, as will be discussed later; (2) If given a choice between being a happy pig or an unhappy human being, many if not most people would choose the unhappy human being—which shows that there is something that we value about being a fully conscious, fully actualized agent *other than* or *in addition to* the happiness such an agent may enjoy. Both these intrinsic values can claim to be as "intuitively obvious" as the intrinsic value of happiness, yet they form the essential basis for the main types of nonutilitarian value systems.

There is, however, one last line of defense for utilitarianism. It begins with Henry Sidgwick, whose thinking ultimately laid the groundwork for 'rule utilitarianism'.

(c) Sidgwick's defense of utilitarianism. At the turn of the twentieth century, Henry Sidgwick realized that Bentham and Mill had not adequately demonstrated on utilitarian grounds that individuals,

primarily concerned with their own happiness (according to the psychological premise of hedonism), should nevertheless in certain instances sacrifice their own happiness for the happiness of others. Sidgwick's *Methods of Ethics* (1901) made three important contributions to the philosophical defense of the system. (i) He gave a more convincing argument than Mill's to show that happiness is the only intrinsic value. (ii) He introduced a subsidiary principle alongside the principle of utility that attempted to show why one person's happiness is no more intrinsically important than another's, in some objective sense, and thus that equity in distribution is prima facie desirable. And (iii) he began the transformation that would eventually be carried further by other philosophers, which led from the extreme version of utilitarianism to the restricted or "rule" variety.

(i) Sidgwick's argument that happiness is the only intrinsic value essentially takes the form of a thought experiment that presumably would yield similar results if carried out by "any reasonable person" in exploring the issues. Imagine, Sidgwick says, a universe in which no conscious beings exist, ever have existed, or ever will exist. Can there be any possible value in such a universe? No. Therefore, only states of consciousness can be intrinsically valuable. This follows, he thinks, because consciousness is the thing on which the existence of any other value whatever must depend. But, clearly, only positive states of consciousness, not negative ones, have value. Thus all value is derived from positive states of consciousness, that is, happiness.

Although this seems a more convincing argument than Mill's, it still has problems. In the first place, the fact that no other value could exist unless consciousness exists does not prove that consciousness *is* the only value. It may show merely that consciousness is a *necessary condition* for the existence of value. Second, in the case of political values, my *consciousness of* the value of a political goal is not in itself the thing that is of primary value to me; the *attainment* of the goal is what I value. For example, I may value the achievement of distributive justice for future generations even though I will not be conscious of it at the time. Granted, no such justice could exist if not for the existence of the conscious beings who will comprise the future generations, but it does not follow that it is only the maximization of their happiness that I value. The notion that the maximization of happiness, well-being, or preference satisfaction for as many people as possible is the *only* intrinsic value remains a very questionable one.

(ii) Sidgwick solves the contradiction between the psychological egoistic hedonism and the ethical nonegoistic hedonism, which existed in Bentham's and Mill's thinking, by introducing a new principle. "It cannot be right for A to treat B in a manner in which it would be wrong for B to treat A, merely on the ground that they are two different individuals, and without there being any difference between the natures or circumstances of the two which can be stated as a reasonable ground for difference of treatment." (See Sidgwick, Book 3, Chapter 5.) Sidgwick appears to believe that this principle follows from pure logic; otherwise, it would become a form of intuitionism. As Kymlicka has noted, this kind of utilitarianism really takes equal treatment of people as the more basic value and then derives the value of utility maximization *from* this basic assumption of equality. Kymlicka summarizes the reasoning this way:

1. People matter, and matter equally; therefore
2. Each person's interests should be given equal weight; therefore
3. Morally right acts will maximize utility. (Kymlicka 1990, 31)

One problem with Sidgwick's principle can be seen from the lack of clarity in its practical implications. A slaveowner would never claim that it is fair for him to own X as a slave but that it would be unfair for X to own him as a slave. He would simply say that it is right that there should be masters and slaves, and that he is simply lucky to have turned out to be a master. By the same reasoning, and equally consistent with Sidgwick's principle, a moderately well-to-do person whose wealth is based largely on inheritance could argue that it is fair for some people to be wealthy and others to be poor, and that he is simply lucky to have turned out to be wealthy. If Sidgwick's principle denies the fairness of slavery, it denies the fairness of inheritance by the same reasoning. But Sidgwick does not seem to want to deny the fairness of things like inheritance. Extending the same reasoning, a complete analysis of the principle would show that not only slavery and inequality of economic resources but, indeed, all other unfair distributions of opportunities and resources are perfectly allowable by the principle, and therefore that the principle really has no tangible meaning. In fact, since the principle is so similar to Kant's 'categorical imperative', it is also vulnerable to essentially the same criticisms as Kant's theory. But utilitarianism was originally intended as an alternative to non-utility-maximizing codes of conduct such as Kant's, not merely as a supplement to them.

Furthermore, the principle that A and B should treat each other as equals (or as having equal rights in relation to each other) often seems to conflict with the greatest happiness principle, as we saw earlier. The priority of equal rights (which is really derived from the principle of fairness in the distribution of the benefits of governmental protection) often conflicts with maximizing the total quantity of happiness or want-satisfaction. In this case, then, we need some further principle to resolve the conflict between the principle of utility and the principle of equity. If the principle of utility is used as the ultimate court of appeal to resolve this conflict, then one might ask how Sidgwick's subsidiary principle can have any claim to validity in the first place. Why not just have the one first principle—the principle of utility maximization—and assume that it always leads to the best possible results in cases of conflict between the two principles? But neither does Sidgwick provide us with any third principle on the basis of which the conflict between his two principles might be resolved (see Kymlicka 1990, 35ff). To this extent, Sidgwick becomes what Frankena (1963) calls a "mixed deontological" theorist rather than a utilitarian, in that he does not really hold that happiness is the only value but also values equity for its own sake.

(iii) While Sidgwick remains an extreme utilitarian, his attempt to reconcile the principle of utility with the principle of fairness in distribution of opportunities and benefits paves the way for still more recent attempts to accomplish the same purpose by claiming that the principle of utility itself *implies* a system of rules—that presumably would be equally binding on everyone. The principle of utility is taken by these theorists as *implying* such a system of equitable rules because such a system would produce the greatest possible amount of general happiness on the whole. It is this "restricted" form of utilitarianism, 'rule utilitarianism', that has been most influential in recent years, especially in the realm of policy analysis. Yet, when we examine its logic carefully, we still find a good deal of logical confusion, resulting in important unanswered questions whose practical implications are absolutely crucial, as the next section will show.

2. Rule Utilitarianism

'Rule utilitarianism' (sometimes also called 'restricted utilitarianism') designates any ethical theory that, on utilitarian grounds, prescribes rules of conduct that should not be violated even if doing so would produce better consequences. As Goodin points out, "There are substantial utilitarian gains ... from being able to enter into long-term commitments in some confidence that they will indeed be carried out" (Goodin 1995, 64). H. J. McCloskey, a critic of rule utilitarianism, defines the doctrine in this way:

> According to restricted utilitarianism we justify particular actions by reference to general rules or practices and the rules by reference to the principle of utility. Hence according to this theory particular actions may be obligatory even though they are not productive to the maximum good possible. (McCloskey 1957, 466)

At first glance, such a theory seems paradoxical. How, one might ask, can a philosophy begin with the assumption that one should do that which produces the greatest happiness and then end up advocating that in some instances we should purposely do something that we know will *not* produce the greatest happiness, merely in order to obey a rule? Such a conclusion might seem more deontic than utilitarian.

The answer to this question hinges on two theses, in light of which rule utilitarians argue that a conception of rules follows from the principle of utility: (1) On the whole, it is better (i.e., conducive to the greatest happiness for the greatest number) to have certain rules than not to have them, but (2) it would be impractical to have the rules and at the same time to allow disobedience of them.

To use a favorite example of the rule utilitarians, it makes absolutely no difference, from a utilitarian point of view, whether everyone drives on the right or on the left. Nonetheless, it makes a great deal of difference whether or not everyone drives on *the same* side, whichever it is. But it cannot be left up to the individual, the rule utilitarians argue, to decide whether to drive on the left or the right, because no one would know which side everyone else was going to choose. Here, then, we apparently have an example of a decision that is better made by the society as a whole, or by some arbitrary authority, than by the individual—and better precisely on utilitarian grounds.

Rule utilitarians would call the law against driving on the left (or right, if in Britain) an "institution." They would call the act of driving on the right in order to conform to the rule a "practice." The purpose of institutions, they argue, is to define practices whose universal or near-universal observance should be expected to be conducive to the general happiness. Because the universal observance of the practice defined by the institution is conducive to the general happiness, on the whole and in the long run, it is, therefore, the responsibility of each individual to conform to the practice *in all instances*, without improvising exceptions as we go along. If there are going to be exceptions allowed, these exceptions should be clearly stated as qualifications of the rule when it is originally formulated, so that the exceptions are equally allowable to everyone. If anyone were to have a right to disobey the rule even in a single instance (other than in ways specified by the stated qualifications of the rule itself), then we must also grant that anyone else in a similar situation also has the right to disobey the rule. But if everyone disobeyed the rule any time they chose, then the rule would become meaningless and, therefore, the rule might as well not exist. The reasoning here is notably similar to Kant's justification of his duty ethic (never act according to any maxim that could not be universalized without logical contradiction); such a similarity is not surprising if we recall that Mill's criticism of Kant, which occurs at the very beginning of Mill's *Utilitarianism,* castigates Kant for not realizing that the justification of rules rests on an unconscious intuition to the effect that rules have utilitarian value, rather than on pure reason or on the logical self-contradictoriness of breaking the rule.

At least two of the most prominent rule utilitarians, Stephen Toulmin and Patrick Nowell-Smith, consider themselves to belong to the group of theorists who are called "linguistic analysts." That is, they believe that the main purpose of philosophy is to clarify the language that people actually use in order to determine the *purpose* that that language is supposed to serve. Frequently, they believe, philosophical problems will reveal themselves as rooted in confusion about the way words are used. They believe that analysis of moral terms will reveal the purpose that is supposed to be served by a value theory, which in turn will reveal what *kind* of theory is capable of serving this purpose best.

In the case of ethical or moral language, Toulmin (1950) argues that we must begin by asking ourselves what the purpose of having ethical language is in the first place. This question can be answered empirically; we simply observe what reasons people have for wanting to have ethical principles. Such a study reveals, Toulmin thinks, that the purpose of ethics is to harmonize people's desires with each other as well as possible—to "correlate our feelings and behavior in such a way as to make the fulfillment of everyone's aims and desires as far as possible compatible" (137). Later he says, "If the adoption of the practice would genuinely reduce conflicts of interest, it is a practice *worthy of adoption,* and if the way of life would genuinely lead to deeper and more consistent happiness, it is one *worthy of pursuit"* (224).

Thus the purpose of institutions is to harmonize people's aims and desires with each other (Goodin 1995, 63–64). An *individual* cannot make a correct moral choice as easily as can the whole society on such an issue, precisely because the individual would be too blinded in favor of self-interest. It is therefore easy to see how such a position would lead to rule utilitarianism. Some other party besides the individual must be entrusted with the responsibility of deciding on moral principles that harmonize the self-interests of various individuals. This other party (usually a government) must then require individuals to conform to the practices defined by its rules, although the purpose of the rules is none other than the maximum happiness of the aggregate of all individuals. Each individual should also realize that the most rational arrangement possible is one in which the institutions demand obedience to rules. Of course, it is completely up to the aggregate of all individuals to decide whether they want to set up this institution or that institution. From this last point one might infer that the people have the right to change or replace an institution if it does not ideally serve the collective self-interest. But in this case, according to rule utilitarians such as John Rawls in his earlier period (see Rawls 1955), one must work toward changing the institution itself, not simply ignore its rules because one disagrees with them.

An objection to this whole line of reasoning arises from the inference that one does not have the right to disobey the rules if one cannot succeed in getting them changed. Does not such a rule-bound value system condone the crushing of small minorities and certain individuals beneath the weight of an 'overbearing majority', as Madison warned in *The Federalist Papers* (especially paper no. 10)? And does it not crush these minorities and individuals even *more* brutally than the simple, extreme utilitarianism of Bentham and Mill? We saw in the last section that one of the strongest motivations for elaborating a rule-oriented system of utilitarianism was to overcome just this type of objection, by establishing rules that equally bind and protect everyone in relation to everyone else and, therefore, that should promote some tendency toward equality or distributive justice. But now it seems that rule utilitarianism is vulnerable to a very similar criticism, although from a different perspective.

McCloskey (1957) pushes this line of criticism even further, charging that the rule utilitarians do not really know what they mean by a "rule in practice"—whether it refers to *real* practices as defined by *real* political and social institutions, with all their imperfections, or whether it refers to *ideal* practices as they *would* be defined by an *ideal* social arrangement, *if* such an ideal arrangement ever did exist. If it refers to real practices, McCloskey insists that one should have no obligation to conform to it if one is powerless to change it; otherwise, the system would be unfair to minorities (i.e., those who are in the minority with regard to any given controversy). On the other hand, if it refers merely to ideal practices—those grounded on a perfect set of social institutions—then the whole question of whether one should conform to it becomes irrelevant to real life, since no such ideal arrangement is even approached by real practices and institutions, nor is it ever likely to be.

Partly because of these kinds of criticisms, *some* rule utilitarians, such as Toulmin, hold that disobedience of a rule *is* allowable, but only in certain very specific circumstances—namely, the kind of circumstances in which disobedience of the rule is most conducive to the general happiness on the whole and in the long run, after taking into consideration all negative or undesirable effects of this disobedience, such as the undesirable effect of weakening general respect for the rule by one's example. For instance, to return to the question of driving on the wrong side of the road, Toulmin says that if I must swerve to the left side of the road in order to avoid, let us say, hitting a child who is playing in my lane, it would be absurd to hit the child simply in order to obey the rule. I am therefore allowed to disobey the rule, but *only* if the consequences of such disobedience are better, on the whole, than the consequences of obedience.

But this issue of exceptions to rules is extremely problematic for rule utilitarianism. A. K. Stout (1954) distinguished two forms of rule utilitarianism, on the basis of the very controversy we have just been discussing. He calls them the "causal" form and the "hypothetical" form of rule utilitarianism. In its *causal* form, the doctrine would say that one should follow a rule if and only if breaking the rule would be likely to have the undesirable consequence of causing other people to lose respect for the rule and feel justified in breaking it more often in the future, *and* if and only if these harmful effects *outweigh* the beneficial effect that one could produce by breaking the rule. Stout is obviously describing such thinkers as Toulmin here. This causal form of rule utilitarianism would therefore prescribe that I should swerve into the wrong lane in order to avoid hitting a child, even if doing so might to some extent make other people feel justified in driving on the wrong side on other occasions, thus ultimately undermining the efficacy of the rule to some tiny extent. The undesirable effects of this do not outweigh the desirable effects of swerving, even when we take into consideration the negative effect on respect for the law, and, therefore, the causal form of the theory prescribes that we should break the rule in this type of instance.

The *hypothetical* form of rule utilitarianism, on the other hand, is quite different, Stout says. Rather than having us ask whether our violation of a given rule would *in fact* cause others to violate it, this form of the theory would have us ask simply what would happen *if* everyone violated the rule, even if we know full well that they are not likely to do so. Hypothetical rule utilitarianism would therefore say that there are some rules whose violation should not be tolerated under any circumstances whatever, even if violating them does produce good consequences. Here Stout surely has in mind such theorists as John Rawls (especially in his earlier period). Of course, in fairness to this position, we should grant that it would not, in all probability, regard the law against driving on the wrong side of the road as one of the rules that are universal in this sense. (Rawls would probably hold that the spirit of the law implies that one would be excused in cases of very drastic consequences, and thus one is not really violating it in such cases. The implicit qualification contained in the rule itself covers the possible exceptions to it.) But other rules would presumably be considered universal. For example, one should never murder, even if murdering a specific individual does appear conducive to the best possible consequences on the whole. Murdering Hitler, obviously, would have had far more beneficial results than not murdering him; nonetheless, an implication of rule utilitarianism in its hypothetical form might well be that one should not murder Hitler or anyone else (unless specific exceptions are stated or implied in the rule itself), regardless of the consequences. (Actually, even in this case the rule utilitarian would more than likely attempt to avoid such a counterintuitive implication, simply by defining Nazi Germany as an unjust institution whose laws, therefore, are not binding. This, in turn, would raise the question as to how to distinguish a just from an unjust institution, and whether one is obligated to obey an unjust institution, which we have already seen is a fuzzy issue, to say the least.) So, in principle, this hypothetical form of rule utilitarianism is much stronger in its insistence that we obey rules regardless of the consequences than is the "causal" form. According to the hypothetical form of the theory, people should obey rules, period. The rules themselves, however, would be judged by whether having the rules is more beneficial than having some other rules, or than not having any rules at all. Thus, in the hypothetical form of the doctrine, I must always ask myself what would happen *if* everyone else were also to disobey the same rule; whether I think they *actually will* disobey it is irrelevant.

J. J. C. Smart, the contemporary *extreme* utilitarian discussed in section 1 above, criticizes rule utilitarianism by building on Stout's distinction between the "causal" form and the "hypothetical" form of rule utilitarianism, maintaining that in its causal form, rule utilitarianism is no different from extreme utilitarianism. Extreme utilitarianism advocates doing whatever produces the best consequences, which in turn would imply that if having rules produces the best consequences, then we should have the rules, and if obeying the rules most of the time produces the best consequences, then we should obey them most of the time. And like extreme utilitarianism, this form of rule utilitarianism also grants that there may be instances in which breaking the rule produces better consequences than not breaking it, in which case one should break it. None of these implications are any different from the implications that Sidgwick, for example, drew from extreme utilitarianism.

"Hypothetical" rule utilitarianism, on the other hand, is not really a form of utilitarianism at all, according to Smart. Smart maintains that no utilitarian reason for having a rule can be provided that would not allow an exception to be made in any instance in which making the exception has better consequences on the whole (including its negative effect on other people's respect for the rule) than not making the exception.

For example, suppose a student is sitting in the back row of an English class, hiding a music assignment on which he is working. The teacher, upon catching him in the act, severely reprimands him, ending her argument with the rhetorical question, "What would happen if everyone wrote music during English class?" Perhaps out of fear the student refrains from giving the logical response: "Obviously, not everyone is *going* to write music in class, since most people cannot write music." According to Smart's thinking, this would be an entirely appropriate response, since the question the student should be asking herself is not "What would happen if *everyone* wrote music during class?" The question, rather, should be "What would happen if *anyone who felt like it* sat in class writing music whenever they chose to do so, *given the fact that most people never will?*" (Of course, what the teacher really meant was that if everyone relaxed discipline *in general,* the utilitarian consequences would be quite undesirable. But in that case she would have become an extreme utilitarian, not a hypothetical rule utilitarian; she would simply be calculating the overall predictable consequences of that particular type of action, not demanding obedience to a rule *regardless* of the consequences.) Smart's question is "*Why* should I base my actions on the assumption, which I know from the outset to be completely false, that my writing music will cause everyone to write music? If there were a moral rule about writing music in class, would the rule state that no one should *ever* write music in class, under any circumstances, regardless of the consequences? Or would it be more consistent with a utilitarian foundation for the rule to let it state that no one should ever violate the rule *unless doing so would produce better consequences on the whole* (that is, after considering the negative consequences of undermining respect for the rule or for the institution in question)?" Since the second alternative seems clearly more consistent with a utilitarian foundation (because it would be more conducive to the greatest happiness for the greatest number in the long run), then whoever prefers the first alternative must prefer it for some other reasons besides utilitarian reasons. Thus, Smart concludes, rule utilitarianism either introduces an arbitrary and essentially nonutilitarian requirement that rules be universally obeyed (i.e., in the form of "hypothetical" rule utilitarianism)—in which case it is not consistent with a utilitarian basis for the rules at all—or else it takes the form of "causal" rule utilitarianism, in which case its outcomes are no different from (and no improvement over) those of extreme utilitarianism.

Those who advocate rule utilitarianism maintain that rule utilitarianism is preferable to extreme utilitarianism because it helps get around some of the strongest objections against utilitarianism. We saw in section 1 above what these objections are. Extreme utilitarianism would sometimes punish the innocent and sometimes refrain from punishing the guilty, in order to do whatever is expedient in terms of producing the best consequences. Nor would extreme utilitarianism always favor a just distribution of the benefits of the society, but instead would advocate whatever policy is likely to produce the greatest *quantity* of benefits, regardless of the question of distribution. Thus it would lead to de Tocqueville's 'tyranny of the majority' or Madison's 'over-bearing majority' that might well trample upon the rights of minorities (i.e., minorities with respect to any controversial issue that might arise) because to do so would produce general happiness (i.e., the happiness of a large majority, but not of the minority in question). Rule utilitarians believe they can get around these objections by showing that having rules tends to put everyone in the society on a more equal footing, since all must obey the same rules. This is clearly the position of John Rawls in his early but influential paper, "Two Concepts of Rules" (1955). But, precisely for this reason, Rawls seems to be a prime example of a philosopher who considered himself at that time to be a utilitarian, but who then gradually shifted toward a nonutilitarian and essentially deontic perspective (in *A Theory of Justice*, 1971, and still more in *Political Liberalism*, 1993). Rawls's early attempt to defend the notion of inviolable rules on utilitarian grounds is exactly what Smart has in mind when he says that rule utilitarianism in its "hypothetical" form can have no utilitarian basis in the first place. The only truly utilitarian conception of rules would treat rules as mere rules of thumb, which are convenient to have in that they prevent us from having to be perpetually calculating consequences of specific actions, and also for reasons such as the advantage offered by everyone's driving on the same side of the road. Such rules of thumb, however, would be breakable by their very nature (which is utilitarian) if breaking them were to produce better consequences on the whole in any specific case.

McCloskey, who is not himself a utilitarian at all, agrees with Smart's criticisms of rule utilitarianism but disagrees with Smart's endorsement of extreme utilitarianism. In McCloskey's view, the criticisms of rule utilitarianism do show that it is either no better than extreme utilitarianism (and therefore subject to all the same criticisms) or else not a form of utilitarianism at all (but rather a deontic view). But, since Smart does not refute the worst of the criticisms of extreme utilitarianism either (particularly that it must remain silent on the issue of equity), McCloskey rejects utilitarianism altogether.

McCloskey also raises two other points about rule utilitarianism that are especially important because they must be addressed in one way or another in *any* coherent value system. (i) Any theory that proposes a system of rules, making the morality of actions dependent upon whether they follow the rules, must account for instances in which the rules turn out to conflict with each other. For example, when the Gestapo comes to the door looking for Jews, one must either avoid being an accomplice to murder by lying to the Gestapo, or one must avoid lying by becoming an accomplice to murder. McCloskey thinks that rule utilitarianism, if it has any claim to association with the principle of utility whatever, must maintain that in cases of conflict between rules, the principle of utility itself must be appealed to for a final decision. However, it would seem both inconsistent and arbitrary to let the principle of utility be the final arbiter in cases of conflict, but not in cases in which obedience to a rule conflicts with the principle of utility itself. Another alternative that the rule utilitarian might choose would be to let cases of conflict between rules be decided by means of some higher order rule that might say, for example, that rule A is always to be preferred to rule B in cases of conflict. But this procedure ignores the probability that in certain specific cases telling the truth might be preferable to, say, protecting private property, and in other situations protecting private property might be more important than truthfulness. For example, it would not be self-contradictory to think that it is wrong to tell a lynch mob that some innocent person is guilty of a crime just in order to avoid the lynch mob's burning down my house, but that it is nonetheless acceptable to tell a burglar that I have a gun, when in reality I have no gun, in order to avoid his burglarizing my house.

(ii) McCloskey also charges that rule utilitarians are confused about whether they mean that rules should be obeyed if they are *in fact* conducive to general happiness, or that rules should be obeyed if the members of the society merely *believe* that the rules are conducive to the general happiness. If it is only necessary for the members of the society to *believe* that the rules are ultimately beneficial, would this not imply a strange kind of ethical relativism? What if a certain member of the society knows that the rules are *not* ultimately beneficial? Is that person, then, free to disobey them? On the other hand, if it is necessary that the rules *really* be ultimately beneficial, then McCloskey charges that rule utilitarianism is irrelevant to whether or not we should obey the rules of any given society with their numerous imperfections, since these rules often result from unjust power relations, and even if not, they often reflect more or less erroneous notions of what kinds of policies are likely to be most beneficial in the long run.

In defense of rule utilitarianism, it might be said that the "rules" it is referring to are not the rules of any existing society, but merely the ideal rules that *should* govern *all* societies. If living in a society in which murder is universally condoned, for example, Rawls would say we still should not commit murder.

But we should note that there are several problems that rule utilitarianism still cannot solve. It does not escape the difficulty that even rule utilitarianism, in either the "hypothetical" or the "causal" form, frequently does not recommend justice by preference over aggregate utility. A rule that is formulated in such a way as to further the happiness or interests of the majority will not necessarily serve the happiness or interests of minorities or distribute opportunities and benefits in a fair way; nor will it necessarily protect any political "rights" that people might be supposed to have. (Bentham, of course, refers to all talk about "rights" as "nonsense on stilts.")

Moreover, the epistemological foundation of rule utilitarianism would depend on the same presuppositions and arguments as extreme utilitarianism, which, as we have already seen, are quite questionable in certain respects, especially in relation to the conflict between its egoistic psychological hedonism (i.e., that people value *their* own happiness) and its nonegoistic ethical hedonism (i.e., that people *should* value *everyone's* happiness). It also seems highly questionable whether happiness is the *only* thing people value (for example, some people seem to intrinsically value justice) and, even if people are this hedonistic, whether it is the only thing that *ought* to be promoted in a good society. We shall see later that there are very good arguments to show that some sort of distributive justice would be preferred by any rational reflector not biased by prejudice or self-interest, and this objective judgment ought to be accepted as the criterion for justice in a society.

And, finally, the charge that rule utilitarianism is either the same as extreme utilitarianism (rule utilitarianism in its "causal" form), or it relies on some altogether different assumption than the principle of utility, such as some sort of deontic principle (rule utilitarianism in its "hypothetical" form), does not seem to have been refuted.

There are many other problems and criticisms that would have to be addressed by any coherent utilitarian value system besides the crucial ones we have considered here. But the all-important problem seems to be that, no matter how the principle of utility maximization is interpreted, dressed up, or sociopolitically contextualized, there is no way to erase the fundamental conflict between the value of maximizing human well-being on the one hand (however 'well-being' is conceived) and on the other hand, the fairness or justice of the way this human well-being is *distributed* among the population, either in the form of desirable benefits and situations for people or in the form of opportunities to achieve these desirable benefits and situations. It seems inevitable that some principle of distributive justice must be included in a coherent value system *in addition to* a principle of utility. The real challenge is not merely to *philosophically ground* such a distributive justice principle (which is not as difficult a project as it might at first seem), but rather to ground it in such a way that the two principles—justice and utility— can be commensurably *weighed against each other* to yield objective and rational (as opposed to seriously questionable or arbitrary) *conflict resolution procedures.* This, then, is what we must now try to do.

4

Crucial Problems with Rights-Based Decision Principles

We have seen that utility-maximizing decision principles such as cost–benefit analysis have tended to attract empirically minded policy analysts primarily because the intrinsic value on which utilitarian decision principles are based—human happiness—is one that can be unambiguously and empirically *demonstrated* to have value. One of the assumptions of this reasoning is that other intrinsic values—such as distributive justice, loyalty, giving people what they "morally deserve" to receive, etc.—are so subjective and controversial that no one could ever provide objective enough arguments to warrant imposing such values on others who do not agree with their importance. That is, objective reasons cannot be given as to why we should regard some preferred nonutilitarian conception of rights or of retributive or distributive justice as having *intrinsic* value (although such things obviously do have *extrinsic* value in a utilitarian system); still less has anyone provided forceful enough arguments to produce enough consensus with regard to some particular concept of rights or justice as *morally binding* the institutions of a society to promote it as an intrinsic value. In the absence of any such objectively valid moral consensus, then, many policy analysts prefer to promote only those values that *can* be clearly demonstrated as having value (for example, Viscusi 1991; Sinden and Worrell 1979; Zeckhauser 1975; Peskin and Seskin 1979; and many others to be discussed later).

This reasoning strikingly resembles the logical structure of the main argument for utilitarianism discussed in the first chapter, which was schematized as follows:

1. It is an empirical fact that each person values his own happiness, at least prima facie.

2. Therefore, each person's happiness has prima facie value (i.e., *unless* some more important value supersedes it).
3. Therefore, *everyone's* happiness has prima facie value.
4. Therefore, maximizing the general happiness has prima facie value.
5. No one can demonstrate that any nonutilitarian value (such as some particular concept of retributive or distributive justice) is the correct concept of nonutilitarian justice *and* that it should supersede the maximization of the general happiness.
6. Therefore, maximizing the general happiness is the *only* intrinsic value, although other values may be *derived from* it as extrinsic values.

Against this whole viewpoint, of course, there is an important strain in political philosophy that emphasizes precisely the thesis that there are fundamental human rights and duties that are more important than the maximization of aggregate happiness. The Bill of Rights in the U.S. Constitution reflects just this kind of assumption, having been directly influenced by John Locke's notion of 'natural rights' that were supposed to be "self-evident," and that all people were supposed to intuitively recognize as a priori truths. Unfortunately, Locke produced no arguments to show why the three natural rights he championed—life, liberty, and property—should take priority over maximizing the general happiness or, indeed, that they were intrinsic values at all. He assumed that everyone was capable of 'intuiting' such truths. Nor did Locke offer any justification as to why the list of rights should be limited to just the three he proposed, rather than also containing other rights—for example, the right to free medical treatment, unemployment compensation, or twice-a-week garbage collection.

This chapter will focus on some of the most rational arguments that have been given to support the idea that rights of some sort should be regarded as having intrinsic and not just extrinsic value, and thus as superseding the mere aggregate maximization of human well-being. What I hope finally to show is that very few of these arguments stand up under logical scrutiny, and that those that do stand up show, at best, only that distributive justice of a certain sort *has* intrinsic value—not *how much* intrinsic value it should be regarded as having in comparison with utility maximization. The main problem that must be solved, then, is how to make the value of justice *commensurable* with the value of utility maximization, so that we can develop a coherent decision principle to guide policy decisions. That is what the remainder of this book will attempt to do.

1. Positive Law and Natural Law: In What Sense Do Rights "Trump" Beneficial Consequences?

The distinction and interrelationship between positive and natural law helps to show the respects in which the consequentialist approach and the justice-oriented approach to policy analysis contradict each other, and the respects in which they need not inevitably contradict each other. 'Positive law' refers to rules that people make for themselves for the sake of accomplishing some purpose. It would include civil legislation as well as unwritten customs and conventions within a specific culture (see Fagothey 1981). Natural law, on the other hand, refers to rules that are not made by people—rules that should be regarded as equally valid and binding whether people believe that they are true or not. It would include objectively true ethical principles, if such exist. The concept 'natural law' in ethics got its name because early philosophers tended to believe that the moral law was analogous to physical law in terms of its universal bindingness, except that humans, because of our free will, had a choice as to whether to obey the moral law. In the case of many Christian philosophers, such as St. Thomas Aquinas, this was the primary distinction between moral and physical law.

Perhaps the most important application of this distinction is in the area of 'rights'. We saw in the last chapter that Bentham, a thoroughgoing and extreme utilitarian, called all talk about rights "nonsense on stilts." Nonutilitarian theorists, by contrast, generally take the notion of rights very seriously, maintaining that people have certain "inalienable" natural rights (rights that should not be taken away or "alienated" from people, regardless of the beneficial consequences of doing so). Such rights would have to be conceived as ends in themselves, not as means toward some other end. As such, it is often supposed that they fall within the scope of social relations prescribed by natural law, as opposed to positive law. Positive laws made by governments may provide the "teeth" to enforce respect for rights, but the thesis that they *should* be respected is presumably not a positive law invented by human beings, but a natural law that exists independently of any human invention.

Thus a distinction can also be maintained between legal rights on the one hand and natural rights on the other. Legal rights are rights that are guaranteed to someone by a government or state. For example, citizens of Great Britain have the right to have their college tuition paid by the government if they cannot afford to pay it themselves. Obviously, a legal right in one nation or state may not be a legal right in another, since not all societies guarantee this right to their members. By contrast, natural rights, if any exist, would be rights that all people everywhere possess and that, from a moral point of view, *should* not be violated. Whether they are in fact violated is a different question. Someone may believe that people have a natural right to be free from slavery, although it is obvious that this right has frequently been violated in various historical situations. This distinction is important because it is possible to show that even a relativistic or utilitarian theory of ethics has room in it for a concept of *legal* rights, though it may eschew any concept of *"natural"* rights in a sense that would include the *intrinsic* value of protecting such rights. Utilitarians, whether extreme or restricted, do believe that the government ought to guarantee each individual that it will act in such a way as to promote the maximum human well-being insofar as possible. Thus each person, even according to utilitarianism, can be said to possess the right to be treated by the government in such a way as to maximize human well-being. But, strictly speaking, all such rights have extrinsic rather than intrinsic value in a utilitarian system.

It is obvious that not all natural rights are legal rights, and not all legal rights must be natural rights. The mere existence of a legal right to a state-financed college education in Britain does not imply that all people everywhere and at all times have a natural right to such an education. Even the truth of the supposition that a given legal right *should* exist in a specific society does not necessarily imply a corresponding natural right. It may be that citizens of New York should be guaranteed the right to have their garbage collected twice a week, but few would claim that the right to have one's garbage collected twice a week is a universal natural right, possessed by all peoples everywhere although violated by 99 percent of the governments in human history.

The main reason why it seems implausible to assign twice-a-week garbage collection as a natural right possessed by all people is that it would probably be impossible, or undesirable, or both, to assign the *duty* to the populations of certain types of countries that they should *pay the amount of taxes* that would be required to implement such a service. But if it would be impossible or undesirable to assign this *duty* to people, then it also becomes impossible or undesirable to assign the corresponding *right,* since a right that it is no one's duty to enforce or respect is no right at all. This correlativity between rights and duties becomes an important device, in many deontic rights theories, for grounding the "mandatory" nature of rights and, therefore, the priority of rights over consequentialists concerns.

A certain ambiguity in ordinary usage of the word 'right' sometimes tends to cause confusion. If we ask whether a person has the 'right' to eat an $80 steak dinner while people who could be helped by the $80 are starving elsewhere, there is one sense of the word 'right' that seems applicable here and another that does not. In one sense, the person has the 'right' to eat the dinner, unless doing so conflicts with some particular moral responsibility she might be demonstrated to have; that is, no one should forcibly prevent her from eating the steak dinner. This would be a *negative* right—the right not to be interfered with while doing something. (We might also remark here that if the person does *not* have the right to eat the $80 dinner in this negative sense—that is, if eating the dinner *does* conflict with her duty—then perhaps someone *should* prevent her from eating it. But that is a different question.) This negative sense of 'right' is a weak one and not the one usually involved in discussions of the most controversial types of rights. In the stronger or *'positive'* sense of 'right', it would be absurd to say that anyone has a 'right' to eat an $80 steak dinner, because this would mean that the society as a whole would have the responsibility to provide each of its members with an $80 steak dinner. In this stronger sense of 'right', to say that one person has a right to X is to say that someone, or everyone aggregately, has the duty to provide each person with X, at least to the greatest degree possible in the given circumstances. For example, medical care is sometimes proposed as a candidate for this type of right. In the weaker or negative sense of 'right', I do have a 'right' to eat an $80 dinner, provided that I can afford to pay for it, if and only if it turns out to be true (as supported by some justifiable value system) that no one else has the 'right' to stop me from doing it, that is, if everyone has the *duty* to *refrain* from stopping me. This in turn could be true only if eating the dinner does not conflict with any given duty that I (along with everyone else) can be demonstrated to have.

The 'inalienable rights' on Locke's list—life, liberty, and property—seem to be purely negative ones. I may have a right to a certain
amount of "freedom of movement" in the negative sense of 'right'; it
is even arguable that I may have a right to retain whatever property
I possess, that is, not to have it stolen or taken from me in the form
of theft or taxation not needed to support equally important rights
(Nozick and Ross, for example, maintain such a right as enjoying a
strong priority over utility maximization and other competing rights).
But, in the strong or positive sense of 'right', this negative "freedom
of movement" does not guarantee that I will have the *power* to make
any given move. Nor did Locke envision guaranteeing each citizen the
actual possession of any property. Whether the rights in question are
positive or negative ones, one thing that seems clear is that to guarantee
someone a right always entails imposing a duty on someone else. $80
steak dinners cannot possibly qualify as rights in the positive sense,
because it would be impossible to guarantee every human being in the
world an $80 steak dinner. To do so would impose too severe a duty
on others.

From this notion of 'rights' as correlative with corresponding
'duties', it follows that one possible approach to the question of whether
we have any natural rights (and if so, which ones and how they can
be clearly established as such) is to begin by asking whether there are
any *duties* that people are bound to obey, regardless of the consequences
of such obedience. If any such nonutilitarian duties can be established,
then the corresponding rights would follow automatically. If we have
a duty not to kill, then everyone else also has a right not to *be* killed.
This is the approach that Kant takes to the issue of rights. According
to Kant, every right implies a corresponding duty (although not every
duty implies a corresponding right—there are duties to oneself, for
example, that entail no right on the part of other people). The leading
concept in Kant's theory of rights is therefore the concept of *duty*.

A very different possible approach to this same question is to think
of rights in terms of a conception of the "best possible arrangement of
society." Whatever the best possible arrangement of society would be,
on the whole, people might be said to have whatever *natural* rights
would necessarily be recognized as *legal* rights *within* such a "best possible" arrangement of society. This seems to be the approach that Rawls
takes, both in *A Theory of Justice* (1971) and in his more recent reformula-
tion of his theory, *Political Liberalism* (1993). By deriving duties from
rights, which are in turn derived from a concept of the best possible
arrangement of society as a whole, Rawls believes that we can avoid

assigning rights to people whose corresponding duties we are not prepared to accept, because if the corresponding duties are unacceptable, then such duties and, therefore, their corresponding rights, have no place in the best possible arrangement of society. Nor, in Rawls's view, does this concept necessarily entail an absurdly utopian concept of rights in the sense of demanding a "best possible arrangement" that is never likely to be attained: The "best possible arrangement" can simply be interpreted to mean the best arrangement that can possibly be attained in the given circumstances. If electricity has not yet been discovered, then the right to have free electrical power to one's home could not be said to have any place in the best possible arrangement of society under the given circumstances—circumstances that preclude electrical power.

An interesting aspect of this second type of approach to the issue of rights is that it would allow the question of rights to be settled by reference to the simpler question as to what ought to be the case in general. This type of approach to the question of rights would therefore be open even to a rule utilitarian, at least in principle, since rule utilitarianism holds that it ought to be the case that society is arranged in such a way as to produce the greatest happiness for the greatest number, and since the establishment of certain legal rights might be necessary or overwhelmingly conducive to such an outcome. It would then follow that these legal rights *ought* to be established, even if a utilitarian value system is assumed. (This was essentially Mill's argument in *On Liberty*, and it was Rawls's position even in his early work, when he was still a rule utilitarian; see Rawls 1955). Such a notion of rights would still count as a notion of "natural" rights rather than merely *legal* rights, since the latter could never be assumed to exist unless the people or their government had *actually* seen fit to bestow such rights. Natural rights, in contrast, can be assumed to exist on this basis *whether or not* the corresponding legal rights actually exist in a particular society; it would be enough to establish that such rights *ought* to be respected and protected. A utilitarian and a deontologist, of course, would disagree as to what the best possible arrangement of society *is*. The utilitarian would say that the best possible arrangement is the one that produces the greatest happiness for the greatest number (and that people therefore have the right to expect their government to promote this outcome), whereas the deontologist would equate the "best possible arrangement" with fairness, justice, or something of that nature (so that the people would correlatively have the right to expect their government to promote *these* outcomes).

The remaining two sections of this chapter will critically reexamine the two very different nonconsequentialist approaches that I have tried to distinguish here for grounding rights and duties as 'mandatory oughts'. Section 2 explores the view, exemplified by Kant, Gewirth, and Nozick, that rights can be sharply distinguished from beneficial or desirable consequences because rights and duties are, for practical purposes, correlative; on this view, respect for rights is mandatory because it is a duty. This approach, then, proceeds by trying to show that there are duties that do not depend for their bindingness on any good consequences to be produced by doing one's duty. I shall then explore some criticisms of this approach, which are crucial for our overall purpose here.

Section 3 then considers the other main nonconsequentialist approach to grounding rights, which in my view is exemplified by Frankena, Rawls, and many other recent theorists: deriving rights from a theory of distributive justice based on a concept of the best possible arrangement of society. We shall see, however, that the epistemic grounding of this approach can be shown to be insufficient to support a sharp distinction between rights and beneficial outcomes, for two main reasons. First, it becomes impossible to determine what the appropriate *balance* might be between the rights so derived on the one hand, and the maximization of the general welfare on the other. Second, the very *notion* of rights as derived from the best possible arrangement of society is not really as sharply distinguished from the maximization of beneficial consequences as it appears to be; 'rights' in this conceptualization seem to be defined as legal rights whose establishment is shown to be conducive to a certain outcome, namely, the achievement of an appropriate balance between distributive justice and utility maximization.

This second approach to rights is very promising, however, because it shows that there is an important place for a notion of rights defined in a way that is conceptually linked to the concept of overall distributive justice, and that if only an adequate theory of the appropriate balance between distributive justice and welfare maximization could be developed, then such a balance would also entail a designation of the appropriate place of rights in an overall political theory. I shall then argue, in the remainder of the book, that there is only one basic natural right whose protection has intrinsic value: the right to have one's society organized in such a way as to achieve an appropriate balance between welfare maximization and distributive justice with regard to all types of goods (both tangible and intangible). Protection of all other types of rights has only extrinsic value to the extent that protecting these rights promotes the one basic right that has intrinsic value—to be governed by a distributively just system in appropriate balance with general welfare maximization. The task of political philosophy then becomes to epistemically ground, and then work out in detail, the formula for such an appropriate balance and the political organization needed to establish and maintain it.

One further possible confusion about the notion of 'rights' must be waylaid before we proceed to the critical discussions of the two main types of nonconsequentialist rights theories. It is important to notice that there is a difference between "the right to X" and "the right to an equal opportunity for X." A newspaper editorial, discussing a proposal to cut federal financial aid programs for students, began with the headline "College Education a Privilege, Not a Right." The author concluded from this premise that the government, therefore, does not have the duty or responsibility to finance students' educations. This argument, however, plays on the ambiguity just mentioned. It may very well be that, even if everyone does not have the right to a college education (in which case the government would have no duty to pay on *this* basis), everyone might still have the right to an *equal opportunity for* a college education, in which case the government might still have a duty to pay on *this* basis. In fact, it was the latter type of reason, not the former, that constituted the rationale behind the liberal U.S. student-aid programs of the 1970s, continuing somewhat into the 1980s. The purpose was not so much to enable everyone to attend college as to enable everyone (including the children of poor parents) to have an equal opportunity to attend college. Another method of achieving the same goal would have been to eliminate poverty altogether; this, however, would have been a roundabout and unlikely-to-succeed approach to the problem of ensuring the right to an equal opportunity. The distinction between the right to X and the right to an *equal opportunity for* X is therefore important to bear in mind throughout any discussion of rights theory.

I suggested above that theories of 'rights'—in a sense strong enough that the rights in some sense are able to "trump" considerations of general utility—can be divided into two types. On the one hand, there are those theories that attempt to demonstrate the existence of rights *indirectly*, by first demonstrating the existence of the corresponding duties. Such theories might be called "conservative" or "minimal" theories of rights, because they prefer to err in the direction of leaving *out* of account any rights claims whose corresponding duties cannot be clearly demonstrated, rather than to proliferate long lists of postulated 'rights' that would require citizens to incur *duties* that cannot be unquestionably justified. Thus such a "duty-based" theory makes no attempt to defend any rights claims except those whose corresponding duties are clearly justifiable. Correlatively, these kinds of theories have the epistemological advantage (their proponents can argue) that they are more clearly *demonstrable* than are more "liberal" theories of rights, because they hold that it is easier to demonstrate the bindingness of a duty than to decide which rights claims are truly worthy of overriding others' claims to freedom from overburdensome duties. Kant's sociopolitical theory, which centers around a theory of the 'ideal social contract' (as opposed to defending an actual, historically existing social contract), is a prime example of such a conservative approach to rights. Kant's approach is to ground the theory as to which rights an ideal social contract would recognize in terms of a theory about which duties can be clearly demonstrated to be morally obligatory.

By contrast, more "liberal" theories of rights ("liberal" in the sense that they advocate a more extensive list of rights as taking priority over conflicting values) take just the opposite approach. They attempt to defend certain rights claims directly, by showing in one way or another that to deny consideration of such rights would be "unfair" or "unjust" in one way or another, appealing to some concept of distributive justice as the immediate basis for the rights claims. Once a specific list of rights claims has been defended successfully, then it follows that whatever duties are required to facilitate respect for these rights should be imposed. Thus the moral bindingness of the duties themselves need not be demonstrated directly. For example, if it is determined that medical care is a right of all citizens (or perhaps even noncitizen residents), then taxes must be collected to put such guarantees in place, and it will thus be someone's duty to pay these taxes. The formidable task facing such "liberal" approaches to rights, however, is to demonstrate with a reasonable degree of certainty that the list of rights claims in question really *is* philosophically supportable, even to the extent that the priority of these rights should be considered to override the corresponding claims to be free from the possibly overburdensome duties required to enact such rights. And, since freedom from overburdensome duties is itself usually considered to be *one of* the rights in question, such theories must successfully defend a set of criteria for deciding the relative priority of the various rights on the list when they conflict in various kinds of situations.

The next section will briefly consider the attempt to show through purely rational argument that certain duties are morally binding and, thus, that the corresponding rights ought to be respected, protected, and accorded priority over other values. The classic spokesman for this kind of argument was Immanuel Kant. Kant's political philosophy began with the premise that if we want rights to truly have priority over other kinds of values, then we must define these rights in terms of values that are mandatory or obligatory rather than merely desirable—that is, in terms of values that everyone is obligated to respect or has a 'duty' to respect. If rights are really to "trump" considerations of what merely produces desirable *consequences,* then the duties corresponding to these rights must be binding in a stronger sense than the sense in which it is merely *desirable* to perform some action that is not morally *mandatory.* For example, to refrain from murdering people seems to be a *mandatory* ought, and thus a duty that people have a right for others to observe. On the other hand, giving 10 percent of my income to the March of Dimes is certainly morally desirable or beneficial in that doing so would produce good consequences, but the March of Dimes can hardly be construed as having a *right* to receive 10 percent of my income, nor do I have a duty to give it to them.

It will not be surprising if a theory that sharply distinguishes rights and duties on the one hand from actions that are "desirable but not mandatory" on the other hand will tend to yield political theories that are conservative and minimalist. If it is *mandatory* that the government respect my *right* to keep my property that has been fairly acquired (as Nozick argues), and if rights really do absolutely "trump" consequentialist concerns (such as helping the poor), then the government has a duty to refrain from taking my property in order to fund welfare benefits for the poor—unless it can be independently demonstrated that helping the poor is a *duty* and not merely an action that would have *beneficial consequences.* In fact, as Posner points out, if the right of autonomy really trumps all other considerations, then it might even be argued that the government ought not to interfere in market transactions at all: "Suppose we consider consent an ethically attractive basis for permitting changes in the allocation of resources, on Kantian grounds. . . . We are led . . . to an ethical defense of market transactions that is unrelated to their effect in promoting efficiency. . . . It is clear that forbidding transactions would reduce both the wealth of society and personal autonomy" (Posner 1983, 89–90).

For similar reasons, the government would lose its authority, in such a conservative approach, to do anything that is merely *beneficial* whenever doing so would require infringing anyone's rights (for example, property rights), because duties (and the protection of the corresponding rights) would be *mandatory*, and oughts that are *mandatory* must take priority over oughts that are merely *desirable* or *beneficial*.

2. Kant, Gewirth, and Nozick: Rights and Duties as Mandatory Rather than Merely Beneficial

a. The basic argument for rights and duties as 'mandatory oughts'. Kant's argument that respect for certain kinds of values is a *duty*— that is, an obligation as opposed to merely desirable—begins with a distinction between two types of principles that can possibly guide human conduct. These two types of principles are 'hypothetical imperatives' and 'categorical imperatives'. An imperative is a statement that tells us that we should do something. Each type of imperative asserts a "should" or "ought," but with very different *meanings* of these terms, depending on whether the imperative takes a hypothetical or categorical form. A *hypothetical* imperative contains an *if* clause. "*If* you want to accomplish X, *then* you ought to do Y." Such a hypothetical imperative does not tell us that we should or should not want to accomplish X in the first place. It simply tells us *how* we could go about accomplishing X *if* it is our goal. A categorical imperative, on the other hand, is very different. It states, "You ought to do Y," not merely in order to produce X or some other consequence, but *regardless* of any consequences—simply because you have a moral obligation to do Y. Y is imperative in its own right, not for the sake of some further goal that it is expected to promote, such as happiness or pleasure or economic efficiency. For example, "You ought to keep promises" would be a categorical imperative if it could be demonstrated to be true.

Notice that this last example would still have the form of a categorical imperative even if it contained a qualification, such as "You ought to keep promises unless you have a good reason not to." In this case, the imperative is still categorical rather than hypothetical, because it contains no conditional. It does not say, "*If* your goal is so-and-so (happiness, for example), *then* you should keep promises unless you have a good reason not to." It asserts something stronger than this mere conditional; it claims unconditionally that we should keep promises unless we have a good reason not to, *regardless* of what our goals in life might be. This shows that an "ought" statement can still be a categorical rather than hypothetical imperative even if the types of instances in which the "ought" applies are limited by means of a qualification. A categorical imperative need not be an absolute state-ment that admits of no exceptions or qualifications (as is often wrongly supposed). A merely prima facie ought can be a categorical imperative, at least in principle, as long as it is not conditional on some further objective to be attained. By contrast, if the entire truth of an "ought" statement is made conditional on our wanting to accomplish some further goal by means of the action, then the imperative it states is not categorical at all, but only hypothetical.

Kant holds that "should" or "ought" in the categorical sense is a moral "should" (and thus can be morally binding in a way that super-sedes nonmoral goals), whereas "should" or "ought" in the hypotheti-cal sense has nothing to do with morality (and thus has no claim to priority over other non-moral goals). "Should" (or "ought") actually has a different *meaning* in the two contexts, and he holds that it is crucial not to confuse these two senses. In Kant's view, no proposed moral system based on a hypothetical imperative can really be a moral system at all, let alone a valid moral system. It would be simply a book of instructions on how to get what we want most efficiently. It would ignore the most fundamental issue of morality: Are there instances in which my duty (and thus someone else's right) *conflicts* with what I want? If there are cases in which my duty and my interest do not coincide, are there grounds for believing that I am obligated to do my duty, regardless of whether doing so conflicts with accomplishing whatever goals I happen to have set for myself, such as happiness or pleasure? In such cases of conflict between duty and self-interest, no theory based on a hypothetical imperative can give us any answer; yet this type of question, Kant says, is the most fundamental question in ethics. Therefore, any theory that simply dodges this question is in reality no ethical theory at all, but only a theory of "prudence"—a set of guidelines on how to accomplish a nonmoral objective. And, of course, this would include not only all utilitarian theories, but all consequentialist theories of any kind.

Kant's argument thus hinges on the idea that if there is going to turn out to be any demonstrably binding categorical imperative, by contrast to a hypothetical imperative, then its bindingness must not be based on any psychological theory of human nature or on any assumption about what kinds of goals a person may have in life. These could only lead to hypothetical imperatives that a person might choose to follow if she found that doing so served her purposes. Such consider-ations could never ground a categorical imperative, which must be universally binding and equally applicable to all people in all circumstances.

On the other hand, no categorical imperative can be binding unless its truth is rationally demonstrable, rather than merely decreed by some arbitrary fiat. To follow rules of conduct that we have no reason to believe are valid would not be to do our duty or even to do what we "ought" to do in any sense, because we would have no reason to think we were any more likely to act rightly than wrongly by following such arbitrary decrees. Only a demonstrably true categorical imperative can be a legitimate one.

The requirement for a categorical imperative is thus quite a tall order. It implies that the rightness of obeying the imperative cannot depend on the consequences of such obedience. This question therefore arises: If we are not to demonstrate the bindingness of duties and the rightness of acting according to these duties on the basis of the good *consequences* to be produced by so acting, then how *can* we demonstrate it?

Kant argues that only *one* such principle is capable of qualifying as a categorical imperative and, at the same time, as a rationally demonstrable one. This principle can be formulated in three ways. The first is that we should "never act in such a way that [we] could not also will that [our] maxim should be a universal law" (Kant 1785–1959, 18). In other words, we should do nothing that we could not consistently be willing for everyone to do if they were in similar circumstances. The other two formulations will be considered in a moment, after we have shown why they are needed.

Notice that Kant's argument hinges on the idea that the *inconsistency* of willing the universalization of a maxim is what makes it unallowable, not our mere *emotional preference* that it not be universalized. Many a classical musician would have difficulty in willing that everyone play rock music, but this does not make "Don't play rock music" a binding rule of conduct. Rather, Kant's point is that we should not do things that we could not *consistently* be willing for everyone to do if they were in our place. For example, he thinks that "Don't tell deliberate falsehoods" does qualify as a binding duty (at least with certain qualifications), because if we were to will that everyone should tell deliberate falsehoods, then we would thereby will a state of affairs in which no one would take anyone else's word for anything, which would defeat our purpose in telling the deliberate falsehoods we wish to tell. We would thus wish something that, when universalized, would become self-contradictory or inconsistent. As another example, suppose there are five pieces of pie to be divided among five people. Before taking a second piece, the categorical imperative demands that we ask ourselves, "Would I be willing for everyone to take two pieces if they could get away with it?" Obviously, we could not will this, because to do so would be to will a self-contradiction; we would have to be willing for someone else to take a piece of pie that we have already committed ourselves to wanting, if that person could get away with it.

How does Kant *demonstrate* that we should act according to no maxim that is not universalizable in this sense, and that this principle, therefore, qualifies as the only valid and universally binding categorical imperative? His initial assumption is that if we ask ourselves whether we would be willing to allow that the world we live in might be devoid of any possibility of a genuinely moral community—and of genuinely moral value—we would find such a notion so repugnant, and so foreign to the sense of our everyday experience, that we *must* elect to live *as if* there were moral principles. But as soon as we accept that there is such a thing as a moral principle, then it is not difficult to demonstrate exactly how such principles would have to be formulated. If hypothetical imperatives cannot qualify as moral principles, then no utilitarian or consequentialist doctrine can count as evidence for any principle. The fact that a maxim promotes the general welfare, our own welfare, or any other ulterior consequence would convert the "ought" of the moral ought into a *hypothetical* "ought." But no hypothetical ought can be accepted until the end on which it is conditional has been shown to have moral value and not merely prudential or self-interested value. Thus every hypothetical imperative, if it is to have any moral relevance, is dependent on the assumption that the end on which it is conditional can be legitimated on the basis of a *categorical* imperative—very much in the same way that an extrinsic or instrumental value can have value only to the extent that the *intrinsic* value that it facilitates has value. Obviously, if the end on which a hypothetical imperative is conditional could not be demonstrated to have moral value, then neither would the hypothetical imperative in question have moral value. But such an end could not be legitimated by showing that it is in turn dependent on some prior hypothetical imperative whose value in turn is conditional on some *other* end, unless these ends themselves are ultimately legitimated on the basis of a value that is *not* conditional—that is, a categorical imperative.

If the consequences of an action cannot ground its morality, then no moral principle can be legitimated by showing that its obedience produces good consequences. But if the validity or bindingness of a principle cannot be demonstrated in this way, then the only other way to do so is to show that to deny the principle would be self-contradictory. And the only principle that it would be self-contradictory to deny is the categorical imperative, whose primary formulation was mentioned above: Act according to no principle that you could not consistently will to be a universal principle of human conduct. If there is to be any moral law whatever, this must be it. Given Kant's initial assumption then—that there must be *some* moral principle or principles—it follows that this categorical imperative is the only reasonable candidate for one. Note that Kant never pretends to prove that there must be some moral principle or principles. The reason for accepting this premise is simply that no one would be willing to live in a society in which there is no such thing as morality; such a life would be intolerable. This assumption is similar to the one made by many other social contract theorists, as Rawls notably makes clear in *Political Liberalism* (1993). A similar use of this kind of assumption in contemporary political philosophy can be found in Baynes's *Normative Grounds of Social Criticism* (1992). Baynes, like Rawls, directly attributes the assumption to Kant, characterizing it as a "constructivist" as opposed to a "foundationalist" approach. "As I understand it," says Baynes, "Kantian constructivism attempts to account for the objectivity of our normative assessments by relating the ideals and principles employed in our critical practices to an expressly normative conception of practical reason or, what I shall argue amounts to the same thing, to a conception of ourselves as free and equal moral persons" (1).

There is a need for a definite specification of the types of actions required and prohibited by the categorical imperative, and this need leads to the second formulation of the principle. At first it might seem that, if it would be logically possible to will that everyone be allowed to do X, then X would be allowable by the categorical imperative. Thus if a mafia hit man could will without self-contradiction that everyone be allowed to try to commit murder (and be responsible to provide their own protection), then murder would be allowed by the categorical imperative. To forestall this type of possibility, Kant argues that the categorical imperative can also be formulated as requiring that we treat others always as ends in themselves and never merely as means toward ends. This formulation follows from the clarification of what it means to will something: An autonomous agent capable of willing according to a moral principle is an end in itself, not merely a means to some other end, because by willing according to a moral principle as governed by reason, the agent causes there to be intrinsic value that otherwise would not have existed. So the categorical imperative requires not only that we treat others as we could will to be treated, but to do so without reducing anyone to a mere means to some end. This requirement is entailed by the categorical imperative because no one who wills according to a moral principle can be willing to be a means only, since to will according to a moral principle is already to *be* an end in itself (Gillroy 1992b, 495–96).

This second formulation in turn entails a third. We should act so as to regard others as ends in themselves only insofar as they are considered *in their capacity as autonomous moral agents*—not necessarily in their capacity as hedonistic subjects. The reasoning here is that it is the other's capacity to will according to a moral principle that we cannot consistently treat as if it did not have intrinsic value. As far as the person's capacity as hedonistic subject is concerned, it would not be logically self-contradictory to will that certain hedonistic interests be frustrated, even though we cannot will that our own hedonistic interests be frustrated. In other words, I can desire an ice cream cone, and desire that someone else *not* get an ice cream cone, without any logical self-contradiction, because I am not necessarily willing that the other's *intrinsic value*, qua morally autonomous agent, be negated or incapacitated. So, in the final analysis, what the categorical imperative prescribes is that we both act positively to facilitate others' autonomous moral agency (since we could not consistently will that our own be thwarted) and, in negative terms, that we refrain from depriving others of the conditions needed to be autonomous moral agents. Ultimately, this entails that everyone's autonomy qua moral agent ought to be respected equally.

b. Criticisms of the Kantian approach. In the chapter on utilitarianism, we saw that some utilitarians, notably Mill, base their criticisms of Kant on a misinterpretation of his reasoning. Mill suggests that Kant fails, "almost grotesquely," to show that there would be any contradiction involved in the universalization of the most immoral imaginable rules of conduct, but shows instead that *undesirable consequences* would follow from the universalization of such rules (*Utilitarianism*, 3–4). This criticism addresses itself only to a straw man caricature of the Kantian view. As we have seen, the categorical imperative does not prohibit actions whose universalization would have undesirable consequences; it prohibits only those actions whose universalization would be self-defeating because it would involve willing a *self-contradictory* or *inherently impossible* state of affairs. For example, to will that anyone should be allowed to exercise so much greed that some others must starve or live under inhuman conditions (i.e., conditions detrimental to their functioning as autonomous agents) would be inconsistent, because it would entail being willing to starve or to live under inhuman conditions myself if the person taking more than an equal share were someone other than myself.

There is another common objection to Kant's view that can be gotten around by appealing to the second and third formulations of the categorical imperative discussed above. We might pose the following dilemma: Suppose we tell a Mafia hit man not to commit murder unless he can will without inconsistency that everyone try to kill other people whenever they think they can get away with it. The hit man might reply something to this effect: "Certainly I can will without inconsistency that anyone who can get away with killing others may do so, because I have provided my own protection against being murdered, as is everyone's responsibility. And, while I realize that my willing the universalization of this kind of action may well involve a certain *risk* that, in spite of all my efforts to protect myself, someone will nonetheless succeed in murdering me, I am prepared to take this risk in exchange for the privilege of murdering others."

While we may consider the hit man's risk an unwise one to take, Kant's critics may argue, it does not seem to involve any self-contradiction, inconsistency, or self-defeatingness. It would seem to follow, then, that if inconsistency is required in order to prohibit a rule of action, then Kant's categorical imperative does not prohibit murder, the most vicious of all crimes. The hit man merely increases his *risk* of death, and there seems to be nothing logically inconsistent about being willing to take a risk. Also, suppose I am getting ready to kill someone whom I hate very much—whom I hate so much that I would be willing to die in order to ensure his death (as many murderers, in fact, do feel, according to Beristain 1977 and Gold 1961). Then my willing the universalization of murder would not be to will something that makes my action self-defeating purely from the standpoint of whether the action accomplishes its goal. I would merely be balancing a stronger motive (to kill the other person) against a weaker motive (to stay alive).

A plausible Kantian response to this objection is that the hit man is not willing a logical inconsistency, *because of his desire to stay alive* (which does not really contradict his desire to kill the other person, as we have seen). Rather, the hit man's *functioning as an autonomous agent* (bringing values into existence out of his rational autonomy rather than merely conforming to hedonistic needs) entails that to be an autonomous agent has intrinsic value, which in turn would contradict his destroying the agency of another person, since that agency too has been granted to have intrinsic value. This implication was discussed earlier with reference to Kant's second and third formulations of the categorical imperative.

A more serious criticism arises from a slight variation on the hit man example: Suppose someone says that he does not believe it is anyone's responsibility to help anyone in times of trouble—that no one has a duty to support relief programs for the unemployed, the aged, the disabled, etc. In fact, let's go to the absolute extreme and imagine that this Scrooge does not believe in helping anyone under any circumstances unless their very physical survival is at stake (and therefore, obviously, such a person would believe in a very conservative, laissez-faire political philosophy). Let's say he justifies this belief on the basis that it is each person's responsibility to save money, have insurance policies, etc., to cover such possibilities. Suppose further that our Scrooge has made all such possible provisions for himself in case of hardship. Then, would there be anything self-contradictory, self-defeating, or inconsistent in his being willing to universalize such an attitude? Granted, he is taking the risk that he himself may need help someday. But considering all the preparations he has made for such a contingency, the risk is small. Thus his uncharitable attitude, when generalized, would not seem self-defeating. What is inconsistent or self-contradictory about being willing to take such a risk?

The problem is that if Kant's second and third formulations are invoked to show that the only intrinsic value that I must respect in other people is their ability to function as moral agents, then there is no duty to benefit them in any way that is not necessary for their existence as moral agents. There can be no duty to merely *benefit* people in any way not required in order to make possible their moral agency, nor to distribute any benefits or opportunities in a just way, except for those necessary to make possible people's moral agency.

On the other hand, if we say that other kinds of benefits not necessary to moral agency must be taken into consideration, then we are back to the original problem that the second and third formulations were meant to avoid. It is not logically inconsistent for me to want an ice cream cone without wanting the other person to have one, because I could will, without inconsistency, that the other person try to get as much ice cream as she can. This would entail a greater *risk* of my not getting any ice cream, but there is nothing logically inconsistent about being willing to take a risk.

So, given the more defensible version of Kant's approach, which includes all three formulations of the basic principle, the problem is that it seems to entail an extremely minimal theory of government, in which there would be no duty to benefit people in any way not required to sustain their ability to exist as moral agents, nor to distribute any opportunities or benefits justly, except those that are required to sustain people's ability to exist as moral agents. If the government wished to take action merely in order to benefit people, this wish would always be overridden by the conflicting need to facilitate autonomy, since the demands of autonomy automatically "trump" considerations of the general welfare.

It might be objected that not all merely beneficial collective actions *would* conflict with some right grounded in the demands of autonomy. But that leads us to a still more important problem with the Kantian approach, insofar as it is to be used as a method for political decision making. The theory does not offer any criterion by which those political rights and duties that *can* be derived from it could be compared in importance to the value of providing services to people simply in order to benefit them per se—for example, by building roads, promoting a productive economy, providing unemployment compensation, or by making effective educational facilities available. Presumably, the Kantian position is that the protection of and facilitation of everyone's moral autonomy, along with all the rights and opportunities required for this purpose, must be guaranteed first, and then government programs meant merely to benefit people can be considered for adoption, as long as they do not conflict with the guarantee of autonomy. But, in concrete terms, it would be very difficult or impossible to make many, if not most, aggregate decisions on this basis. For example, how should the government decide how many deaths from auto accidents are to be tolerated for the sake of fast transportation, which is needed to move people effectively enough to make an urban-industrial economic system feasible? How many cancer deaths are to be tolerated for the sake of the production of goods whose purpose is to make life's hardships more tolerable? There seems to be no criterion by which to make the value of services that facilitate moral autonomy commensurable with the value of services which facilitate other intrinsic values such as happiness, personal fulfillment, and the just distribution of such values or the opportunity to achieve them. And there are many government programs—education, welfare, free medical care, etc.—that have a *tendency* to facilitate moral agency, at least for some, but still may not be strictly *necessary* to people's autonomy.

In terms of concrete policy decisions, the crucial question is whether Kant means that respecting all people as ends in themselves includes (a) respecting all the ends that those people intrinsically value (for example, their happiness) as ends in themselves, or only (b) respecting the *autonomous moral agency* of those people as ends in themselves, but *not* necessarily respecting other things that those people intrinsically value (such as their happiness) as ends in themselves. If (a) is our interpretation, then the Scrooge in our example can consistently will that others be deprived of happiness and distributive justice due to his greed, because his own happiness is also an end in itself, and it is not logically self-contradictory for him to assert that his happiness has more value than the other's (for the reasons we have already discussed). But if (b) is the correct interpretation, then the promotion of autonomy would seem to take such absolute priority over other values (such as the happiness and well-being of people) as to lead to a very minimalist theory of government—one in which demands arise from what is needed for moral autonomy, leading to minimal interference with people's freedom (except where needed for others' moral autonomy). It would then never be justified for the government to interfere with X's exercise of her freedom in order to facilitate improving Y's material conditions of well-being in any instance, except for two types of cases: (1) those in which X is not exercising her freedom in the interest of moral ends; or (2) those in which Y's autonomy depends on certain minimal material conditions (for example, so that it would not be absolutely impossible for her to get enough to eat or to avoid growing up in a neighborhood completely dominated by street gangs, etc.).

It may be true that the Kantian system limits its protection of 'freedoms' to just those freedoms needed to facilitate moral autonomy. But then any instance of any such freedom would automatically enjoy absolute priority over any other consideration whatever. And we would still lack a way to make the value of liberty in the *broader* sense (i.e., not just freedom to follow the moral law, but also freedom to do *other* kinds of things, such as run industrial operations or engineer the merger of corporations) *commensurable* with the value of promoting people's welfare in order to compare the relative importance of *these* values in various contexts. Thus there are still many priority decisions for which this interpretation of Kant does not yield an answer.

Gillroy's (1992b) solution to this last type of problem is to point out that there are many instances of *material and psychological well-being* that need to be in place in order to foster the *development* of moral autonomy (for example, freedom from extreme, continuous hunger, from completely gang-dominated neighborhoods, and from autonomy-destroying child abuse; access to certain educational opportunities; etc.). But this seems to imply that access to these needed conditions can be present to greater or lesser extents, and that this access can be distributed in various ways, some just and some unjust—and perhaps even that autonomous agency *itself* can be present to greater or lesser degrees (as, in fact, I suggested in *Theories of Criminal Justice*). And this would mean that some theory of *distributive* justice is needed by which we can determine the relative importance of *maximizing* the availability of such resources on the one hand, and of *distributing them fairly* on the other.

Once we stretch a Kantian approach far enough to admit that the conditions required for agency are quantifiable and can be either maximized or justly distributed or some balance between the two, then we may as well take the next step and regard responsible human agency or moral autonomy as an *outcome* to be promoted, just as a personalist or self-actualizationist system would advocate. By seeing agency as an outcome to be promoted, we can then reopen the question as to what is the appropriate balance between maximizing the conditions needed for this outcome on the one hand, and justly distributing those conditions on the other. But for this purpose, as I shall try to show in the remainder of this book, we need a consequentialist approach, although not a purely utilitarian one.

A related problem, as William Frankena points out, is that those duties *can* be established by means of the categorical imperative seem to be too strictly universal. For example, the duty not to lie seems immune to the above criticisms, because the categorical imperative would imply that the universalization of lying would be self-defeating (since one's own lies would not be believed). But this would then imply that one should *never* lie, which seems counterintuitive. When the Gestapo comes to the door looking for Jews, is the moral course of action to tell the truth? This would seem to be what Kant's theory implies, *unless* we try to make room for exceptions in ways that Kant himself did not do. For example, we might say that the telling of lies in specific types of exceptional cases could be universalized without becoming self-defeating. There would be nothing self-defeating about being willing for everyone to lie only in those cases in which it is necessary to do so in order to help someone. Thus we could let our universal rule of conduct be: "Never lie, except to help someone." Such a move would not make the rule hypothetical, as we noted at the beginning of our overall discussion of Kant, because it is possible to qualify a rule without making it hypothetical.

But then other problems arise. If we allow one type of exception to be stipulated, we inadvertently drag in numerous others by the same token. Suppose we let the rule say, "Never lie, except to trick someone after having told the truth enough times in a row that your lie becomes believable." This could be universalized without becoming self-defeating. Or we could say, "Only lie when you can be reasonably sure that the lie won't be detected," or "Only lie 10 percent of the time." These are the kinds of principles most criminals follow when dealing with each other, after all, so why should there be any inconsistency in their being willing for everyone else to follow them as well? In fact, Max Scheler thinks that if we went on long enough with these kinds of examples, we could show that there are no actual rules of conduct that strictly follow from the categorical imperative at all. The principle is too formal and abstract to have any specifiable practical consequences.

Another problem with the categorical imperative is that it is difficult to know whether it means that we should not do something that we could not be willing for *everyone* to do, or that we should not do something that we could not be willing for *anyone who pleased* to do. As in the discussion of rule utilitarianism in the last chapter, Smart's objection would apply here too. If the categorical imperative means that we should not do something that we could not be willing for *everyone* to do, then it would seem to have strange consequences. For example, no one should become a philosophy teacher, because if everyone became a philosophy teacher, then everyone would starve, thus defeating the purpose of teaching philosophy. But if the categorical imperative means that we should not do something that we could not be willing for *anyone who pleased* to do, then such a principle would allow that it is all right to write music during English class since, if everyone *who is likely to want do so* were to write music in class, no problem would result. By the same token, it would become all right to lie if we happen to know that not very many people are going to want to lie as a result of our lies, all right to steal if we know that not very many people will want to steal, etc. The universalization of the rule of conduct to cover all those who find themselves wanting to engage in the immoral behavior would entail no inconsistency: The number of lies told would, then, not defeat my purpose in lying; the number of thefts would not greatly increase my chances of being robbed; etc.

c. Contemporary versions of Kant's proof of mandatory rights and duties. Kant's theory serves as a paradigm for the notion that a concept of justice and a theory of rights can be based on rules of conduct derived from a principle of moral obligation. Other theorists have tried to make nonutilitarian value principles follow from purely logical analyses or from the "dialectical" need to maintain consistency in the rights and duties we assert for ourselves and for others. For example, Alan Gewirth (1978, 1984) has recently attempted to stand Kant on his head by deriving rules of obligation from rights claims, rather than deriving rights claims from rules of obligation. Gewirth argues that we must all *claim* to have certain rights, and that in order to be logically consistent, we must then allow that others are just as entitled to claim such rights as we are. Thus we must acknowledge any rights we might wish to claim as being universal rights belonging to all people.

But the problems here are similar to Kant's problems. Just as it could be objected against Kant that a mafioso need not be unwilling for others to try to steal, so could it be objected against Gewirth that a thief need not claim any 'right' not to be stolen from. He could simply take the position that "it would be better, all else being equal, if people didn't steal from each other." Or he could simply take the necessary precautions against being robbed, while denying that anyone has any *right* not to be robbed. Moreover, even if it is "dialectically necessary" for people to *claim* to have certain rights, the fact that someone claims something does not necessarily make it so. People might claim to have a right to smoke cigarettes in public (and be willing to universalize the claim), but this does not prove that such a rights claim is legitimate or philosophically justifiable. Such a person, to be consistent by Gewirth's criterion, would, of course, also have to admit that she is willing for others to jeopardize her own health to the same extent that she jeopardizes the health of others. But such people typically *are* willing to universalize a diminished concern for health risks.

Perhaps the most decisive objection against Gewirth's argument, however, is that although it might be dialectically necessary for each person to make certain claims to the effect that *it would be better* for people to treat each other in certain ways, it is impossible to infer from the claim that *it would be better* for people to be treated in these ways, to the conclusion that people have a *right* to be treated in those ways. For example, *it would be better*, all else being equal, if I were to give 20 percent of my income to the poor, but this does not imply that the poor have a *right* to receive 20 percent of my income. So, granted that it would be beneficial for the poor to be helped, it would be a much stronger claim to say that the poor have a *right* to be helped. (These criticisms are formulated very forcefully in Regis 1984.)

Correlatively, the mere fact that someone needs or wants something does not necessarily make it "dialectically necessary" for that person to assert that whatever is needed or wanted is due her as a *right*. I may want or even need a new roof on my house, but does this fact logically entail that I must assert a right to have my roof replaced at government expense?

This objection (as discussed more fully in Ellis 1992) leads to a corresponding problem with the concrete applicability of Gewirth's theory in a way that is very analogous to the problems in applying Kant's theory. If one person feels that it is dialectically necessary for her to assert a right to state-sponsored medical care (and thus is willing to extend this same right to everyone), whereas someone else does not assert such a right (and is not willing to extend the same right to everyone), how do we decide whether this rights claim should be extended to everyone or not? In the same way, this crucial question would seem to be irresolvable in the case of every proposed rights claim.

In defense against this objection, Gewirth takes the position that only that which is necessary to a person's free agency can be considered a legitimate rights claim (Gewirth 1984). For example, in order to be a free agent, it is necessary to have the minimal requirements for survival, a modicum of human dignity, and a certain amount of freedom of movement. The emphasis on the notion that the value of free agency "trumps" all other considerations, and is thus a mandatory right, is similar to the Kantian argument that the moral autonomy of each person is an inviolable principle that must trump all consequentialist calculations, as Gillroy (1992b) points out. But in this case we run into another problem that is analogous to one of the above criticisms of Kant: If only the crucial conditions for free agency can form the basis for rights claims, then the duties of the government become severely limited; and if rights really "trump" considerations of the general welfare, then the freedom of people (which presumably is a right) would seem to take automatic priority over the goal of benefiting people whenever these interests conflict. And these interests very often do conflict. Thus the freedom of businessmen would take priority over merely beneficial regulatory policies; the freedom of manufacturers to use their preferred technologies would take priority over merely beneficial regulatory policies; etc. If we limit inalienable rights to just those cases in which the rights claim in question is dialectically necessary for a person's free agency, while at the same time holding that rights automatically "trump" consequentialist concerns, then we are again left with an ultraconservative and minimalist role for government, an extreme laissez-faire philosophy, just as in the theories of Kant and Nozick—although such practical consequences are, of course, far from what Gewirth originally intended.

It might be responded here that the business practices and technologies in the examples just mentioned *do* affect other people in ways that jeopardize their ability to exist and function as free agents (for example, pollution kills them, and unregulated business activities, by allowing unfair labor practices, impair the survival and human dignity of workers). But it would be impossible to illegalize all practices on the part of business and industry that would create even the least degree of *risk* of death, unemployment, or poverty to any workers, consumers, or citizens exposed to pollution. To do so would require eliminating all automobile transportation (which entails risk of death), athletic activities (which also entail such a risk), and most other activities in which human beings engage (since they all involve some degree of risk). In the final analysis, it remains very unclear what the appropriate *balance* might be, in Gewirth's theory just as in Kant's, between consumer protection and the freedom of business, between protection from hazardous wastes and the freedom of manufacturers, etc. Instead of a theory that initially seemed to offer a concept of rights that were to "trump" merely beneficial outcomes, we are left with a theory in which the distinction between a right and a merely beneficial outcome is essentially a quantitative rather than qualitative one (i.e., whether a given practice infringes the rights of others depends on the *degree of risk* to which it exposes them and on the *extent* to which it tends to deprive them of freedom, of human dignity, of the means of survival, and thus of the ability to exist and function as 'free agents'). Yet no quantitative formula seems capable of facilitating such priority decisions.

Any attempt to logically prove the existence of rights by means of a rigid distinction between mandatory oughts (i.e., rights and duties) and merely desirable oughts (i.e., beneficial social policies) will ultimately confront essentially the same problem that Kant confronted: If we wish to demonstrate the truth of a value statement by means of a purely logical proof, then to do so would require that the denial of the value statement in question must be logically self-contradictory. But it is possible to maintain outrageously immoral rules of conduct without contradicting oneself. An immoral value system may be false, arbitrary, lacking in epistemic justification, or even incoherent, without thereby becoming logically self-contradictory. Even if it is unwise to be willing for everyone to go around stealing from other people, it is not logically self-contradictory to will such a state of affairs. Any proof that stealing is wrong must therefore rely on more than the demand for logical consistency. It must rely on a demonstration that stealing is indeed harmful. But in this case the admonition against stealing must ultimately be justified in consequentialist terms, not in terms of a logical proof that stealing entails some sort of self-contradiction or dialectical inconsistency.

Even if it could be shown that some short list of logically or dialectically necessary rights and duties take absolute priority over consequentialist concerns, the fact that such a list would be extremely short and would involve only the most negative sorts of rights, combined with the fact that these negative rights would take absolute priority over all other concerns, could lead only to a very minimal theory of the role of government—essentially, a Lockean type of theory, in which the only roles of government would be to prevent people from killing each other; stealing each other's property; or enslaving, kidnapping, or imprisoning each other without due process of law.

Nozick (1974) and Machan (1989) are the ultimate expressions of such a minimalist conception, in which freedom takes absolute priority over the values of benefiting people or of distributive equity. Any concept of equality that remains is merely one of equal freedom. But as Gillroy points out, there can be no equal freedom among people whose resources are vastly different or who lack certain conditions needed to actualize their potential as free agents in the context of a complex, technologically sophisticated society (for example, access to jobs, freedom from domination by street gangs, etc.). Merely negative rights have little meaning devoid of the resources needed to exercise them in concrete contexts.

On the other hand, if we wanted to make the list of logically or dialectically necessary rights and duties longer, and make it include some positive as well as negative rights, then we could do so only by maintaining, with Gewirth, that the exercise of 'free agency' is a basic right that entails extensive constraints on activities that would conflict with the possibility of this free agency. But in this case the question as to how much someone's action conflicts with the possibility of someone else's free agency becomes, in most cases, a quantitative one, and the distinction becomes correspondingly blurred between socially beneficial policies on the one hand, and policies that are necessary to protect inalienable rights on the other.

What is needed for a viable theory of rights and duties, then, is a theory that makes the assessment of the importance of rights and duties *commensurable* with the assessment of the importance of consequentialist concerns. And this commensurability can be achieved only if the concept of distributive justice is first established as the ultimate basis from which rights claims can be derived. Distributive justice, after all, can be conceived as a *consequence* to be achieved, so that there is no need to insist on the absolute priority of certain types of rights (no matter how frivolous the example) over all other considerations of human welfare (no matter how cataclysmic the example). Instead, such a theory would try to show that distributive justice in general enjoys a certain priority in relation to utility maximization, and that rights must be considered as "inalienable" only to the extent that protection of the rights can be derived from the need to ensure the appropriate balance between distributive justice and utility maximization, again with distributive justice enjoying a certain priority. William Frankena and John Rawls are instructive examples of the attempt to establish such an integrative approach under the broad umbrella of a "distributive justice" theory.

3. Frankena and Rawls: The Need for a Commensurability of Justice and Utility

a. William Frankena's "mixed deontological" approach to the theory of justice attempts to build on the criticisms of both the deontic and the utilitarian approaches by creatively synthesizing the two. The main problem with utilitarianism, according to Frankena (1963), is that it cannot ground an adequate theory of distributive justice. There will always be conflict between what tends to generate the greatest happiness for the greatest number (or the greatest quantity of good consequences in general) on the one hand, and on the other hand, what tends to *distribute* these good consequences equitably. If utilitarianism remains consistent, it cannot prefer 100 units of happiness distributed among 100 people over 101 units distributed among 10 people. Deontic theories, by contrast, argue for some list of rules of obligation designed to ensure that justice does not always take a back seat to utility. Deontology's main problem, however, is that its plurality of principles cannot provide a clear criterion by which to decide the relative priority of these principles in cases of conflict.

Frankena hopes to provide such a unified criterion. We should unite the principle of beneficence (or utility maximization) with the principle of justice, he says, forming one coherent principle: Always act in such a way as to contribute an *equal* amount of goodness to all people's lives. Included in this is the principle of utility (produce the greatest possible quantity of good), as well as the principle of equity or distributive justice (distribute this good as equally as possible).

One might at first assume that Frankena means that we are to work toward a greater degree of social equality. But while it is true that Frankena believes that there should be a minimum living standard below which none are allowed to fall, beyond this point his theory not only does not lead to social equality, but directly contradicts any such goal (although Frankena does not acknowledge this implication). The theory does not imply a movement toward greater equality because if we contribute an equal amount of good to each person's life, then we end up helping the fortunate exactly as much as the unfortunate, thus leaving the discrepancy between them exactly the same as when we began.

This implication with regard to social inequality immediately raises a criticism of Frankena's view. If we give welfare to the poor, must we contribute some equivalent amount of goodness to the rich? If a millionaire and a penniless pauper sit down to play cards, would not this principle require that if I wish to donate $5 to the pauper's stake, I must also give an equal amount to the millionaire? This would seem to have a marked tendency to arbitrarily perpetuate whatever degree of social equality or inequality happens to exist at the present moment. Frankena explicitly rejects the principle of "to each according to his needs":

> Are we always prima facie unjust if we help A in proportion to his needs but not B, or if we make demands of C in proportion to his abilities but not of D? It seems to me that the basic question is whether or not in so doing we are showing an equal concern

for the goodness of the lives of A and B or of C and D. Whether we should treat them in proportion to their needs and abilities depends, as far as *justice* is concerned, on whether doing so helps or hinders them equally in the achievement of the good life. If helping them in proportion to their needs is necessary for making an equal contribution to the goodness of their lives, then and only then is it unjust to do otherwise. (Frankena 1963, 40–41)

In spite of this problem in the conceptualization of equality, there are limited respects in which Frankena's approach does recommend policies that would have some tendency to lead to social equality. By "treating all people equally," we would try to establish programs to increase the degree of equality of "economic opportunity." Yet even this limited increase of equality creates two additional problems for the theory. (1) The notion of "economic opportunity" seems unclear. To return to our example of the card game, suppose the rules of the game are such that the winner takes all the loser's property, leaving him with neither house, car, nor livelihood, yet each player has an "equal opportunity" to win or lose. Suppose further that neither player has a choice as to whether to engage in the game (as is generally true in the economic game). Would this really be a "fair" game? Obviously not. Equally obviously, a society in which the gap between the "winners" and "losers" is extremely great must be deemed unjust even if "equality of opportunity" does exist. But Frankena's theory does not condemn this kind of unfairness.

In current political discussion about balancing the budgets of governments, one frequently hears calls for "everyone's bearing a share" of the burden—implying that it is only fair to reduce such items as medical care for the aged and the indigent, social security benefits, and unemployment compensation if the wealthy are also to be expected to pay higher taxes or give up some of their tax deductions. But the same problem exists here as in Frankena's theory: To ask the poor to give up a substantial part of what little they have in exchange for the rich's giving up an equal amount is not a fair exchange.

There is still another problem with Frankena's formula for combining utilitarian and deontic values within one overarching principle. Consider the following passage:

We must remember here that this equality of treatment, though it is a basic obligation, is only a *prima facie* one, and that it may on occasion (and there is no formula for determining the occasions) be overruled by the principles of benevolence or beneficence. We may claim, however, that in distributing goods and evils, help, tasks, roles, and so forth, people are to be treated equally in the sense indicated, except when unequal treatment can be justified by considerations of benevolence (including utility) or on the ground that it will promote greater equality in the long run. Unequal treatment always requires justification and only certain kinds of justification suffice. (Frankena 1963, 41–42)

If this passage is taken at its word, then Frankena no longer really seems to overcome the criticisms of earlier deontic theories such as the ones discussed in the previous section. The reason is that there is now no longer any clear criterion by which to determine in which cases utility should take precedence over equity or vice versa.

In spite of these difficulties, Frankena's theory still seems to be pointing toward a fruitful direction, if only the difficulties can be resolved (and, in essence, I intend to show in the remainder of the book that they can be). In the first place, Frankena's theory is more coherent than a purely nonconsequentialist deontic theory of rights, since in Frankena's case we have only two principles between which to decide in cases of conflict. In purely deontic theories of rights, there are as many principles as there are rights and duties, *plus* the principle of beneficence, all to be balanced against each other in cases of conflict. Frankena also has two advantages over Kant: (i) Since he incorporates the principle of utility, Frankena's theory does not have the counterintuitive implication that we must do our duty even if doing it produces disastrous consequences for people. Doing one's duty in Frankena's sense can never produce disastrous consequences for people as a whole, but must, by definition, produce good consequences. (ii) Because the rule Frankena gives us can be applied without the tortured complexities of reasoning in which the application of Kant's categorical imperative appears to enmesh us, Frankena does not have to worry about the many possible criticisms that we saw in the previous section to arise from the problem of how the categorical imperative is to be applied.

In addition, Frankena's approach may well enjoy still another advantage over purely deontic theories in general: Purely deontic theories typically require that actions be judged not only by their consequences or intended consequences, but also according to whether they were committed freely and for the right motives. Since "ought implies can," the agent must possess free will in order for an action to be adjudicable on this basis. Frankena remains remarkably free of the "ought implies can" can of worms, because he does not need to specify what kind of motive must lead us to conform to his principle in order for our action to be considered morally justified. All human actions could be completely predetermined (although Frankena does not say that they are) without altering the truth value of Frankena's theory in the least. We either follow the correct ethical principle or we do not, but whether we are led to do so by superior reasoning ability, by environmental factors (such as education), or by any other predetermining cause, does not alter the correctness of the principle.

Although Frankena does not, in the final analysis, provide a workable and defensible decision principle for balancing deontic and utilitarian concerns, his approach does point in the general direction of one. What is required, essentially, in order to counter all the criticisms of Frankena just mentioned, is to make room for the principle of diminishing marginal utility. It was failure to account for diminishing marginal utility, after all, that led to the criticism that it is absurd to make an "equal" contribution to the rich and to the poor. In other words, contributing $100's worth of value to a rich person's life is not the same as contributing $100 to a penniless vagrant, because the principle of diminishing marginal utility implies that the same $100 is much less important for the rich person than for the poor one. But what would the consequences be if "equal" here is moderated to allow *compensating* for diminishing marginal utility? The principle of diminishing marginal utility states that as we acquire more and more goods, the additional goods have less and less value. Thus $100 to a very poor person would have much more *true* value (i.e., use value, defined as the amount of difference the $100 makes to its user's total sense of happiness or well-being) than the same $100 would have for a very rich person. To contribute "equal" amounts of goodness to everyone's life could therefore be modified to entail contributing different exchange values to people who are at different levels of well-being to begin with.

In essence, diminishing marginal utility requires that, in order to contribute "equitable" amounts of *use* value to people's lives, it is necessary to contribute much *more* to the needy than to the fortunate when these contributions are measured in terms of *exchange* values. Moreover, the sum total of goodness is increased, all else being equal, if we redistribute goods in such a way that their use value is increased due to their being possessed by those for whom the same exchange value has greater use value (as Hare 1997 in effect suggests). This prima facie principle is commensurable with the principle that inequality is justifiable when needed to provide incentives for people to work effectively to increase the total amount of goods to *be* distributed. Thus, in principle, it should be possible to calculate the best possible amount of distributive equality needed to maximize productivity on the one hand, while on the other hand taking account of the extent to which redistributing goods toward greater equality tends to increase their use value (because of diminishing marginal utility). And this would be as true for intangible goods such as human dignity, freedom of religion, etc., as it is for economic goods such as job opportunities, medical insurance, or tax burdens. In my interpretation, to allow for the effect of the principle of diminishing marginal utility, and to draw out the implications of this adjustment for a coherent account of distributive justice and decision theory, is the major advance of Rawls over Frankena.

b. Rawls's theory of justice is based on the argument that any rational person, examining a society from the standpoint of the "original position" (i.e., knowing that she is going to occupy some position in the society but not knowing which one), would necessarily tend to prefer a somewhat egalitarian arrangement of the society and a high priority assigned to the protection of certain crucial rights. Otherwise, the person in the original position would *risk* occupying an unacceptable position for the sake of an outside chance of being extremely well-off. Every gambler knows that when betting "double or nothing," one eventually reaches the point at which the *risk* of losing everything on the next game outweighs the *gain* of doubling one's stake. The rational thing to do is to set aside a certain amount, saying to oneself in effect, "Even if I lose everything else, I will not touch this amount for gambling purposes." Financial advisers, too, know how to modify their cost–benefit analyses in accordance with this principle, so that investors will not only maximize the chance of gain, but also, and more importantly, minimize the risk of large losses. The general idea is that *most* of one's capital should always be invested in *safe* but not very profitable ventures, while only a *small* portion of it is invested in very lucrative but very risky ventures. Diversifying investments is another means toward this end. The formulas used in such determinations are simply mathematical determinations of the proportion of risks to possible gains. The same kind of determination is used by a football coach when deciding whether to punt on fourth down. With fourth down and twenty-five yards to go, and with the ball on one's own one-yard line, the chance of earning the first down is not worth the risk. Rawls's point is that this same reasoning would necessarily be used by the rational person in the original position, in determining exactly *how* equally the members of the society should be related to each other. Social positions should not be so *unequal* that the chances of fabulous wealth are only one in a billion, whereas the chances of destitute poverty are one in eight. Nor should they be so *equal* that the cost (in terms of limitations of personal freedom) would outweigh the benefits of equality. The advantage of this theory is that it gives the traditional "impartial observer" in ethical thought experiments—now conceived of as the person in the original position—a definite and rational *reason* for preferring one alternative over the others, rather than relying merely on "moral intuitions."

During the years since Rawls published *A Theory of Justice*, many criticisms have been raised against this reasoning—so many, in fact, that Rawls (in a series of separate essays finally culminating in *Political Liberalism)* has now fallen back into a position of asserting only the "dialectical" necessity of his concept of distributive justice, not its literal truth. Why does Rawls feel compelled, in the light of criticisms, to abandon the claim that distributive justice as he characterized it in *A Theory of Justice* is simply a true account of the way opportunities and resources in a society *ought* to be distributed? In my view, this move on Rawls's part is simply the wrong move. Rather than arguing for a theory whose truth is not claimed—which undercuts its persuasive power—it would be better to change the theory in those ways that are needed to make it more epistemically defensible. One neo-Rawlsian who would seem to agree with this assessment is David Richards (1971), since he extends Rawls's reasoning beyond the context of a political hypothetical contract, and instead uses Rawlsian distributive justice as a foundation of the whole of morality.

The theory proposed in the remainder of this book can be viewed as an attempt (1) to defend the philosophical *truth* of the thesis that distributive justice, conceived in a way that is similar in many ways to Rawls's conception, *has intrinsic value,* and (2) to assess the comparative *importance* of this principle of distributive justice on the one hand, and the maximization of the general welfare on the other. It is thus important for our purposes to take account of the force of several types of criticisms of Rawls's concept of justice.

One criticism follows from the problem that desires are not rational phenomena, yet Rawls's decision formula requires that certain desires be considered "irrational." There is no rational reason why an aspiring actor should sacrifice everything for the sake of a one-in-a-million chance of success, yet actors routinely do so. How does this problem affect Rawls's view? It affects it in several ways: (i) Emotions arise *from* a concrete life situation. It is therefore meaningless, some would argue, to ask what a person in the original position, divorced from her concrete situation, would want. The protagonist in Faulkner's novel *Absolom! Absolom!* is told that he must enter a rich friend's mansion by the back door, and from that moment forward his life's all-consuming passion is to own that particular mansion—at any risk, any price, or any hardship to himself. While such a sentiment may be ignoble, can Rawls's person in the original position, who has not experienced these concrete emotions (because to do so would require knowledge of her particular station in life), really say that such emotions are *irrational*, and that certain alternative ways of feeling about the risks involved here would be more rational?

(ii) For the same reason, the person in the original position may not really know what genuine abject poverty would be like. It can be argued that only a person *living in* a situation can really know how it feels to be in that situation. Even those who have actually lived in the ghetto and have suffered all its slings and arrows, including hopelessness of escape, but who have somehow managed to escape, may *forget* all too easily what it was really like, condemning their former friends for not "pulling themselves up by their bootstraps." If it is this difficult to understand what it would be like to be in a particular position without actually *being* in that position, then how can the person in the original position, who is not allowed to know that she is in a particular position, really understand the alternatives that must be compared with each other in order to construct a cost–benefit analysis?

(iii) A crucial implication of the nonrationality of emotions follows from the fact that *feelings about risk taking* are themselves emotions. The problem arises as to how the person in the original position is to decide *how much* risk is to be considered "irrational." Much contemporary discussion of Rawls has centered on this point (see Kymlicka 1990, 66ff). Rawls's analysis of the kind of decision that would be made by a person in the original position is based on a principle taken from game theory: The rule for decision making under conditions of risk that is chosen by Rawls is the *"maximin* rule" (so designated by game theorists). The *maximin* rule says that, in any risk-taking situation, we should begin by determining the worst that can possibly result from each possible decision and then pick the decision that is "least worst," that is, whose worst possible outcome is the least disastrous when compared with the worst possible outcome of each of the other possible choices.

But as David Kaye, among others, has pointed out, the *maximin* rule is not the only rational one that could be chosen by the person in the original position. Several other decision-making rules are highly respected among game theorists, but would yield more or less different sociopolitical consequences if used by the person in the original position. For example, there is the *"maximax* rule," which calls for the decision that offers the possibility of most gain; the *"pessimism-optimism* rule," which suggests that we *average* the minimum and maximum payoffs of each decision; the *"equiprobability* rule," which says that we must average *all* the possible outcomes of all the possible choices, not just the highest and lowest possible outcomes; and then there is the *"minimax regret* rule," which says that we should choose the strategy whose largest possible cost of error is a minimum compared with the other possible decisions. Kaye and other critics who take this line insist that Rawls gives us no rational reason to prefer the *maximin* rule over any of the others. This is just another way of saying that some people might be more daring risk takers than others, and that the rational reflector in the original position has no way of knowing how daring a risk taker she might be, because the notion of the original position prevents the rational reflector from knowing what her personal emotional preferences might be. In short, it has not been adequately demonstrated that an extremely conservative risk-taking rule, such as *maximin*, is more rational than some of the less conservative ones that are available. But the amount of social inequality that would be tolerated by the person in the original position hinges directly on the degree of conservatism in her attitudes toward risk taking. Moreover, since even the priority of certain rights and procedural rules also depends on the original-position argument, whether or not these rights and rules really should be inviolable would again depend on how daring a risk taker the person in the original position is presumed to be.

In spite of these objections—and they do appear to be serious ones—Rawls's theory still holds a strong attraction for many political philosophers. There seems to be a hunch or feeling that the objections could conceivably be overcome, while still preserving the essential core of the theory. Even though no exact rule of risk taking has yet been demonstrated to be intrinsically preferable from the standpoint of the original position, there is still a meaningful sense in which rationality in the original position would tend to dictate a *somewhat* egalitarian society, although *how* egalitarian it must be might still be up in the air. Also, one is hesitant to condemn a young theory that shows promise and has some logical appeal because it has not worked out all of its problems. The objections may not be decisively devastating, even though they do show that the theory needs work.

The remainder of this book can be viewed as building on the criticisms of Rawls's use of the principle of diminishing marginal utility. The problem of determining how daring a risk taker the person in the original position would be is analogous to the problem of determining the quantitative *rate at which* marginal utilities decline in true value. Is $100 worth five times as much to a pauper as to a millionaire, or ten times as much, or a hundred times as much? If the person in the original position could make a purely rational determination of the rate at which marginal utilities decline, then she would know whether $100 lost by the poorest member of a given community is more valuable or less valuable than $1,000 gained by the richest member. This determination could then be developed into a criterion for saying that a $100 gain or loss to the poorest member has more importance or less importance than a $1,000 gain or loss to the richest member. And from this prioritization of relative importance of gains and losses at various levels of marginal utility (or economic status), not only can a principle of distributive justice be developed, but also a principle for determining the appropriate balance between distributive justice and utility maximization, since in this case both will be quantifiable in commensurable terms.

5

Toward a Nonutilitarian Consequentialist Concept of Distributive Justice

If the problems just discussed are to be given any practically applicable solution, a workable criterion must be developed for balancing the prima facie value of distributive justice against the prima facie value of maximizing the general welfare. We have assumed that injustice arises from distributive inequity with regard to all types of benefits, burdens, opportunities, and resources—not only material ones such as income and jobs, but also intangible ones such as health, happiness, access to the political process, and opportunities to actualize one's self-development as a human being, or even as a self-responsible moral agent (as Gillroy 1992b stresses). According to Fried, "There are material conditions for the development and maintenance of the integrity of the self, just as there are material conditions for the maintenance of self-respect. Given the priority of the concept of self, it should not be surprising that the interest in those material conditions is of a wholly different order from the interest in other conditions for the realization of other goods" (Fried 1992, 226). As Fried points out, we must, of course, guard against excessive paternalism here (220), but as I have suggested elsewhere (Ellis 1989, 1991), *opportunities* for personal development can be provided in a way that does not coerce and brainwash people, or unjustly limit their freedom of thought. Voluntary choice itself can be viewed as a good that gets distributed in a society: Gillroy writes, "If it is the case that the initial endowments of the individuals involved in an exchange are greatly asymmetric (which is very possible within a policy framework), then it is the case that voluntary choice is also asymmetrically distributed" (Gillroy 1992a, 201).

Even if all the various types of goods just mentioned can be thematized in terms of just or unjust distribution, the assumption that justice can be defined by a completely distributive type of conceptualization is far from controversial, and the attempt to apply such a conceptualization in practical contexts also raises questions that can be answered only by providing a more careful philosophical clarification of the conceptualization itself. We have therefore reached the point at which more detailed and rigorous philosophical grounding is needed. In the remaining chapters I shall attempt to provide adequately systematic arguments and analysis to demonstrate, within the limits of reasonable philosophical conclusiveness, that a concept of distributive justice based on a nonutilitarian form of consequentialism can be appropriately balanced with utilitarian concerns to yield a philosophically defensible, yet practically applicable, principle for aggregate policy decisions.

1. The Effect of Diminishing Marginal Utility

It is often taken for granted that the social and political implications of a consequentialist philosophy will conflict with theories of distributive justice such as Rawls's, in which the utilitarian maximization of value must sometimes be sacrificed for the sake of a just distribution of the value (Rawls 1971, 1993; Ellis 1992; Sterba 1980; Sandel 1982; Heller 1987). For example, one hears that the practical application of a consequentialist decision principle entails the use of cost–benefit analysis in social decision making (see Gillroy and Wade 1992; Sagoff 1984). I would now like to suggest, on the contrary, that one very viable type of consequentialism—I shall call it 'nonutilitarian consequentialism'—does imply a principle of distributive fairness of just the kind that contemporary justice theorists would like to use and, in fact, that Rawls's theory of justice is only one special case of a nonutilitarian consequentialism, differing from the other possible types not on normative grounds, but on empirical ones.

On the surface it appears that if consequentialism's only interest is to maximize good consequences, then it should make no difference how this good is to be distributed, as long as the total amount of good is maximized. However, this surface impression rests on a confusion about the way "goods" are to be quantified. In the case of an individual, there seems to be a sense in which it would be irrational to incur, say, a 50-percent risk of losing "very necessary" goods (in some sense that must be clarified) in exchange for a 50-percent chance of gaining even much larger amounts of very "superfluous" or "nonessential" goods. Such preferences seem to be obvious phenomenological data, and are regarded as completely noncontroversial by many authors (Rawls 1971; Pareto 1971; Jaffe 1972; Kohler 1979, Chapter 2). Pareto, for example, defines a principle of 'diminishing utility of marginal goods', meaning that the same good diminishes in value as the person who possesses it acquires more and more additional goods. As we saw in the last chapter, given $10, a poor person will use it to buy the most important goods that have not yet been provided for (i.e., "essential" or "necessary" goods, such as a meal), whereas a rich person, whose most important needs and wants will have already been provided for, can only use the money for goods that contribute proportionately less to the person's total happiness or well-being—frivolous goods for which the same person would not have traded adequate nutrition, clothing, shelter, or any of the other goods for which the person has already provided prior to receiving the money in question. There seem to be goods that, to a given user in given circumstances, are more "necessary" or "essential" than others, and that it would not be rational to trade for any amount whatever (or at least for very large amounts) of "unnecessary" or "superfluous" goods. Goods that have equal *exchange values* on the open market may therefore have different "use values" in different circumstances, depending on how "necessary" or "unnecessary" they are for the user. Here I use the term "use value" to mean the actual amount of well-being a good contributes to its user, as opposed to the good's exchange value on the open market, the latter being determined by the average "willingness to pay" for that good. In short, a given dollar amount of necessary goods is worth more than that same dollar amount of less-necessary goods.

This same principle is a key assumption for Rawls's *Theory of Justice* (1971). Why is it "irrational" for the person in the original position to risk abject misery, poverty, or loss of crucial legal rights in exchange for a chance to be filthy rich? The reason is the same as the reason a rational gambler would never bet his right arm on a hand of cards, no matter what the stakes or odds (as explained, for example, in Kymlicka 1990, 50–76; Wolff 1977, 77ff). As Fried (1992) suggests, there are certain necessary or essential goods whose permanent loss results in greater disvalue than the positive value of *any* amount of unnecessary goods could ever add up to (or at least greater than *comparatively much larger* amounts of unnecessary goods, as measured in terms of their exchange value).

If the aggregate good were measured by the same standards as individual goods, and if the individual good for one person is considered no more or less aggregately important than the same amount of individual good for another, then it would follow that a greater amount of pain for one person ought not to be exchanged for a lesser amount of pleasure for someone else. This is the standard assumption of the traditional utilitarian calculus, as reflected in typical cost–benefit analyses. But if we add to this principle the principle of the priority of necessary goods, as Hare (1997) suggests, it seems to follow that one person's necessary goods, at least prima facie, should not be sacrificed in exchange for an "equivalent amount" (as measured in exchange value) of unnecessary goods for someone else. This generally neglected complication would result in a type of consequentialist calculus very different from cost–benefit analysis as usually conceived. Let's consider what this alternative calculus would amount to and whether it would have any philosophical justification.

First we must note that, in reality, the distinction between necessary and unnecessary goods is not a sharp one. Instead, the extent to which a given good under given circumstances is "necessary" is a matter of degree. Some goods are more "necessary" than others. Thus it would be inadequate to merely make some sharp, absolute distinction between "needs" on the one hand and "wants" on the other. A need differs from a want in that it is more necessary; also, one "want" can be more necessary than another, and one "need" can be more necessary than another. This means that, at all points along the continuum from "very necessary" to "very unnecessary" goods, a distinction must be accommodated between "use value" and "exchange value." This distinction prevents the aggregate good from being equal to the mere sum of individual goods (as measured in exchange values), for the following reason: In the context of aggregate value measurement, it is important to distinguish between "use value" and "exchange value," whereas in the context of value for one individual it is not necessary to take this distinction into account; in the latter case, we are comparing goods at one particular marginal level of utility (because the person is at one particular economic status). But when we are assessing the value of the same goods to different people, who may have different economic statuses, we must take diminishing marginal utility into account. The exchange value of a good is determined by the amount of other goods that all members of the given market, on average (in some sense), would be willing to exchange for the good in question. Suppose all exchange values are measured on a scale from 1 to 10, and suppose that for any given individual the "minimal standard" below which one would not risk falling is 2. Any given individual will thus consider the difference between 1 and 2 to be far more important than the difference between 7 and 8. As one ascends the scale, a difference of "one" is less and less important. However, in terms of *exchange* value, people on the average are willing to pay just one unit for any difference of one unit (Weimer 1991; Gillroy and Wade 1992; Kohler 1979).

For example, a given type of car may be worth less, in terms of individual *use value,* when used as a family's second car than when used as some other family's primary car. But the *exchange value* is simply the average amount of money that *people in general* could be induced to exchange for the car. The fact that for one family the car may be a very necessary good whereas for another it is a less necessary good figures into its use value but not its exchange value. The concept of exchange value recognizes no distinction between more-necessary and less-necessary goods.

Nonutilitarian consequentialism can be conceived of as a type of consequentialism that measures value in terms of use value rather than exchange value. This means that if a given exchange value has more use value to one person than to another, then, all else being equal, one person at least prima facie ought to have that same good to a greater extent than another person ought to have it. Even if the "good" in question is an intrinsic value, such as happiness or well-being, the same point still applies in principle, although it is difficult to measure such a parameter. The difference between one unit of happiness and two must be regarded as more important than the difference between seven and eight. The reason is that no rational gambler would consider these two differences as having equal importance in her own life, and would not as willingly risk the former as the latter.

Notice also that this point remains true in spite of 'threshold effects' (Pojman 1997, 288ff). As an example of a threshold effect, under certain circumstances, if I need an immediate $100,000 to avoid bankruptcy and can only get $90,000, the $90,000 might be as worthless as nothing at all. Such threshold effects sometimes make it misleading to assume diminishing marginal utility with regard to extrinsic values, such as money. But when it comes to *intrinsic* values, such as a person's overall well-being, it would be self-contradictory to say that nine units are no better than none, since this would mean that I would be no better off with nine units of "well-offness" than with none.

The remainder of this chapter will develop the notion that diminishing marginal utility can be used as a method of characterizing the degree to which distributive justice exists. We can then make distributive justice commensurable with the value of maximizing utility. If all principles of justice (for example, rights, responsibilities, procedural rules, etc.) can be derived from the basic value of distributive justice, we can then develop a coherent decision principle for aggregate policy decisions that is equipped to allow each of these potentially conflicting values their appropriate place.

2. Nonutilitarian Consequentialist Distributive Justice and the Utility–Justice Conflict

If the person who ought to have a certain good to a lesser extent has it, whereas someone who ought to have it to a greater extent does not have it, it follows that goods are (prima facie) not distributed as they ought to be distributed. In this sense, we can say that nonutilitarian consequentialist distributive "justice" is the condition in which all goods are had by those who ought to have them—which essentially implies an allocation of resources in favor of those for whom the resources would be used to supply the most "necessary" goods possible, and thus an allocation essentially favoring the least advantaged, just as Rawls would require (as we shall see more fully in a moment). But this is exactly the same as a condition in which existing goods are distributed so as simply to *maximize use value* (in contrast to exchange value). Thus those who have the most pressing use for any given $100 would have the $100, and those who have the least pressing use for any given $100 would not have it. And the distribution of all $100 units of goods would be accordingly in proportion to the pressingness with which people need the goods (i.e., have a use for them).

This nonutilitarian consequentialism would also be similar to Rawls's system in that deviations from the distribution of goods in proportion to people's needs (i.e., use for the goods) would be justified if such deviations led to an increase in the total quantity of *use* value (in contrast to exchange value) and if this additional use value could in turn be distributed "fairly" according to the same criteria, that is, if the additional goods so produced can be distributed so as to increase the amount of use value available to people generally according to the just distribution system as defined above. This criterion creates an internal conflict, of course (just as in Rawls's system), which we must consider in a moment—the conflict between just distribution and growth in the total quantity of use value.

There is therefore one concept of 'justice as fairness' or 'distributive justice' that can be summarized by the injunction "Maximize use value!" The ultimate difference between this system, which strongly prioritizes distributive justice, and utilitarianism, which as normally conceived does not, is that utilitarians generally tend to think in terms of maximizing value without realizing that they were to maximize use value, they would end up agreeing that a type of "fairness" (essentially, a quasi-Rawlsian type of fairness) in the distribution of goods has intrinsic value, not merely extrinsic value, yet this distributive principle creates an alternative and conflicting way to increase the total quantity of use value.

To be sure, the injunction "Maximize use value!" *does* engender a fundamental moral conflict. On the one hand, it implies that we ought to distribute the valuable goods in existence according to their use value rather than their exchange value—that is, allot goods to each person in proportion to her need for them. On the other hand, the same injunction of "Maximize use value!" implies that we ought to *increase* the quantity of valuable goods that *do* exist (as measured by their use value). But there are many situations in which certain inequalities in the distribution of use values can facilitate the creation of a greater quantity of use value. To the extent that capitalist economic relations (which lead to distributive inequality by definition) are useful in creating greater and greater quantities of valuable things (capitalism, of course, is *sometimes* counterproductive to this end), we can say that the entire capitalist period of the history of humankind dramatizes more than anything else the conflict between these two principles. It is the classic conflict between distributive justice on the one hand, and on the other hand, the traditional utilitarian goal of maximizing value— although utilitarianism has really been misunderstood by its own advocates, because they see themselves as recommending the maximization of exchange value rather than of use value.

Now let's see if we can refine the mathematicization of use value in such a way as to accommodate these conflicting demands. In the process, we shall also see that the Rawlsian system of distributive justice is really, in principle, only a special case of nonutilitarian consequentialism. Suppose a society consists of four families: A, B, C, and D. Family A has three cars; B and C have two each; and D has only one. Obviously, a nonutilitarian consequentialist would say that an economic growth policy that would create an additional car and give it to family D would be better (all else being equal) than a merely redistributive policy that would simply give one of A's cars to D, thus making the number of cars equal. The reason is that D would be as well off as a result of the growth policy as of the redistributive policy, whereas A would be *better* off as a result of the growth policy rather than the redistributive policy. The total amount of use value would be increased more by the growth policy than by the redistributive one. Although A's third car has less use value than anyone's first and second cars, it still has some value. On the other hand, if the initial distribution of cars is as described at the outset, then a merely redistributive policy that would simply give A's third car to D, so that D would have two cars rather than one, may well be better than an economic growth policy that would create a fourth car for the already well-to-do A. The reason is that D's second car may well have more use value than A's *third and fourth cars combined.*

Whether or not D's second car has more use value than A's third and fourth cars combined depends on the mathematical *rate* at which additional marginal goods decline in use value compared with goods that already exist. If a second car is worth half as much as a first car, a third car half as much as a second, and a fourth car half as much as a third, then someone's second car will indeed be worth more than someone else's third and fourth cars combined. But if each additional car is worth, say, 90 percent of the use value of the previous car, then D's second car is *not worth as much* as A's third and fourth cars combined. If the value of additional cars declines at this rate, rather than at the 50 percent rate assumed above, then a third car has 90 percent of the use value of a second car, and a fourth car has 81 percent of the use value of a second car. Thus A's third and fourth cars combined have 171 percent of the use value of D's second car. The question, then, is whether the use value of newly created goods (or 'marginal utilities') declines arithmetically, or geometrically, or exponentially, or in some more complex pattern, as compared with previously existing goods.

But now consider an additional question that might shed some further light on this one. Suppose a Rawlsian reflector in the original position asks herself which of the above outcomes she would prefer. The basis for the decision will be a risk analysis in which she will consider the *probability* of being benefited or harmed, and the *amount* of benefit or harm, with the loss or gain of *more necessary* goods weighing more heavily in the analysis than *less necessary* goods, and with the probability of benefit or harm determined by the *number of people* in the total society, combined with the *extent* to which each one is benefited or harmed. In the case in which we assumed that each car is worth *half* the value of that family's previous car, the person in the original position will calculate that a growth policy that would produce an additional car for the already well-to-do A would give the person in the original position a 25 percent chance of ending up with *four* cars (if she turns out to occupy A's position), but also a 25 percent chance of having only *one* car (if she turns out to occupy D's position). Alternately, the merely redistributive policy that would simply give A's third car to D would lead to everyone's having two cars, so that the person in the original position could count on a 100 percent chance of enjoying exactly 1.5 units of use value (defining the first car as one unit). From the standpoint of Rawls's original position, the difference between the redistributive policy and the growth policy just described (which results in a fourth car for the already well-to-do A) would be viewed as follows: The growth policy would offer, from the standpoint of the original position, a 25-percent chance of occupying well-to-do A's position, a 50-percent chance of occupying B's or C's positions (which are equivalent), and a 25-percent chance of occupying poor D's position. Now, given the growth policy just described, which would create an additional car for A, and given the assumption that each additional car has 50 percent of the value of the previous car, the following outcomes would be obtained: B and C would continue to possess their second cars, valued at 0.5 unit, in addition to their first cars, valued at 1.0 unit, yielding a net value of 1.5 units for both B and C. But A, in addition to the first two cars (valued at 1.5 units) would now possess a third car, valued at half the value of the second car (i.e., half of 0.5 = 0.25), and a fourth car, valued at half the value of the third car (i.e., half of 0.25 = 0.12). Thus the total value possessed by A in this case would be 1.0 + 0.5 + 0.25 + 0.12, or 1.87 units. If the growth policy in question (which creates a fourth car for A) is adopted, then the person in the original position has a 25-percent chance of occupying A's position (thus possessing 1.87 units of value), a 50-percent chance of occupying B's or C's position (thus possessing 1.5 units), and a 25-percent chance of occupying D's position (thus possessing only 1.0 unit of value, corresponding to D's one car). In sum, from the standpoint of the person in the original position, this growth policy would offer a 25-percent chance of enjoying 1.87 units (i.e., if she occupies A's position, thus possessing four cars), a 50-percent chance of 1.5 units (i.e., if she occupies B's or C's position, thus possessing two cars), and a 25-percent chance of only 1.0 unit (i.e., if she occupies D's position, thus possessing only one car). This means that A would stand to be 0.37 units better off in the growth policy than the redistributive policy (which yields her only 2 cars); and D would stand to be 0.5 unit better off with the redistributive policy (which yields her a second car) than with the growth policy (which leaves her with only one car). Now it would be irrational to incur a 25-percent chance of gaining 0.37 unit in exchange for a 25-percent chance of losing 0.5 unit. In this case, then, the Rawlsian reflector would recommend the same policy as would the nonutilitarian consequentialist in our formulation. It would be better to have a 25-percent chance of gaining what D gains via the redistributive policy than to have a 25-percent chance of gaining what A gains via the growth policy. Note that the distinction between necessary and unnecessary goods has already been taken into consideration when we determined that D's second car had more use value than A's third and fourth cars combined; thus there is no need for the rational reflector to reintroduce this distinction after the use values have been assigned. If two goods have equal *use* values (as opposed to exchange values), there is no reason for a Rawlsian reflector to prefer one over the other.

On the other hand, how would a Rawlsian reflector assess the same set of options if the use value of additional goods diminishes at a *small algebraic rate* rather than a large one? For example, suppose a second car is worth 90 percent as much as a first car; a third car is worth 90 percent as much as a second; etc. Then to simply reassign A's third car to D is to increase the amount of use value by the difference between 0.81 (the car's value as A's third car) and 0.9 (the same car's value as D's second car)—a net increase of only 0.09. But a policy that would let everyone keep all the cars they have, but create one additional car to be assigned to the already well-to-do A as a fourth car, would increase the total amount of use value by 0.73 (the value of anyone's fourth car). This policy, then, would increase the total amount of use value more than would the redistributive policy mentioned above, even though it does not benefit the least advantaged (D) at all, whereas the redistributive policy *would* benefit D. The question is: How would the Rawlsian rational reflector assess these options? By insisting that the rational reflector would necessarily use *"maximin"* rather than some other decision principle, Rawls assumes that the use value of additional (less-necessary) goods diminishes *very rapidly*, rather than at the small algebraic rate that this last example assumed (Rawls 1985, 1982). *If*, on the other hand, it *were* to be granted (contrary to Rawls's assumption) that the use value of additional goods increases only at a small algebraic rate, *then the rational reflector would not use "maximin."* Instead, she would often prefer policies that benefit the privileged classes, even though they do not benefit the least advantaged at all, or conceivably even demand a small sacrifice from the least advantaged.

Rawls's essential reason for assuming that the rational reflector would use *"maximin"* is the way the distinction between necessary and less-necessary goods affects risk taking in conditions of extreme uncertainty (Kaye 1980). His key point is that no rational person would risk necessary goods for the chance of gaining unnecessary ones (as we have defined these terms here). But if the distinction between necessary and unnecessary were a matter of *degree* rather than a rigid either-or, then this gradual distinction could be mathematicized in terms of what we have called use value. When Rawls insists on *"maximin,"* what he is saying is that the value of additional goods always diminishes very exponentially, so it would never be rational to risk goods that are as necessary as those owned by the least-advantaged person for the sake of gaining *any amount* of goods that are unnecessary enough to be added to those that most people already possess. This represents a *very* exponentially diminishing value indeed for additional marginal goods. But then, *"maximin"* is a *very* conservative risk principle.

For our purposes here, the important points to be drawn from this analysis are the following: (1) Rawls's system is equivalent to a nonutilitarian consequentialism with a very exponentially diminishing use value for additional marginal goods. (2) Whether the use value for additional marginal goods diminishes exponentially, algebraically, or in some other pattern is neither a *normative* nor a *logical* question. It is a *factual, empirical* question. As such, it is a question to be answered by means of empirical assessment or phenomenological reflection on the emotional and motivational dimension of human consciousness. We must somehow determine, using empirical or phenomenological methods or both, *to what extent* marginal goods are less-and-less valuable to people as they acquire more and more. And this must be determined in a manner that accounts in some appropriate way for the apparent differences between the rates at which marginal utilities diminish in value *for different people and in different contexts.* The next section will address this crucial problem. (3) When Rawls asks which decision principle would be used by the rational reflector in the original position, he is asking essentially the same question that nonutilitarian consequentialists are posing when they ask whether the use value of additional goods decreases arithmetically, algebraically, exponentially, or in some other pattern. Thus nonutilitarian consequentialism, in contrast to traditional utilitarianism, does entail an inviolable principle of distributive justice. And at the same time, systems of distributive justice of the Rawlsian type are special cases or particular types of nonutilitarian consequentialism.

3. The Problem of Individual Differences in the Rate of Diminishing Marginal Utility

If diminishing marginal utility is to provide a basis for assessing distributive justice, the problem arises that marginal utility does not decline at the same *rate* for different people under different circumstances. Two main types of difficulties arise from these individual differences. First, some people might require larger amounts of goods than others to attain the same degree of well-being ('happiness', for example); thus marginal utilities would also decline more slowly or in a different pattern for these different people. For instance, a more self-indulgent person or a person suffering from 'anhedonia' requires more than a stoic or a "good-natured" person requires to be happy (Pojman and Westmoreland 1997, 10). A variant of this same difficulty is that some people have special problems (for example, medical problems) that entail a need for greater *resources* in order to attain the same degree of *well-being* (Fried 1992, 223). Still another variant, discussed by Nozick (1974), is the person who wastes resources when it is within her power not to do so. Suppose we give everyone an equitable share of the resources, and then one person throws hers into the ocean: Should we redivide all the others' resources so that this person again has an equitable share, perhaps only to be thrown into the ocean again? How many times should we be prepared to repeat this process if she continues doing so? At a more general level, Sagoff (1992) points out that preference satisfaction does not necessarily correlate with happiness, although it may correlate with people's *expectations* that certain things will make them happy.

The second difficulty is that some people may be more "desperate" than others to acquire a given good and, therefore, may be more willing to pay for it. So to regard that type of good as having the amount of value that one person is willing to pay for it may be to "accept as proxies for the rest of us the choices of people who do not have many choices or who are exceptional risk seekers" (Kelman 1992,

159). I shall consider the effects of these two types of difficulties separately.

(a) *Diminishing marginal utility for self-indulgent or particularly needy people.* As Pojman puts it, "A monk needs far less than a corporate executive to meet his needs. . . . Some people, optimists and cheerful folk, are better converters of resources to utility than pessimists and morose people. Some are stoics, who are able to handle adversity nobly. . . . Some people, who are grumpy, greedy, or masochistic, may misuse resources to enhance their suffering" (Pojman 1997, 288). Yet it would seem unreasonable to provide the anhedonic or unreasonable person with greater resources in order to bring her level of well-being up to the level prescribed by a theory of distributive justice.

This argument focuses on the fact that some people have more self-discipline than others, and others are more self-indulgent. However, it must be remembered that it is in the interest of the society as a whole for self-indulgent people to cultivate more self-discipline (so that they can learn to be happy with less). Moreover, not only maximal utility but also distributive justice would be facilitated by fostering conditions that encourage people to cultivate self-discipline, by requiring that they learn how to condition themselves to find enjoyment in activities that do not require unreasonable sacrifices from others. This means that, at least prima facie, people should be required to accept the predictable consequences of their own actions in enough instances to allow them to learn to take responsibility for themselves (excepting, of course, those few mentally ill people who are genuinely unable to learn such coping skills). For example, a person who knows how to take responsibility for herself in this sense will not cultivate a heroin addiction, because she knows that it is within her power not to cultivate it and predicts that there will be negative consequences for herself if she does cultivate it. As Rakowski says, "Our present preferences, even if they have arisen through processes largely beyond our power to control, are now within our control in the sense that we could now undertake actions, at greater or lesser cost, that would change our preferences in ways that we can foresee" (Rakowski 1997, 248). Thus autonomous agency and a self-disciplined character structure are important goods that any consequentialist value system should seek to promote. A nonutilitarian consequentialist decision principle that makes utility maximization and distributive justice commensurable with each other must therefore attempt not only to *maximize*, but also to *equitably distribute* the opportunities people need to actualize their potential as autonomous agents, that is, as self-disciplined, non-anhedonic persons who are able to accept the predictable consequences of their own actions.

It is also important to emphasize that, as Kymlicka (1989) points out, not only things that affect people's level of *happiness* must be distributed equitably (i.e., things that people can be said to *"have"* or *"not have"*), but also the conditions that create power relations that, in turn, can affect and distort people's capacity for *doing* and *being* in ways that can be found valuable.

> Rawls and Dworkin often write as if the most obvious or likely result of implementing their conceptions of justice would be to increase the level of transfer payments between occupants of existing social roles. . . . But . . . another important result would be to change the way existing roles are defined. As they both recognize, an important component of the primary goods or resources available to a person is opportunity for skill-development, for personal accomplishment, and for exercising responsibility. . . . People would not choose to enter social relations that deny these opportunities, that put them in a position of subjection or degradation, if they were able to choose from a position of equality. (Kymlicka 1989, 93)

Moreover, Charles Taylor (1985) suggests that certain material and social conditions are needed to promote a sense of "cultural community," which is an outcome that should be promoted, not because "cultural practices and traditions" are the arbitrary presuppositions needed to ground value assumptions and thus policy opinions, but rather because, for nonarbitrary and nonrelativistic reasons (as I discussed in Chapter 2 above), people's psychological capacities are strongly affected by the influence of their cultural environment.

It would therefore seem that the society prima facie ought not to provide each person with whatever amount of goods is required to make that person as happy or well off as the next, but rather should equitably distribute *opportunities and resources* to be used for that purpose, so as to hold people responsible for their own choices, including the choice to cultivate inordinate appetites by letting people know that there will be no special benefits for people with inordinate appetites. This would seem true, however, only in those cases in which it is *possible* for people to cultivate less self-indulgent tastes and behavior patterns.

But, as Fried points out, some people have *inalterable* problems that cause them to need more resources than others for a similar level of well-being—for example, special health problems requiring very expensive treatments. In these cases, both justice and utility are served by distributing *actual welfare* equitably, rather than by distributing mere *opportunities and resources* (i.e., means toward the end of welfare) equitably.

So it would seem that, in general, both distributive justice and the general welfare are served best by distributing *resources* and *opportunities* equitably only in those cases in which it is *within people's power* to use those resources to achieve a given level of well-being, and then to expect people to use that power wisely; thus people would be provided with an incentive to motivate themselves to use it wisely. But on the other hand, when it is *not* within a person's power to change the efficiency with which she uses resources (for example, in the case of an expensive medical problem), then correspondingly greater resources ought to be available for this person's special problem (as Rakowski 1991 argues). Using the principle of diminishing marginal utility as a criterion to distribute only *resources* for those who have the power to use them efficiently, while using diminishing marginal utility to distribute *actual welfare* for those who do not have the power to affect the efficiency of their resource usage, would thus resolve the difficulty posed by this type of individual difference. It would account not only for Fried's problem of people with greater needs, but also for Nozick's and Pojman's problem of people who waste resources when they have the power not to do so.

In sum, it can be argued that (1) equitable distribution of welfare has prima facie intrinsic value, and (2) people's cultivating non-self-indulgent and non-anhedonic personality patterns has prima facie extrinsic value (and *perhaps* intrinsic value, if we believe certain philosophers). Thus, with the notable exception of those who do not have the power to affect the efficiency of their own resource usage, equitable distribution of *resources* promotes both values (1) and (2), while at the same time it promotes the best possible balance between them. So, in the final analysis, diminishing marginal utility should be used as a criterion for determining the most equitable distribution of resources rather than of actual welfare (with the notable types of exceptions just mentioned).

(b) Diminishing marginal utility as affected by the "desperation" problem. If an aggregate distribution system is to determine the best

and most just way to distribute a variety of different kinds of goods (resources, opportunities, or actual welfare), the question arises as to how interpersonal comparisons are to be made in order to establish whether, for example, one person's desire for a motor boat is more or less good for that person than another person's desire to have a place to live, or a third person's desire to subscribe to a symphony concert season, assuming that the exchange value of these goods is the same. The real value of Adam Smith's "invisible hand" concept was that it freed the policy analyst from having to worry about these interpersonal comparisons, since if the person with the motor boat was willing to exchange it for the symphony tickets, then this fact in itself was enough to show that the symphony tickets were more valuable to her; if the other person was willing to trade them, this willingness could be taken as an assessment of the value of the goods in question for her (assuming that the parties to the transaction are knowledgeable, reasonable, not in the clutches of self-deception or psychosis, etc.). So, as long as pure utilitarianism was assumed as the value system, the process of exchange could take care of the problem of interpersonal comparison between different utilities for different people. It was unnecessary for the policy analyst to determine whether X is as valuable to A as Y is to B.

We have seen, however, that aggregate utility maximization should not be the only outcome that governments and societies strive to promote, but rather that principles of distributive justice should also be promoted. And if government is in the business of distribution, then by definition distribution is not being left up to a process of free exchange, so the problem of interpersonal comparison again arises for the policy maker. How do we know whether Smith's summer house is more or less good for Smith than the Jones children's college educa-tion is for them?

Classical utilitarianism of the Adam Smith type relied on willing-ness to pay as the criterion for interpersonal comparison of utilities. If A was willing to exchange more of her other goods for X than B was for Y, then X had more value for A than Y had for B. The crucial problem with this willingness-to-pay criterion is that people in more desperate circumstances are willing to incur greater risks in exchange for a given pay increment than a well-to-do person would incur for that same pay increment (Kelman 1992). The empirical basis for this claim will be discussed more extensively in the next chapter. The im-portant point for now is that two people who value a certain good equally (for example, something to eat when hungry, or the pleasure derived from a motor boat) often may *not* be willing to pay the same amount for that good. So the willingness-to-pay criterion cannot establish whether X is worth as much to A as Y is to B.

But if we adjust for the extent to which the good in question is necessary or unnecessary, then we should be able to resolve this problem. The poorer worker is willing to take risks (i.e., "willing to pay") in exchange for a given pay increase more than a well-to-do worker would be, because the goods for which the poorer worker hopes to use the additional money are more necessary (i.e., more important to his general well-being). So the goods for which a poorer worker uses a marginal $100 are more valuable (for him) than the goods for which the more-well-to-do worker would use a marginal $100 would be (for him). The marginal $100 contributes, correspondingly, more value to the poor person's life than it does to the well-to-do person's, because the degree of necessity of the marginal $100 is greater for the poor person than for the well-to-do person. So, when A is willing to take a greater risk in exchange for some outcome than B is, one of the main reasons is that this outcome has greater necessity for A than for B due to A's more desperate circumstances.

It might be, of course, that A's *personality* constitution is simply more risk oriented than B's. But, in the first place, this problem can be handled in the same way as the problem of inefficient resource users was handled above; that is, only *resources* and *opportunities* are to be distributed in accordance with diminishing marginal utility, not welfare per se (with the same notable exception of those whose unusual circumstances cause them to require more). So, if someone is unusually willing to risk her equitable share of *resources* (as in Nozick's example), that person can legitimately be expected to learn to accept the predictable consequences of that risk-taking behavior or change it, except where it is beyond the person's control to do so. But, in the second place, we should also note that the *personality* variable that supposedly reflects a strong *"willingness"* to take risks, as Golec and Tamarkin (1995) show on empirical grounds, can really be seen as a form of *ignorance* of the true risk involved. In other words, gamblers who are more prone to take risks do so not because they are more willing to take the risk, but because they feel or have become convinced that, in that particular instance, their risk of losing is smaller than it really is, or that the negative consequences of not winning that particular payoff are greater than they really are. In this case, the person may be no more willing to take the risk *as she perceives it at that moment* than anyone else would be. This point is important for our purposes because it would imply that if the person were well informed and thinking logically, her risk behavior would be different from the way it empirically appears to be. This and other relevant individual differences relating to the "irrationality" of risk-taking behavior will be discussed more fully in the next chapter.

The important point for now is that if equitable distribution is the goal, then individual differences in the rate of diminishing marginal utility are primarily attributable to either the "greediness/neediness" type of difference accounted for in *a* above, or to different degrees of "desperation," which can be accounted for by compensating for the rate at which people become more desperate (and thus a given exchange value has more use value for them) as their economic circumstances worsen, and become less desperate (and thus the same exchange value has less use value for them) as their economic circumstances get better. This rate can actually be approximately measured in terms of the "wealth effect" in occupational risk studies (Siebert and Wei 1994; Viscusi 1978b, 1993; Garen 1988; Biddle and Zarkin 1989; Robinson 1988), as the next chapter will discuss in more detail.

As soon as we compensate for the varying degrees of necessity of similarly priced goods for people in different circumstances (some more desperate than others), then we can again use willingness to pay (as adjusted in this way) as an indication of how valuable a good in question is for that person. For example, it may be true that, in our current society, people are willing to pay more for a yacht than for a college education. The reason is that most people who buy yachts already have college educations, and a few do not need them. But if we compare the willingness to pay for a yacht or a college education on the part of two people who have neither of these two goods and whose circumstances are similar, yet who can afford to buy only one of the two goods in question, the college education is chosen by most, and some of those who make the opposite choice predictably regret it later (so that their choice cannot be counted as a well-informed one).

It is true, of course, that there are a few people for whom a yacht *is* more important (more "necessary") than a college education—that is, people who would actually benefit more by the yacht, even if they must choose between the two. This means that the government should not be in the business of legislating that a specific commodity A is more valuable than a specific commodity B, without regard to individual differences. But what the government *can* do is to help ensure that A's ability to do or acquire whatever has the greatest use value for A (not exchange value) is not unjustly different from B's ability to do or acquire whatever has the greatest use value (not exchange value) for B.

It would be utopian to hope for absolute precision in promoting such just results. The political process is too complex, and the human psyche is too difficult an object of scientific inquiry, to know how to achieve an exactly perfect balance between different people's access to the things that are valuable for them to do, to have, or to be. But it is better to achieve distributive justice with minimal error variance than to resign ourselves to extreme injustice. In the most extreme instances certainly (and thus the most important ones), it *is* possible to know that certain people (for example, those whose parents cannot afford to send them to college) do have such different amounts of access to something that would be good for them (for example, to attend college, for those who could benefit from such an experience) that the difference is on the whole undesirable as a consequence purely of the distributive injustice of it (and not because of considerations of *maximization* of the availability of the good in question). And in such extreme cases, there is little difficulty in figuring out how the government *could* use its various powers to ameliorate the injustice.

The main purpose of this brief chapter has been to define in bare outline the possibility of a nonutilitarian consequentialism as a method of rendering commensurable with each other the maximization of the general welfare on the one hand, and on the other hand, distributive justice and the correspondingly necessary rights and duties, all under the broad umbrella of one coherent principle. I have also tried to show that the basic intuition of Rawls's original position argument already pointed us in this direction but mistakenly committed itself to the *maximin* principle as a way of mathematicizing the comparative importance of goods at different levels of marginal utility. This extremely conservative risk principle in turn led Rawls to absolutize certain rights to the point at which even relatively inconsequential instances of them could not be made commensurable with the value of equitably distributing other opportunities and resources, so that by 1993 Rawls had backed away from discussing the latter at all. Such considerations now had to be "trumped" by considerations of rights, which of course included freedom, which thus could not be infringed merely to benefit others, or at least there was no clear criterion by which to decide when to do so.

The attempt to elaborate nonutilitarian consequentialism as an approach to aggregate or political policy analysis raises a plethora of questions. What is the place of rights in such a system? How much authority should the government have to regulate business practices, industrial activities, and, in general, people's daily lives in order to further the aims of a nonutilitarian consequentialist concept of distributive justice? How are redistributive policies that are meant to promote distributive justice to be integrated with the obvious need to encourage and require people to take responsibility for the consequences of their own actions? How would such a concept affect the executive, judiciary, and/or legislative branches of government? The remaining two chapters will make a beginning toward addressing these questions. In the process, I shall attempt to show, in further defense of the nonutilitarian consequentialist distributive justice principle, that its application results in policy guidelines that are much more practically applicable than purely deontic, "rights-based" approaches, yet are more just from a philosophical point of view than traditional utilitarian cost–benefit analysis.

The next chapter will therefore attempt a more detailed philosophical defense and mathematical working-out of the type of nonutilitarian consequentialism that I believe needs to be developed in order to address these problems.

6

A Method for Quantifying
Distributive Justice

Cost–benefit analysis has been widely criticized as a method for policy decisions, especially those involving "unpriced values" such as life, health, and safety (Campen 1986; Baier 1986; MacLean 1986; Gibson 1985). Yet, realistically speaking, government agencies are unlikely to allow personnel to make decisions involving such value judgments without some fairly precisely spelled-out decision principle, which therefore needs to be quantitative enough to provide for definitely enforceable guidelines for daily operation. John Quarles (1976) and John Drysek (1987, 96ff), for example, emphasize this point with regard to government bureaus, notably the U.S. Environmental Protection Agency. The economist W. K. Viscusi voices a concern prevalent not only among recent economists, but also among policy analysts and government decision makers when he says that, in spite of the questionable aspects of such quantitative methods as cost–benefit analysis, "A greater danger is that these tradeoffs will be made without systematic analysis. Society may then be paying a substantial implicit price in lives sacrificed in an effort to preserve popular illusions" (Viscusi 1983, 113).

This chapter will attempt to spell out in concrete detail a more philosophically defensible decision principle than traditional cost–benefit analysis for aggregate social decisions, but one that is equally precise and quantifiable in its formulation. My hope is that once the most essential philosophical objections against cost–benefit analysis have been clearly enough elaborated, it will be possible to develop an alternative economic formula that makes room for the competing values whose neglect has been the most serious philosophical shortcoming not only of cost–benefit analysis, but indeed of all mathematical decision principles used at the aggregate level, especially when involving unpriced values. We shall see that the problem really centers around one of the most traditional of all moral problems: If utility could be maximized by unjustly distributing the necessary burdens, would it then be right to do so?

Accordingly, section 1 below will clarify the most fundamental philosophical objections to cost–benefit analysis, showing that the essential problem is that cost–benefit analysis fails to account for the distinction between more-necessary and less-necessary benefits (or between what some would call "needs" and "wants"—for example, see Simpson 1982; Gillroy and Wade 1992). It therefore also fails to recognize the lack of direct proportionality between exchange value and use value, let alone between economically measurable value in general and any philosophically defensible notion of value in the context of ethical theory. For example, traditional cost–benefit analysis provides no way to avoid trading off a few cancer deaths in exchange for a more cost-effective but also more hazardous technology that provides cheaper paper or plastic products for the many.

Section 2 will then attempt to orient economic notions of value to philosophical ones, showing how the notion of diminishing marginal utility in economics can serve as a measure of the degree of necessity of various kinds of goods under various kinds of circumstances. Since unjust distribution of benefits and burdens results primarily from the failure to prefer "needs" (such as health and safety) over mere "wants" (such as cheaper plastic razors), we shall see that a correct calculation of the rate at which marginal utilities diminish in value can determine "degrees of necessity" and thus the most just possible distribution of benefits and burdens. Of course, the fact that the initial income distribution will *already* be somewhat unjust at the point when a government agency becomes involved in an aggregate decision is a separate but interrelated problem. That lower-income workers are willing to take greater risks than their better-paid counterparts in exchange for a given amount of economic gain (Siebert and Wei 1994; Viscusi 1978b, 1991; Biddle and Zarkin 1989; Robinson 1988) is an issue whose implications for our analysis will become crucial. The important point for now is simply that administrative agencies such as the EPA should be equipped with a decision principle that (unlike traditional cost–benefit analysis) will refrain from allowing, within its domain of political authority, that unfair burdens be imposed on a few so that the many can enjoy relatively superficial economic benefits. For example, it must know how to avoid imposing an unjust burden of cancer risk on a certain population so that someone (either within or outside of that same population) can buy cheaper plastic razors produced with a more hazardous technology. The crucial point for our purposes here is that traditional cost–benefit analysis inappropriately allows such trade-offs between important and superficial kinds of goods without reference to this notion of distributive justice.

Section 3 will then show that the "wealth effect" in occupational risk studies serves as a measure of the rate of diminishing marginal utility, not only for unpriced values such as life and limb, but for all types of values. Here again, the role of the initial income distribution in occupational risk studies is crucial. In simple terms, a wealthier worker will not assume the same risk in exchange for a given salary increment (which to him is not very necessary) as a poorer worker would assume for that same salary increment (which to him is more necessary) (Siebert and Wei 1994; Viscusi 1978b, 1991; Biddle and Zarkin 1989; Robinson 1988; Kelman 1992). The essential issue here is that the poorer worker hopes to use the additional income for goods that to him are more necessary—goods that thus have more *value* to the poorer worker than a monetarily equivalent amount of less-necessary goods would have for the wealthier worker.

Finally, section 4 will attempt to construct a mathematical model for the effect of necessity/nonnecessity on quantitative decision principles for aggregate and risk-related public policy. This will then provide grounds for weighting a given amount of more-necessary goods (including health and safety) as having more importance than a monetarily equivalent amount of less-necessary goods (such as price increments on plastic razors).

1. Why Cost–Benefit Analysis Fails: The Distinction between Necessary and Less-Necessary Benefits

Some objections against cost–benefit analysis address the inherent uncertainties in its application, whereas others attack it for essentially philosophical reasons. In the former category fall criticisms to the effect that methods of determining the value of life and injury are diverse, controversial, and inaccurate by their very nature. A forceful critique of these methods is in Leigh (1989), and an indication of the variety of such methods can be found in Weimer (1991), Lanoie et. al. (1995), and Zeckhauser (1975). Critics of this aspect of cost–benefit analysis also emphasize that risk decisions, on which unpriced values tend to be based, are notoriously idiosyncratic and irrational (Anderson 1988; Nelkin and Brown 1984; Leigh 1989). These are not the primary problems with which we must concern ourselves here, except where they affect the second and more fundamental type of objection, that is, the criticisms of the philosophical validity of cost–benefit analysis per se. It is these latter types of criticisms that, when pursued carefully enough, will lead to the formulation of an *alternative* decision principle that is quantifiable enough to be applied by bureaucratic agencies.

Given the technical nature of many of the relevant social problems (notably environmental and pollution-control decisions), these agencies inevitably will be involved in the implementation of such decisions at the concrete level. Our earlier example about the production of plastic razors illustrates this point: An agency like the EPA will lack both the moral and the political authority to regulate effectively unless it can define in a coherent way what it means to say that a certain amount of health risk posed to the public by this technology is "too great" to be warranted by the economic gains it makes available to consumers, taxpayers, or workers. Without a clear way to state how much risk is "too much," even the EPA's ability to negotiate with an offending polluter is weakened, and the polluter can then argue that its inalienable right to freedom of action is being infringed without just cause (for example, see Findley and Farber 1988; Georgia Bar Association 1991). Moreover, this method must address itself to a clear definition not only of the criteria for the cost effectiveness of the *means* to achieving its policy objectives, but also the criteria for the judgment of the comparative importance of the *ends* to be achieved as well. The reason for this is that, if the importance of the ends cannot be compared in some way to the importance of the sacrifices needed to accomplish those ends, then here again the government will often be unable to clearly justify enforcing the needed sacrifices—for example, regulating a given method of producing plastic razors. The question will remain unanswered as to whether the policy objective is "important enough" to clearly warrant infringing the manufacturer's right to freedom of action.

But the serious limitations of traditional cost–benefit analysis in addressing this problem become clear when we consider concrete examples in which aggregate risk decisions must be reached regarding the unpriced values of life, health, safety, and environmental protection. Unfortunately, the primary coherent decision principle currently available for making value priority decisions in the realm of environmental management is cost–benefit analysis. This is made clear by Peskin and Seskin (1975) in a cost–benefit study mandated by the 1972 amendment to the Federal Water Pollution Control Act, as well as by Brian Wynne (1987, 404ff), Andreas Faludi (1987, 120–25), former EPA official John Quarles (1976), and presidential directives such as the one issued by Reagan requiring that a cost–benefit analysis must accompany every policy decision by agencies in his administration (Sagoff 1984, 172). In 1994, the U.S. House of Representatives attempted to legislate such a requirement for every federal agency; such a legislation would effectually subject all social policy decisions to a utilitarian cost–benefit analysis. Faludi argues that the "certiori" power of courts, especially in the United States, virtually forces agencies to show tangible evidence that an action is justified and not "unreasonable, arbitrary, or capricious" (Faludi 1987, 118).

However, when people's health, safety, and lives are being compared in value with economic considerations aggregately distributed, there are strong reasons to believe that cost–benefit analysis is an inappropriate and philosophically invalid basis on which to reach decisions. A dramatic illustration of this point is the example of the California referendum that proposed to forcibly quarantine all AIDS victims. In net terms, such a policy would surely be extremely beneficial in cost–benefit terms, since it would save many thousands of lives by infringing the liberty only of a few thousand, but at the expense of extreme injustice (hence the obvious unconstitutionality of such a legislative action were it to pass). Another obvious example was the cost–benefit analysis conducted by the Ford Motor Company to decide whether to go through with the production of the "exploding Pinto," reported by Charles McCaghy (1980, 296) in a standard criminology textbook. According to McCaghy, the value of the lives (as assessed by means of figures used by the New York Highway Traffic Safety Board) was simply compared with the cost (to consumers) of redesigning the Pinto gas tank, with no attempt to consider whether it is fair to compare in aggregate terms a difference in the sticker price of automobiles with a similar amount of value in human lives. I choose these extreme examples in order to illustrate as clearly as possible the seriousness of the problem of reconciling cost–benefit analysis with the concept of distributive fairness. But the same problem exists when cost–benefit analysis is applied to more commonplace examples, such as the decision whether to mandate safer production of plastic razors even if at considerable economic expense to consumers or taxpayers.

The basis for the intuitive sense that a simple cost–benefit tradeoff is inappropriate can be seen clearly by considering the implications of the principle of diminishing marginal utility: An equal monetary value (or exchange value) of extremely necessary goods, such as food, shelter, or health, has more actual value (or use value) to the user of such goods than an equal monetary amount of less-necessary goods, such as yachts or luxury automobiles would have for their users (Kohler 1979, Ch. 2; Sinden and Worrell 1979, 470–84). The reason is that no rational person would willingly sacrifice a given amount of necessary goods in exchange for an equal monetary amount of less-necessary goods. (In fact, it is for this very reason that we perceive some goods as more "necessary" than others.) Thus, as one acquires more and more goods, it becomes less and less important (or valuable) to acquire more. In short, a given dollar amount of necessary goods is worth more than that same dollar amount of less-necessary goods. Yet, as Anderson (1988) points out, this fact is completely ignored in traditional cost–benefit analysis. "The market does not recognize any distinction between wants and principles or needs" (56). (See also Ellis 1992, Chapters 5–6.)

   The problem as yet to be solved, however, is that there is no way to mathematically calculate *how much* more valuable a given amount of goods is for someone to whom the goods are very necessary, as compared with the same amount of goods for someone to whom the goods are less necessary, since the degree of "necessity" of marginal amounts of goods to users with different economic status cannot be accurately quantified or measured. Thus no one has yet discovered a way to construct a mathematical decision principle, even in theory, that could be used as a substitute for traditional cost–benefit analysis. While it is true that some policy analysts recommend non-utility-maximizing decision principles for some situations, such as the *"maximin"* and *"minimax regret"* rules (see Sinden and Worrell, Chapter 16)— in fact, the latter alternative has been popularized by Rawls (1971)— it remains true in the case of each of these decision principles that the value of the utilities being compared with each other, according to whichever decision principle one uses, is still being assessed in terms of *exchange* values, so that the value of $1,000's worth of very-necessary goods would be plugged into one's chosen formula just the same as the value of $1,000's worth of less-necessary goods (as Sinden and Worrell's many examples clearly show). Also, no coherent philosophical justification can be given for preferring one of these formulas over the others. Even if Rawls's "original position" argument is assumed, there is no way of knowing how conservative or liberal the rational person in the original position would be in risk-taking behavior and, thus, no reason for this rational person's preferring one decision principle over the others, as Kymlicka (1990), Kaye (1980), and others have shown quite clearly.

Moreover, there are serious internal-validity problems with non-utility-maximizing decision principles that are currently available. Rawls's use of the "maximin" principle, for example, would imply that the least advantaged position in a decision situation must always be improved, regardless of the expense to the more advantaged positions (see Wolff 1977; Kymlicka 1990). But this reasoning ultimately would seem to imply zero-risk policies, since the least advantaged person in a policy decision regarding automobile traffic safety, for example, is the one who will die in an accident; thus one would forgo the economic benefits of auto transportation in order to avoid traffic fatalities altogether—an obvious reductio ad absurdum of the zero-risk option in public policy. The question is a quantitative one: *How much* risk of death, disease, or injury should be tolerated for the sake of *how much* economic benefit? Thus, when push comes to shove, it is usually cost–benefit analysis that policy makers tend to resort to when they need an accurate way to compare competing values.

This problem is especially acute in the realm of environmental policy. While life, health, and safety are the most necessary goods imaginable, the practical reality is that government bureaucracies tend to operate according to established, written policy that must spell out decision principles precisely, rather than leaving the decisions to the subjective judgment of individuals within the agency. Thus, until a better decision method is formulated, environmental decisions will have a strong tendency to be subjected to traditional cost–benefit analysis, so that the error of comparing the lives of people with economic benefits will also continue to operate when it comes to environmental management and pollution control issues. The task that must be addressed, therefore, is to work toward the formulation of a more appropriate decision principle, yet one that is precise enough to be actually used by government agencies and by firms attempting to comply with appropriate public policy guidelines.

However, before proceeding farther in the direction of an alternative principle, we need first to discuss the philosophical notion of value in general, as applied to quantifying unpriced values, such as life and limb. We shall see in the next section that a careful application of the principle of diminishing marginal utility can be used as a method for measuring the degree of necessity or nonnecessity of values, and that the "wealth effect" in occupational risk studies can lead to the assign-ment of a definite magnitude to the rate at which less-necessary (or marginal) utilities decline in value, and thus also of the rate at which very-necessary ones (such as life and limb) increase in value, compared with their respective monetary values. Traditionally, however, such studies have failed to take account of this problem, assuming instead that the value of a life is determined by the fatality risk that workers *on average* would assume in exchange for a given pay increment (Kniesner and Leeth 1995; Haigh et al. 1992; Viscusi 1983, 93–113; 1991; 1993; Zeckhauser 1975; this is also evident from the other economic studies cited below), and forgetting that the heterogeneity of workers' risk averseness depends largely on the degree of necessity (to them and their families) of the goods for which they need the additional money obtained by risking their lives or limbs. In plain terms, poorer workers are more willing to risk life and limb precisely to the extent that they need the resulting pay increments to buy the more-necessary types of goods. This is just the crucial issue that must somehow be quantified if we want to be able to determine public risks in a *just way*, that is, without unfairly distributing the burdens of trivial economic benefits to those who would not have chosen to risk death for such trivial benefits if they had been given a fair choice. We must find a way to measure the difference between a person's willingness to risk death in exchange for benefits she considers very *necessary* on the one hand, and on the other hand, her willingness to risk death in exchange for comparatively *trivial* benefits.

Moreover, we must avoid simply imposing on everyone the amount of risk that the *average* worker would be willing to assume in exchange for some given amount of economic benefit. The reason for this is that, as indicated above, the average worker may be willing to incur a greater risk than some for a given economic gain and a lesser risk than others, because the degree of necessity (for him or her) of the goods bought with the additional money will be greater than for some and less than for others, depending largely on their economic status. To take account of this problem, the society as a whole should be willing to assume greater risks in exchange for benefits that are very necessary (for its members)—such as life, health, and the most basic kinds of needs—and lesser risks in exchange for benefits that are not very necessary (for its members)—such as a 3-percent savings in the price of radio equipment for yachts.

Of course, assessing the degree of necessity of the marginal values of goods is never a clean or simple matter; we shall therefore see that it is also important to ensure that, if a given risk is borne by the society generally in exchange for a certain economic gain (defined in terms of its degree of necessity for people at the *average* economic status), then programs must be in place to see to it that these risks are not borne disproportionately by individuals whose economic status is *below* the average. For example, if a few workers must lose their jobs to facilitate pollution-control devices to protect the lives of others, these workers must be compensated in the form of job retraining, relocation, and financial assistance to ensure that risks and burdens have been distributed equitably. (All these problems will be considered in more depth as we develop the concepts needed to address them.) Such quantifications are necessary if we are to incorporate a justice factor into the formula for cost–benefit analysis for aggregate decisions involving risks distributed to the public. In the final analysis, the formula we end up using will be very different from cost–benefit analysis as normally understood; it will be a formula geared not toward demanding risks from the public in proportion to the exchange value of the economic benefits attained through this risk, but rather toward reconciling the degree of necessity of the utilities whose loss is risked by the public (for example, life and limb) with the degree of necessity of the economic gains to be made. We shall see how this works out mathematically as we proceed.

2. Measuring the Degree of Necessity

If value is defined in terms of benefits to people, then it is clear that the same exchange value may have greater or less actual value. I shall use the term "use value" to denote actual value, in contrast to exchange value. Obviously, a family's first car contributes more to the family's well-being than does its second car and therefore has more use value, even though the exchange value of the two cars may be the same. It follows also that it is more valuable to provide a homeless family with a house than to provide a well-to-do family with a second house of equal exchange value. Generally speaking, the more necessary a good is (for its user), the more use value it has, whereas goods of different degrees of necessity (for their users) may have the same exchange value. This phenomenon can be described in economic terms by using the principle of diminishing marginal utility, which as we have seen states essentially that, as one acquires more and more additional goods, still further additional goods become less and less valuable.

This principle is the very cornerstone of any analysis that hopes to measure use value by contrast to exchange value, and thus take account of the "needs–wants" distinction stressed by philosophical theories of justice, so that goods with equal exchange values may be more or less valuable depending on how necessary or unnecessary they are for their users. As Wolff (1977), Kymlicka (1990), and others point out, the fact that a rational reflector in a Rawlsian "original position" prefers to safeguard necessary goods rather than risk them for a chance to gain less-necessary goods leads the rational reflector to choose a very conservative risk principle and, thus, to favor distributive justice over utility maximization. We shall pursue this point more precisely in a moment.

At this juncture, we should note that since the value of life is one of our most crucial concerns here, there are several prevalent ways to measure this value. The method currently most often used in court cases is the "future-earnings" criterion (Anderson 1988; Viscusi 1983, 1991, 1993; Zeckhauser 1975). By this criterion, a deceased person's life is valued at the amount of money the person would have been expected to earn had the person survived. Clearly, however, this criterion bears little relation to any coherent philosophical notion of the actual value of life. If value is defined in terms of benefiting people, then the value of a person's life must be conceived in terms of the extent to which it is more beneficial to that person to remain alive than to die. The future-earnings criterion ignores the question of assessing the worth of the person's life *to him or to her,* and instead tries to measure the worth of the person's life *to society* or *to the person's family,* assuming (perhaps erroneously, in any event) that a person's value to society or to the person's family is determined by her earnings. Perhaps such a criterion is not entirely out of place in damages suits, since it is not the dead person who will be awarded the damages, thus the value of the person's life *to herself* is not really the issue. But when making government policy, the latter is precisely the crucial issue. In spite of the obvious philosophical problems with this future-earnings criterion as a measure of the actual value of life, it initially began to be used in court cases primarily because, at that time, no one could think of a better way to precisely quantify the value of life for purposes of litigation. The history of this process again highlights the problem that government decision makers (such as judges in court cases) prefer that a decision principle be fairly precise and as quantitative as possible. Yet the question remains as to whether a mathematically precise method for decision making is preferable over one that is philosophically more defensible but cannot be as accurately quantified.

Nonetheless, later economists were able to refine a very different criterion for the value of life, often called the "willingness-to-pay" criterion (Lanoie et al. 1995; Anderson 1988; Viscusi 1983, 96ff; 1991; 1993; Zeckhauser 1975; MacLean 1986). Assuming that the extent to which a person values something is determined by the amount the person is willing to pay for it, this criterion proceeds to measure one's willingness to pay for one's own life in terms of the amount of income one would be willing to forgo in order to decrease one's occupational death risk by a given amount. If a person would demand an extra $5,000 in earnings in exchange for a 0.5-percent increase in the probability of occupational death, then the person's life is valued at $1 million by this criterion. Of course, no one would willingly exchange her own life for $1 million, but the assumption is that when policy decisions concern aggregate, small *risks* of death (as, for example, with pollution-control policy), the society values each person's life in the same way that one would value one's own life, by tolerating the same risk of death that this same person would tolerate in exchange for a certain amount of economic benefit.

Although the willingness-to-pay criterion is obviously more nearly philosophically defensible than the future-earnings criterion as a standard for the *actual value* of a life (and thus for public policy purposes), it still has problems. Some of these problems affect the conceptual basis of the notion that willingness to pay adequately assesses value in a philosophically defensible way (Anderson 1988; Simpson 1982; Leigh 1989; MacLean 1986; Gibson 1985); I shall return to them in a moment. Other criticisms merely address the point that it is difficult to *measure* the amount that people are willing to pay, because of uncertainties in the empirical methods that must be used to obtain the information, as well as people's own irrationality when it comes to assessing risks (Lanoie et al. 1995). The latter type of problem is largely beyond our scope here, since the failure to solve it would, in the final analysis, be equally devastating to any method of cost–benefit analysis, and certainly to any quantitative value-of-life determination that aspires to philosophical validity. Anderson (1988), Sen (1973), and Nelkin and Brown (1984) summarize these types of objections nicely in criticizing the assumption that people act primarily as rational consumers when they choose among risks. Also, an abundance of empirical psychological studies have established considerable irrationality and ambiguity in people's attitudes toward risk (Lanoie et al. 1995; Golec and Tamarkin 1995; Hersch and Pickton 1995; Ettenson and Coughlin 1982; Lafferty 1974; Fishbain, Fletcher, and Aldrich 1987; Sahoo 1985; Hoyos 1988; Ladouceur, Mayrand, and Tourigny 1987). This point has considerable importance for the way we interpret the value-of-life implications of occupational risk analyses.

The reason these kinds of criticisms are largely beyond our scope here is that we have taken as our starting point that the bureaucratic nature of government agencies, such as the U.S. Environmental Protection Agency, will always demand that a fairly precise and essentially quantifiable decision principle be used; otherwise, each field worker in the agency would be entrusted to make value decisions on the spur of each moment, and the higher-level administrators would therefore lose control of the operations and decisions within their own agencies, for which they are held accountable. However, we shall also see as we proceed that many of the imprecisions in estimating people's genuine preferences can be substantially reduced by compensating for those factors that *cause* people to take irrational attitudes toward risk or cause them to take risks that they would not take if their choices were less constrained. For example, the extent to which poorer workers are less averse to risk than wealthier ones is essentially a measure of one of the most important of the factors that prevent their risk choices from being unconstrained. By using adequate experimental controls to compensate for these kinds of considerations, it should be possible to minimize in practice the amount of error that results from them, if only we can also address the more conceptual types of objections alluded to above, which are really more fundamental and strike at the heart of the *philosophical* basis for using risk behavior to ground a willingness-to-pay criterion at all. Let's consider these more fundamental objections next.

Anderson (1988) discusses some of these more fundamental objections in the following terms: "The market does not recognize any distinction between wants and principles or needs." (56) We have already emphasized this point as an objection to cost–benefit analysis in general. Anderson goes on, as a consequence of this problem, to challenge the assumption of cost–benefit analysis that public bodies should, like the market, "accept the consequences of letting people with vastly unequal powers of self-protection fend for themselves, and even reproduce these consequences in public decisions. . . . Cost–benefit analysis improperly takes the alienation of workers' control over their own lives and health for granted, and thus ignores the way this lack of voice influences the acceptability of the risks they encounter." (57)

I am wholly in sympathy with this type of criticism of the willingness-to-pay criterion as it relates to *traditional* cost–benefit analysis. However, if the distinction between needs and wants can be quantified, and if we can compensate for those constraints that force workers to accept risks that they would not accept under a more nearly ideal social system, then it will be possible to develop an alternative to traditional cost–benefit analysis that mathematically incorporates these kinds of considerations into the formula for the decision principle itself. That is what the following discussion will attempt to do.

3. The "Wealth Effect" in Occupational Risk-Aversion Studies as a Measure of the Rate of Diminishing Marginal Utility and Thus of the "Degree of Necessity" of Both Priced and Unpriced Values

The most serious of the problems with the willingness-to-pay criterion for assessing the value of unpriced values such as life and limb stems from the heterogeneity in the amounts of use value that correspond to given amounts of exchange value at different levels of necessity or nonnecessity. A low-income person might be willing to incur a 0.5-percent greater occupational death risk for a $5,000 salary increase if this $5,000 is to be spent on very necessary goods (i.e., goods that he considers very necessary to his family's well-being), whereas a middle-income person remains unwilling to incur this same increased risk because he knows that his additional $5,000 would be spent on less-necessary goods (i.e., goods that he does not consider so necessary to his family's well-being). It is thus reasonable to hypothesize that wealthier workers will be more averse to risk in their occupational decisions than poorer workers. In fact, the existence of this "wealth effect" on people's occupational risk averseness has been empirically confirmed by several economists (Siebert and Wei 1994; Viscusi 1978b; Garen 1988; Biddle and Zarkin 1989; Robinson 1988) and is statistically significant, although the research designs of these studies vary considerably and have not been constructed in such a way as to accurately reflect the *magnitude* of the effect. For example, Garen (1988) and Biddle and Zarkin (1989), who use nonlabor income as the measure of worker wealth, and Robinson (1988), who uses income per se, find much stronger correlations between wealth and risk averseness than does

Viscusi (1978b), who uses workers' *assets* as the measure of their wealth. Apparently, income is a more accurate reflector of economic security than assets when it comes to the effect of economic security on workers' willingness to take occupational risks. This problem of determining the magnitude of the wealth effect will be discussed further below.

The fact that poorer workers tend to use any additional pay increments in ways that they perceive as more *necessary* to their well-being, in comparison to wealthier workers, may not be the *only* important factor that causes wealthier workers to be more averse to risk. Other reasons that have been proposed are that wealthier workers are better educated about risks (Siebert and Wei 1994; Savage 1993; Viscusi 1978b); that different cultural traditions in the different social classes promote different attitudes toward risk-taking behavior (Leigh 1989; Zeckhauser 1975); that different personality types may lead to different attitudes toward risk, while at the same time certain personality types are more prone to end up in certain social classes or occupations (Liu and Hsieh 1995; Leigh 1989; Krishna 1981; Ansari 1977); or that the different circumstances of wealthier and poorer workers affect their attitudes toward risk—for example, their insurance coverage, the support networks available to them in case of emergencies, etc. However, even though such factors may well play a role in people's risk-taking behavior, the question for our purposes is to what extent these considerations are capable of accounting for the wealth effect. For example, although it is true that wealthier workers tend to be better insured, this could not play a part in accounting for why poorer workers would be prone to take greater risks; if anything, poor insurance coverage would motivate them to take *lesser* risks—which would in no way account for their *greater* willingness to take risks. As for the notion that poorer workers are not as well informed as wealthier ones about the occupational risks they assume, this has been discounted as an explanation both by Robinson (1988) and by Nelkin and Brown (1984). Both these studies empirically surveyed workers, finding that low-paid workers were very well informed about the health hazards of the work they do and that willingness to assume occupational risks did not correlate with ignorance of the health risks of the work, although workers did suspect that these risks may have been *greater* than their employers had publicly acknowledged.

With regard to personality differences that might correlate with socioeconomic class, there does seem to be evidence that certain personality characteristics do correlate with risk averseness, but the personality characteristics in question do not seem to correlate with socioeconomic class. Studies by Fishbain, Fletcher, and Aldrich (1987); Sahoo (1985); Ladouceur, Mayrand, and Tourigny (1987); Hersch and Pickton (1995); Krishna (1981); and Ansari (1977) found that risk taking correlates with such personality characteristics as internal versus external control, personality maturity, and self-esteem. These studies used paper-and-pencil personality tests such as the Eysenck Personality Inventory and such risk-behavior measures as the Choice Dilemmas Questionnaire, as well as actual behavioral observations such as smoking and automobile traffic behavior. The most important point for our purposes is that none of these studies found any correlation between social class and risk averseness as a *personality* characteristic, which would be reflected in the Choice Dilemmas Questionnaire and in smoking and auto-driving behavior. The correlations between social class and risk behavior thus seem to show up significantly in correlational studies primarily when the risk behavior either involves *occupational* health and safety, or ignorance of the amount of risk being chosen (as Savage 1993, Golec and Tamarkin 1995, and Liu and Hsieh 1995 found empirically).

It therefore seems likely that the wealth effect on occupational risk averseness is attributable primarily to the principle of diminishing marginal utility, which causes workers to weigh equal monetary amounts of more-necessary goods (for their perceived well-being) as more important than less-necessary ones (for their perceived well-being). The supposed lack of education or socially relative values of lower-class people does not seem to lead to a greater willingness to take *non-occupational* risks, such as failure to wear seatbelts or cigarette smoking, for example (Krishna 1981; Ansari 1977), except where the ignorance of the level of risk is involved (as the above studies show). These studies found no particular personality variable that would lead lower-income or lower-class people to be more cavalier about taking risks in general than anyone else. On the contrary, the poorer people are more desperate to improve their lot than are their wealthier counterparts primarily because the goods for which they need the additional income are, for them, *more-necessary goods.*

It seems reasonable to conclude from these considerations that the magnitude of the wealth effect on occupational risk behavior is roughly equivalent to the rate at which marginal utilities diminish in value. This follows because we have seen that marginal utilities diminish in value in proportion as they are used in ways that the user considers less and less necessary, and increasing risk averseness among workers corresponds to workers' perception that additional pay increments would be used in ways that they would consider less and less necessary. Thus workers' perceptions that additional pay increments would be used in ways that they would consider less and less necessary can be used as a measure of the rate at which marginal utilities diminish. If so, then we have in principle available to us an empirically observable way to measure the rate of diminution of marginal utility, and therefore to quantify what Kelman (1992), Simpson (1982), and others want to call the "needs-wants distinction." This measure would be the extent to which goods perceived as more necessary (to the user), such as life, health, and safety, are more valuable (in terms of use value) than an equal exchange value's worth of economic benefits aggregated across the society as a whole—that is, the extent to which the goods perceived as more necessary have more use value as compared with their exchange value. Also, Nau (1995) and Chateauneuf and Cohen (1994) have shown an (inverse) empirical correlation between *perceived* diminishing marginal utility and willingness to take risks among workers surveyed about their risk attitudes.

Of course, we must be cautious in equating the amount that people *on the average* would pay for something with the amount that any particular individual would pay, and this distinction is very important for social values, for which the question always arises as to whether some people's assessment of a value should be allowed to regulate other people's behavior or to impact other people's health and welfare. Specifically, if people on the average tend to value a certain type of benefit—for example, health or safety—ten times as highly as they do equivalent monetary amounts of other goods on the market, does this allow us to make governmental policy decisions on the assumption that such benefits are ten times as valuable as the equivalent monetary amounts of those other goods? To completely resolve this question would be beyond our scope here, although I did suggest in the previous chapter some ways of taking individual differences into account. Our main purpose here is not to determine the society's moral or political right to make aggregate decisions that impact people's well-being, but to determine what formula should be used *if* such decisions are to be made.

We saw earlier that if such decisions are to be made, it is more appropriate to make them according to the use values of the benefits involved than according to their *exchange* values. We then saw that the difference between the use values of goods (to their users) and the exchange values of these same goods depends on the rate of diminishing marginal utility, and that the rate of diminishing marginal utility can be measured approximately by the extent of the wealth effect on occupational risk taking. Thus the wealth effect can be used to measure the difference between the use value and the exchange value of any type of good, provided that we know the extent to which people consider that type of good to be necessary to their well-being. For example, if workers are willing to take ten times as much occupational risk to increase their income from $21,000 to $22,000 as they would to increase their income from $31,000 to $32,000, this tells us that the use value of the additional thousand dollars in the latter scenario is proportionally less than the use value of the additional thousand dollars in the former scenario. Working out an exact formula for this is not an easy matter, and I shall attempt to make a beginning in this direction in the next section. But clearly, we have established that no cost–benefit formula should be used at the aggregate level if it determines the comparative values of things merely in terms of their exchange values. An attempt must be made to convert these exchange values into use values. Of course, the philosophical justification for making aggregate decisions at the governmental level per se would be strengthened in general if we knew that different people would similarly assess a given good's necessity (to them) if their circumstances were similar (Ellis 1992, Chapter 6). But this issue is mostly beyond our scope here.

Incorporating the magnitude of the wealth effect can compensate (if it is appropriately operationalized) for much of the inaccuracy in the willingness-to-pay criterion that stems from the heterogeneity in the exchange values for the sake of which people are willing to take various levels of risk. Once the exchange value in question has been modified to account for the greater or lesser degree of necessity of different goods (to their users), the result will be a truer measure of the use value of the good in question (to its user) rather than its mere exchange value, and thus approaches a better approximation to its genuine value in a philosophically defensible sense of 'value'. The mere fact that workers *on average* are willing to incur a 0.5-percent risk of death for $5,000 in economic benefits, so that the *exchange value* of human lives in aggregate risk–oriented policies comes to between $1 million and $6 million (in Viscusi's estimates in 1978 currency), does not imply that this is the *true* extent to which people value their lives. We must devise a formula to compensate for the diminishing value of marginal utility, so as to count the use value of more-necessary goods (to their users) as being greater than their exchange value would lead us to believe. We must count the use value of more-necessary goods as being greater than the use value of an equal monetary amount of less-necessary goods (to their users). Since human life is the most necessary of all benefits, it will be risked only in exchange for other extremely necessary benefits, not in exchange for marginal or less-necessary benefits such as plastic razors. It would therefore be inappropriate simply to judge a $1-million savings in the production cost of plastic razors as equivalent in value to a $1-million death risk to workers, as measured by the exchange value of human lives reflected by average willingness to take occupational death risks. Although the willingness to take risks of life and limb shows up as an "average" willingness among workers in a given sample, the reality is that workers who are desperate for very-necessary goods, and whose options are extremely constrained, are the ones who would purposely accept an increased risk of death or serious ill health in exchange for a pay increment above what could be earned with the lesser degree of such risk in an otherwise comparable job setting. In aggregate analyses, then, $1-million's worth of human life should not be sacrificed in exchange for $1-million's worth of marginal or less-necessary economic benefits to society.

If workers on average would risk their lives for a given amount of very-necessary goods (to them), then they would take a proportionately *smaller* death risk to obtain goods that are *less* necessary (to them). Thus the society as a whole ought not to impose any more than this same proportionately smaller death risk to obtain less-necessary goods. *How much* smaller a risk this should be is determined by the magnitude of diminishing marginal utility, which in turn can be measured by the magnitude of the wealth effect (again, if appropriately operationalized) on occupational risk averseness. In the next section we shall try to express this relationship in terms of an economic formula. It should be obvious already that if the average aggregate exchange value of a human life is $1 million, then its use value, or true value in a philosophically legitimate sense, is going to turn out to be much *greater* than this amount, due to the greater-than-average degree of *necessity* of a human life when it is being compared with the degree of necessity of the *average* economic benefits for which policy decisions are going to trade risks to these lives. Similarly, the true value of all other types of benefits to be balanced in any public-policy cost–benefit equation must be determined by both the exchange value of the type of benefit in question *and* its degree of necessity compared with other types of benefits.

4. A Mathematical Model for the Effect of Necessity/ Nonnecessity on Quantitative Decision Principles

Sinden and Worrell distinguish between a "monetary" and a "utility" approach to estimating comparative values for public policy purposes (Sinden and Worrell 1979, 470–84). In the monetary approach, value is simply assumed to be equal to exchange value. We have now seen the philosophical confusion involved in this assumption. In the utility approach, on the other hand, the values of different outcomes are "weighted" by means of ascertaining the estimates of the subjective *importance* of different considerations, usually in the opinion either of the policy maker or of a sample of the population affected. These weightings are used to modify the exchange values of different outcomes according to the following formula:

$$Vi = \sum_{j=1}^{n} (Uij \times WTj)$$

where n stands for the number of objectives involved in the policy decision, i for each alternative available, j for each objective, U for the utility of each outcome as measured in exchange value, and most important, WT stands for the "importance weighting" of each outcome (480).

Sinden and Worrell point out that since economists have traditionally measured the utility of outcomes in terms of monetary or exchange value, which is not a measure of true value (i.e., the extent to which the good in question affects someone's overall well-being), policy analysts and politicians have found it necessary to include the WT factor to allow for other influences on the true value than mere exchange value. For our present purposes, the important point is that since "needs" are more important than "wants" according to the above reasoning (i.e., more-necessary goods are more important than less-necessary ones of equal exchange value), the degree of necessity of each objective will determine the quantity of WT for that objective in the Sinden–Worrell utility formula. This degree of necessity is determined, in turn, by the rate at which marginal utilities diminish in value, which is an empirical question, and is proportional to the magnitude of the wealth effect on occupational risk averseness, that is, the extent to which wealthier workers are more averse to risk than poorer ones.

If we use a worker's total family income level (both labor and nonlabor, including income from assets, spouse's income, etc.) to approximate an operationalization for the concept of 'economic well-being' (as do Garen 1988, Biddle and Zarkin 1989, and Robinson 1988), and if the additional risks workers are willing to incur are determined by their economic well-being, then the income level at which a worker would choose to incur an additional risk corresponds to the degree of necessity of the goods for which the additional money will be used. For example, food, a commodity for which money is used at low-income levels, is very necessary to its user's well being. A yacht, a commodity for which money is used at high-income levels, is not very necessary to its user's well being. Thus, as we have seen, the risk a low-income person would take for a $1,000 pay increment is not equal to the risk a high-income person would take for a $1,000 pay increment. It therefore becomes possible to assign a "degree of necessity" to goods (i.e., their degree of necessity to users in general), based on the income level at which a given amount of increased risk would be incurred by a given person for a given amount of pay increment, since we have seen that the income level in question will correspond to the degree of necessity of the goods for which money is spent marginally at that income level. In simpler terms, the degree of necessity of a good is proportional to the increased occupational risk a worker would be willing to incur in order to obtain the additional money she needs to buy that particular good. This can be ascertained empirically, either by observing the consuming behavior of workers as their incomes go up and down (noting which items are purchased or not purchased by preference over others as income changes must be managed), or by devising questionnaires to determine whether a pay increment at a given income level would be used for one item in preference to another. To be sure, to make either of these methods accurate would be difficult and complex, but it would be no more difficult or complex than the kinds of empirical questionnaires and behavior measurements already recommended by Sinden and Worrell to determine their *WT* factor. The additional problem would, of course, remain, as mentioned earlier, that whether and to what extent governments should make political decisions on the basis of the priority rankings of people *on the average,* even though these rankings will inevitably differ from those of atypical individuals, involves political-philosophical issues that are beyond our scope here (see Ellis 1992). The important point for our purposes is that when governments *do* choose to take the responsibility to make such decisions (and there are times when they almost inevitably must), they should consider the relative *importance* or *degree of necessity* of different outcomes, not simply the average exchange value they would have in an open market. Of course, we must also address the question as to when the government should and should not assume responsibility to take action. This question will be discussed in the next chapter.

I have emphasized all along that the degree of necessity of a good or outcome means, by definition, the extent to which that good or outcome contributes to the subjectively experienced well-being of a given consumer. For example, many welfare recipients own or rent TV sets, whereas they neglect severe dental problems. This only means that, for most people, a certain amount of entertainment is extremely necessary. But as the amount of money that has been spent on entertainment increases, the value that one places on *additional* entertainment expenditures, compared with other types of goods, diminishes rapidly. So a worker who incurs an additional work hazard in order to buy a TV set, if she owns few other entertainment goods, is really incurring that risk for the sake of quite necessary goods (again, from the standpoint of that worker's experienced overall well-being). We cannot say in general, then, that TV sets are more or less necessary than dental work, for example, although we can determine that a family's second TV set is usually less valuable than its first, and that the second TV set will usually be considered less necessary than the dental work, although the first TV set may be more necessary than the dental work. The importance of a good, then, can be defined only in terms of the importance it would have marginally at a given income level; the same item will have a different degree of necessity depending on the economic status of its user.

If we could accurately assess the magnitude of the "wealth effect" on occupational risk averseness, then we would in effect be measuring (approximately, and all else being equal) the rate at which the degree of necessity of goods increases in accordance with the increased occupational risk workers are willing to incur to acquire those goods. The poorer the worker, the more necessary are the goods for the sake of which she is electing to risk life, health, or safety, and therefore the greater the risk she is willing to incur. We could therefore assign a quantitative measure of "degree of necessity" (or *DN*) to various kinds of goods, as determined by the extent to which workers choose to incur the increased risks necessary to obtain those kinds of goods. The curve that describes the wealth effect on occupational risk averseness, in short, will also describe (inversely) the rate at which more-necessary goods increase in value compared with less-necessary goods of equal exchange value or monetary value on the open market. The true value, or use value, of any good or outcome would be determined by both the exchange value of that good or outcome in monetary terms, *and* the degree of necessity of that good or outcome. We could therefore amend the Sinden–Worrell utility formula so that the *WT* factor— which until now has been based on subjective evaluations of the relative "importance" of different objectives and outcomes, and ultimately has tended to be based on considerations of political expediency (as Dryzek 1987 emphasizes), as well as tending toward an unjust 'tyranny of the majority'—can now be more objectively determined. We could simply replace the term *WT* with our new term, *DN*, resulting in the formula,

$$Vi = \sum_{j=1}^{n} (Uij \times DNj)$$

Intuitively, what this means is that, for example, housing for the home-less is more necessary than improvements in housing conditions for people of average means, and thus when policy decisions are being made, this greater degree of necessity ought to be figured into the assessment of the true values of the two competing objectives. Similarly, energy assistance for the poor is more necessary than redecoration of the governor's office; people's health and safety are more necessary than increased cost effectiveness in manufacturing plastic razors; and the lives of victims of cancer caused by dioxin in drinking water are more necessary than the equivalent amount (in exchange value) of savings in the cost of bleached paper (which necessitates disposing of dioxin given off as a by-product of the bleaching process). This is not to say, of course, that redecoration of the governor's office, cheaper plastic razors, and savings in the cost of bleaching paper have no value, but only that their *DN* is considerably smaller.

In practical terms, how do we measure *DN*? To do this, we must measure the magnitude of the wealth effect on occupational risk averse-ness. And here we run into a plethora of problems relating to both empirical measurement and economic theory. At the present time, little empirical research has been done regarding this wealth effect, and what little has been done is quite controversial in terms of the way the relevant concepts have been operationally defined, the kinds of assumptions that must be made about risk information available to workers, the degree to which their occupational choices are really unconstrained, the extent to which extraneous variables such as personality characteristics or social background might contaminate the research, and many other such problems (as mentioned in Hersch and Pickton 1995 and in Leigh 1989). However, both theory and research seem to indicate that, all else being equal, risk averseness is approximately directly proportional to worker "wealth" or economic well-being, if the latter is defined in terms of the worker's total income as discussed above. (Siebert and Wei 1994; Garen 1988; Robinson 1986; and Biddle and Zarkin 1989 find this much correlation empirically. That theory would predict it is evident from Gregory 1980, as well as from Viscusi 1978a, 1978b, and 1993.) Studies that use workers' *assets* as the operational definition of "wealth" find smaller correlations between risk averseness and wealth, but the correlations are still found to be statistically significant (Viscusi 1978b). Economic theory, using such notions as gambling strategy and the Friedman–Savage utility function, would seem to predict a curve that, if the concavity and convexity at different points were smoothed out, would approximate to a direct proportionality between wealth and risk averseness (Gregory 1980). There are, however, some reasons to believe that the wealth effect may be even stronger than a direct proportionality—that risk averseness may in fact increase geometrically rather than arithmetically with respect to worker wealth, as touched upon further below.

Since the magnitude of the wealth effect is so important for our purposes, perhaps a little further discussion of the problems involved in ascertaining it would not be out of place here. Although we have seen that economists have already begun trying to estimate the magnitude of the effect, it would be premature at this point to regard this quantity as precisely established by the research to date. The danger of doing so would be that the strength of the effect might be greatly underestimated (as Viscusi 1978b emphasizes), given the systematic sources of error that prevent the full impact of the effect from being observed. For example, it is likely that workers, though informed about the risks of *their own* jobs (Robinson 1988; Nelkin and Brown 1984), may not be very well informed about the *comparative* risks of different jobs (Savage 1993); that, even if they were, their decisions would not be absolutely mathematically precise; that the threat of unemployment and other such factors prevent workers from making job changes that such a perfectly rational calculation might otherwise dictate; and that a variety of other rational and nonrational extra-economic factors might induce workers to remain in jobs that a pure risk assessment would dictate that they quit (Leigh 1989; Nelkin and Brown 1984). But any extraneous or unmeasured factor that might prevent a worker from quitting a risky job will therefore make that worker appear more willing to take risks than she really is. The impact of many of these kinds of factors is discussed extensively in the above-cited works by Hersch and Pickton (1995), Nelkin and Brown (1984), Leigh (1989), and Robinson (1988). Any estimation of the value of life or safety based on occupational risk studies will thus have a serious tendency to *underestimate* these values (although it will not underestimate the value of life nearly as much as other currently used methods, such as the future-earnings criterion).

On the other hand, these inaccuracies will affect our estimates of the *wealth effect* much less than they will affect the value of life itself. The reason for this is that the irrationality and ill-informedness of risk decisions are probably not too different for different income levels, as Robinson (1986, 1988) and Nelkin and Brown (1984) have empirically shown. And, although the risk of unemployment might be a more serious influence on poorer workers (whether it is or not is an empirical question), this relationship could be used as a control variable in occupational risk studies.

As far as the underestimation of the *exchange* values of life and limb are concerned, the important point for practical purposes is that present policies already underestimate this value. Indeed, policies using future-earnings rather than willingness-to-pay criteria underestimate it substantially more. So the incorporation of a "justice factor" such as the one we are proposing here (i.e., the *DN* factor in the revised version of the Sinden–Worrell utility formula) can only lead us to value human lives more accurately (and more highly) than we already do, since, as explained above, life is a more necessary good than other types of goods for which policy decisions have tended to trade off the risk of human lives. Our position at the present time is simply that, given current political realities, the refusal to use a precise decision principle would probably lead to worse consequences than to do so with as much justice incorporated into the formula as possible; and that, in any event, government agencies, realistically speaking, will tend to demand precise decision principles rather than let such decisions be taken subjectively, for the reasons indicated earlier.

With regard to research on the magnitude of the wealth effect, the most serious problem seems to be that there are two conflicting effects that tend to mask each other, given the empirical methods used to observe them. On the one hand, there is a "premium-for-risks" effect in that a given worker tends to demand a higher wage for a riskier job. But on the other hand, there is the "wealth effect" in that wealthier (and thus better-paid) workers are *less* willing to take additional risks than their poorer counterparts. Hence the paradox that the *riskier* jobs are filled with workers from the *lower* socioeconomic ranks (Robinson 1988, 247–48, 250; Siebert and Wei 1994), a fact that tends to mask the "premiums-for-risks" effect to such an extent that some economists still question the very possibility of isolating such an effect, arguing that even the demonstrations of its existence, let alone its magnitude, contain unacceptable statistical design problems (Leigh 1989, 832–36). It will be difficult (though not impossible) to study empirically the way these two opposing tendencies interact. Some progress is certainly being made. The consensus among economists seems to be that, currently, demonstrations of at least the existence of both effects have been replicated reliably. As to their magnitude and interaction, further research needs to be done. Viscusi (1978a, 1983, 1993) and others have shown that the value of life based on "risk premiums" is reliably *at least* about $3 million for the safest 75 percent of occupations, and *at least* $500,000 for the riskiest 25 percent (in 1978 dollars). These figures will increase as researchers learn to control more effectively for the contravening wealth effect and other sources of error variance.

Since the only aspect of these studies that is important for our purposes is the wealth effect, which determines degree of necessity (or *DN* in the above formula), and since the dangers of error for its measurement all involve the possibility that its magnitude may have been *underestimated*, we can say with confidence that risk averseness is *at least* directly proportional to worker wealth or economic well-being, as defined in terms of the worker's total income. We can therefore be confident that subsequent research can only increase the value of the *DN* factor and, in light of the kinds of error involved, will do so to an extent that is relatively slight compared with the total magnitude of the wealth effect itself. This already enables us to improve substantially the validity of policy decisions that must compare the values of different kinds of goods and outcomes, because we can now compare these values in a way that takes into consideration the difference in their degree of necessity (for those whom they affect), rather than merely assessing their value in terms of exchange values.

For example, it is important to remember that Viscusi's value-of-life estimates just cited represent *exchange* values for human life. To convert this exchange value to use value, or true value, we must take into consideration the degree of necessity of life as compared with the average level of necessity of goods for which public policies are going to trade these lives. This point is crucial because we have seen that workers tend to risk their lives to obtain goods not *at the average level of necessity*, but only for goods *at extremely high levels of necessity*. Thus the general population should not be expected to risk their lives to as great an extent for goods *at the average level of necessity* as the workers in risk studies have done for goods *at extremely high levels of necessity*. Viscusi notes that the average worker receives only about $400 per year in risk premiums (in some studies, up to $900). No doubt this figure would be considerably higher if it were not for the wealth effect. The riskiest quartile of professions, which were studied in the now-famous Thaler and Rosen study (1976), seems to involve about *ten times* as much risk as the other three quartiles of the professions, investigated in other studies such as Viscusi's. Thus value-of-life estimates using Thaler and Rosen will grotesquely underestimate even the *exchange* value of a life. More important, since an average risk premium of only $400 or $900 per year can hardly account for a tenfold discrepancy in the riskiness of the lowest quartile of professions, and since, as we have seen, noneconomic factors (such as individual psychological characteristics) cannot account for such discrepancies in risk-taking behavior, we can only assume that the wealth effect accounts for a considerable proportion of it. If we combine this point with the fact that risky jobs tend to pay considerably *less* (Robinson 1988, 247–48, 250; Siebert and Wei 1994) in spite of the "premiums-for-risks" effect; the finding of Garen (1988) that the "strong, negative and significant effect of non-labor income on risk . . . reinforces the interpretation of the demand for safety rising with income;" (13) and the finding of Biddle and Zarkin (1989) that "[a]s we increase the amount of nonlabor income, we must compensate the worker more for increases in risk. . . . Although the estimated income elasticities vary over a wide range, 70% are less than 2 in absolute value" (666–67); it seems safe to conclude, tentatively at this point, that risk averseness is *at least* directly proportional to worker wealth. That is, a worker's risk averseness increases at least as rapidly as does her wealth or economic well-being, as Garen (1988), Robinson (1988), Siebert and Wei (1994), and Biddle and Zarkin (1989) found in the studies discussed earlier.

There are some reasons, in fact, to believe that risk averseness may even increase geometrically with respect to worker wealth. Viscusi

(1983, 1993) and Kniesner and Leeth (1991) show that the percentage of the population incurring a given occupational risk is inversely proportional to the amount of risk involved. That is, as job riskiness increases, the number of people willing to incur that risk diminishes proportionately, and the curve describing this diminution is linear. This would seem to imply that, as we ascend along the risk-averseness continuum, there are more and more people exhibiting each increased amount of risk averseness. Thus it might be reasonable to infer that, as worker wealth increases at a constant rate, risk averseness increases at a greater rate, so that more and more people are included at each increased level of risk averseness. This would mean that risk averseness increases faster than worker wealth, so that the increase in risk averseness would be geometric rather than arithmetic with respect to worker wealth, but again with an overall elasticity somewhere between 1 and 2, as indicated above.

We have engaged in what might seem a lengthy digression into empirical economic literature because it is important to see what is involved in determining the all-important *DN* figure in our revision of the utility formula to be used in place of cost–benefit analysis per se. Now let's see how the assessment of *DN* would operate. It must be emphasized that when we assess the degree of necessity of any good or outcome (availability of parks, widening of roads, cleaner air, safer cars, etc.), we are determining only the necessity of one good or outcome compared with another good or outcome. Thus it may turn out that availability of parks has a higher degree of necessity than widening of roads or vice versa. Which one has the greater degree of necessity depends on the income level at which people would spend additional incremental amounts to obtain that good or outcome. If people with a very low income would spend an additional incremental amount to support the widening of roads, whereas only people with high income would spend an additional incremental amount to make more parks available, then the widening of roads is correspondingly more "necessary" than the availability of additional parks. The difference between the degree of necessity of widening roads and of additional parks is determined by the difference between the income levels at which people would spend additional incremental amounts to promote these two outcomes. Intuitively speaking, this means that goods for which money would be spent at low income levels are more necessary than those for which money would not be spent until a higher income level had been achieved.

For example, suppose that the magnitude of the wealth effect is X per \$1,000 in pay increment; that is, a person earning \$1,000 less in income than someone else is willing to take X times as much risk in order to increase her income by a certain increment. And suppose (merely for the sake of simplicity in this example) that the shape of the wealth-effect curve is a steady increase, so that for every \$1,000 increase in earnings, a worker becomes X times as averse to risk. This would mean that the diminishing value of marginal utilities is described by the same curve, so that one's first \$1,000 is worth X times as much as one's second \$1,000, which is worth X times as much as one's third \$1,000, etc. It would then follow that, all else being equal, the importance weightings for outcomes, or WT in the Sinden–Worrell formula, is equal to DN, which is determined by X. Thus, for instance, a \$1,000 benefit that accrues to the *average* family, whose income, let us say, is \$24,000, would be worth much less than a \$1,000 benefit that accrues only to families earning \$10,000. (In a moment we shall see how to calculate *how much* less.) Of course, many policy decisions involve goods and services that are available to people of all income levels, but the degree of necessity of these goods and services can be compared by determining the income level at which they would become marginal expenditures.

In fact, we are now prepared to see how to determine *how much* greater. There are two ways to do it. One is to begin with a person's first \$1,000 in income, and then determine how much less necessary each additional \$1,000 would be. The other is to begin with the average income and then determine how much *less* necessary each additional \$1,000 would be, and how much *more* necessary each \$1,000 subtracted from the average income would be. I shall use the first method here to simplify the numbers. If each additional \$1,000 is worth $1/X$ as much as the previous \$1,000, then one's second \$1,000 is worth \$1,000 $(1/X)^2$, etc. Thus one's nth \$1,000 is worth $(1/X)^n$ times as much as one's first \$1,000. Similarly, if we take the exchange value of a dollar to be its *average* value (i.e., as used to purchase goods at the *average* degree of necessity), then someone's first \$1,000 must be weighted in true value or utility such that this first \$1,000 is worth X^n times as much as someone's nth \$1,000.

To try to become absolutely precise with these calculations at this point would be premature. As I have indicated throughout this discussion, the value of the wealth effect in occupational risk studies has not yet been measured precisely enough for this purpose. Also, other variables that might affect the occupational risk-taking behavior of the workers in these studies need to be taken into consideration. The purpose of the admittedly approximate calculations in the example just considered is merely to illustrate the conceptual point at issue. The idea is that, in principle, *it is possible* to calculate the degree of necessity of different kinds of benefits relative to each other, using the magnitude of the wealth effect as a good approximation to the rate of diminishing marginal utility, and thus to incorporate a justice factor (the *DN* factor) into the formula for cost–benefit analysis that traditionally has conspicuously lacked such consideration to the concept of justice.

Besides allowing a more adequate assessment of the value of life for aggregate policy purposes, the modified formula would apply equally well to aggregate policy decisions for competing benefits whose value has been determined straightforwardly by market prices. Suppose, for example, that a government is weighting whether to spend $10 million on housing subsidies for people at the average income level or for people at the poverty level, which, let us assume, is $14,000 below the median family income. If the *DN* for average benefits is defined as 1, then the *DN* for the low-income housing in this example (again assuming the magnitude of the wealth effect to be 1.1 per $1,000 in income) would come to 1.1^{14}, or about 3.8. In other words, the use value of the low-income housing is 3.8 times the use value of the average-income housing, even though their exchange values are the same. Clearly, then, the money would be more beneficially employed if spent on the low-income than the average-income housing in this example.

5. Conclusion

We have seen that the main shortcomings of cost–benefit analysis for public policy purposes stem from the unjust burdens it imposes on some people in order to benefit others, often in rather frivolous ways. The reason for this injustice is that very-necessary benefits are counted the same as less-necessary benefits in traditional cost–benefit analysis. To correct for this injustice, we have developed a "justice factor," defined in terms of the inclusion of a measure of the "degree of necessity" in the decision formula for policy decisions. Calculating degrees of necessity allows policy makers to count very-necessary benefits—such as health, safety, life, and environmental preservation (which is necessary to future lives and their health)—as having more actual value, or use value, than their mere exchange value would appear to indicate. No zero-risk option is realistic or desirable in public policy, but at least by incorporating the justice factor, policy makers can avoid inappropriate trade-offs between extremely important values and comparatively frivolous economic benefits.

Finally, we have suggested that the degree of necessity of benefits is determined by the rate at which marginal utilities diminish in value, which can be determined by the extent to which wealthier workers are more averse to occupational risk than poorer ones. By taking the degree of necessity of benefits into account, public-policy decisions can incorporate more justice (and therefore also can be seen by the public as more just) than is currently the case. The difference this makes is especially obvious when those decisions involve environmental preservation, pollution control, and other aggregate risk–oriented issues involving unpriced values, since these issues are so apt to provoke controversies over whether it is appropriate to risk simply "trading off" these unpriced values for the sake of more straightforwardly economic benefits. But it is equally important to realize that even "priced" values must be adjusted to convert their exchange values into use values.

Realistically speaking, legislators are constrained from micromanaging such technical matters as pollution emissions standards and other highly specific aggregate risk decisions. They are constrained by the lack of well-informedness of the voting public; by the problem of the "tyranny of the majority" as it affects externalities and competition between local areas and economic interests; by the public's fear of job loss (which is heightened by public relations campaigns engineered by vested interests, but is a real problem that must be addressed nonetheless, as Robinson 1986 and 1988, emphasizes in the above-cited study); by the cumbersomeness of governmental processes; and by a plethora of other factors. What is needed—and, in fact, what is demanded by the executive agencies responsible for elaborating the exact quantitative parameters of these standards—is a decision principle precise enough to clearly spell out appropriate guidelines, approved *in general principle* by the legislature, that would set forth strict rules as to how decisions are to be made, but would allow the technical application to be accomplished by experts, with broad legislative oversight. The use of traditional cost–benefit analysis, however, leads to gross and highly visible injustice in many instances. That is why a precisely defined justice factor such as the one proposed here needs to be explicitly incorporated into the decision formula used by policy makers.

7

The Problem of
Empirical Uncertainties

In order to translate the above considerations about the appropriate balance between general utility and the concerns of justice into specific political policy guidelines, we must take account of the effect of empirical uncertainties on the process of policy making. Scientific research is never more uncertain than when it serves as a battleground for conflicting political agendas, and this problem is nowhere more acute than in the very realms in which empirical research is most necessary for the making of policy—for example, in environmental policy. We shall see, in fact, that the uncertainties revealed by the sociology of scientific research in these areas are so pronounced that these uncertainties themselves influence the direction that political philosophy must take if such problems are to be addressed in a way that is both philosophically defensible and practically effective. In addressing collective problems (such as pollution and environmental destruction, welfare and social security programs, protection of public health, and even crime and unemployment problems), it makes a big difference whether we begin with a consequentialist political theory emphasizing a strong role for government, or with a predominantly rights-based and minimalist-government theory such as the theory of Locke, which in the United States was exemplified almost in its classic form by the Reagan and Bush administrations, and in the United Kingdom by Thatcher. This rights-based theory tends to be ineffectual in collective problem-solving contexts, such as regulating the environment or addressing the causes of crime and poverty, because a purely rights-based approach would severely limit governmental power; would require a stricter standard of scientific proof to justify governmental intervention than is attainable in an unavoidably probabilistic scientific methodology; and (as we shall see) would be consistent with the fragmentation of local governments and of government functions (see Railton 1985; Lessnoff 1986).

A rights-based approach in its purest form interprets the role of government as protecting citizens from having their "inalienable rights" violated either by each other or by their government; these rights are "inalienable" in the sense that they cannot be violated even if doing so would be beneficial from the standpoint of the general welfare. A major problem with this approach is that if freedom itself is a right, then, in order to prevent someone from violating someone else's 'rights', the government must first have "proof" that the action *is* a rights violation. Otherwise the government would violate the rights of the agent of the supposedly harmful action by unjustly limiting her freedom to act. But the kind of "proof" required to justify such a limitation of freedom often would be a much stricter kind of proof than science would be capable of providing. A consequentialist political theory, as we shall see, is more flexible in accepting probabilities and statistically significant correlations in the absence of absolute *proof* of harm, because a consequentialist theory's first priority is to produce the best possible overall *outcome*, taking people's freedom of action into consideration simply as *one* of the important kinds of outcomes that must be balanced against others. It would not regard as an 'inalienable right' the freedom to engage in actions that are substantially likely to seriously impede the general welfare.

The distinction between a rights-based approach and a consequentialist one is not as rigid as is sometimes supposed. Theoretically, a rights-based approach is one in which rights are "inalienable" and in some sense "trump" consequentialist considerations. The government may pursue consequentialist concerns, but only when and if it can do so without infringing on anyone's rights. On the other hand, a consequentialist approach is, in principle, one in which legal rights must be justified by consequentialist concerns, but fairness or distributive justice may be counted as one of the legitimate consequences to be promoted. That is, in a consequentialist approach, one has the 'right' not to be saddled with a *distributively unjust* burden for the sake of aggregate benefits. Since the rights themselves are justified by the desirability of distributively just consequences, no right can "trump" the importance of promoting distributive justice itself. On the contrary, it is easy to imagine instances in which the importance of distributive justice might "trump" property rights or the right of freedom—for example, the freedom to do business in a certain way or to pollute, where such freedoms are in conflict with distributive justice and/or the general welfare. Obviously, consequentialist approaches are not necessarily utilitarian.

One of the most intractable problems with a predominantly rights-based and minimalist approach is that it tends to require a naive-realist notion of scientific verification, as if it were possible to "prove" scientifically whether someone has been harmed by an ostensibly hazardous technology or substance, or by a merger of corporations or an act of environmental destruction, and to do so conclusively enough to clearly warrant curtailing someone else's right to do the action in question—for example, to use the technology or substance at issue (Findley and Farber 1988). By contrast, a consequentialist political philosophy can operate effectively given a considerable degree of scientific uncertainty and variability of ideological motivations as they affect the direction and outcomes of scientific research, since in this approach it is only necessary that legislators and administrators believe that a business activity, substance, or technology is *somewhat likely* to be harmful. The importance of this scientific uncertainty as interrelated with political biases in the sociology of science has been emphasized, for example, by Brian Wynne (1987), who insists that the interpretation of facts is inevitably politically driven. We shall see that the rights-based, minimal-government approach allows pollution to be considered "innocent until proven guilty," as John Quarles (1976, 224) has put it, whereas the sociology of science is such that this "proof" will all too seldom be *conclusive* enough to drive a minimalist and purely rights-based government to action. The same problem arises with regard to proving that growing up in abject poverty or in gang-ridden neighborhoods causes a sufficiently unfair set of opportunities to constitute a "rights-violation"; social scientists cannot even prove to *everyone's* satisfaction that poverty is a cause of crime (for example, see Vold 1967).

A consequentialist and strongly centralized approach, on the other hand, requires only that science establish a modest probability of the harmfulness of a technology or substance in order to motivate legislators to control or ban it. As will become more clear below, the reason *centralized* power becomes important here is that in a decentralized system, local areas often compete to see which one can provide the *least* protection to the public interest in order to provide regulatory and tax incentives for business interests to relocate (Peterson 1981).

Similarly, a centralized government is better able than a small district to address the problems of the poor without motivating those whose taxes support such programs to "vote with their feet" by moving to a jurisdiction whose benefit/tax ratio is more favorable to them.

Some environmental advocates may initially support almost the exact opposite view, fearing that a strong central government operating under a consequentialist philosophy will tend to reach decisions by means of a utilitarian cost–benefit analysis, so that aggregate economic benefits will all too often outweigh environmental and pollution-control considerations, especially when the life or health of relatively small numbers of people are involved. For example, Elizabeth Anderson (1988) and Annette Baier (1986) have expressed such a concern. Too ruthless a utilitarianism, they fear, might be willing to sacrifice a few to cancer in exchange for cheaper plastic razors for the many. It is an empirical fact, of course, that many strongly centralized governments based on consequentialist philosophies (such as the "Eastern-bloc" nations) have been considerably less than friendly to the environment (Drysek 1987, 96ff). We shall show, however, that such failures can be avoided if the consequences to be promoted are arrived at by means of a more appropriate decision principle than those that have been used by such governments in the past.

The largest problem to be solved in order to make a consequentialist approach tenable in the light of these concerns is to show that it does not conflict with principles of just distribution of benefits and burdens simply in order to maximize aggregate benefits. This problem has all too often been ignored by strongly centralized decision makers. To use simple cost–benefit analysis, which presupposes a philosophy of pure utilitarianism, as an environmental decision principle would violate even the most conservative notions of the place of justice in political theory. On the other hand, to insist on zero-risk policies, as some environmentalists sometimes sound as if they were trying to do (for example, as the director of the Georgia Environmental Project suggested in an informal discussion recently), would render impossible any use whatever of even the most primitive technologies. Every time we drive our cars, use a stove, or light a fireplace, we assume some ill-health or death risk in exchange for some expected benefit. It is therefore necessary to formulate a philosophically justifiable synthesis that would provide a better alternative to either of these antitheses. In short, a sound consequentialist theory must find a more legitimate way to calculate outcomes than cost–benefit analysis, but it cannot insist on absolutely minimizing risks at any cost whatever. And it must ground a notion of legal 'rights', at least in the sense that avoiding distributively unjust imposition of burdens enjoys priority over mere utility maximization.

This chapter will argue first that, given the sociology of science and the importance of scientific uncertainties, a purely rights-based and minimalist government cannot adequately address collective problems such as environmental destruction because science is seldom able to *prove* satisfactorily that people are being seriously enough harmed by a given act of pollution or environmental destruction to override someone else's freedom to act. The nature of science is such that in many instances only modest probabilities of harm can be established. Since the right of the polluter or developer to do business is also important, stricter proof of harm than is frequently available would be needed to justify curtailing this right (for example, see Georgia Bar Association, 1991). For this reason, a strong central government must be entrusted with the power to reach decisions on a consequentialist basis, taking the 'rights' of developers and polluters into consideration only as one of the many competing outcomes that must be balanced against each other in the total calculation of which policy is most beneficial on the whole. Such a government would be empowered to take action if even a modest probability of harmfulness of a technology or substance had been reasonably demonstrated, provided that such action does not impose a distributively unjust burden on someone.

Second, a consequentialist system must develop an applicable decision principle that makes room for a principle of *just distribution* of benefits and burdens, in contrast to the traditional utility-maximizing approaches such as cost–benefit analysis, which neglect to consider this problem and thus end up imposing unfair burdens to facilitate frivolous economic gains. In a carefully worked out consequentialist approach, to say that someone's rights had been violated could simply mean that an unfair burden had been imposed. Thus it would only be necessary for the government to calculate the best way to accomplish the most beneficial possible objectives, taking into account the value that should be placed on just distribution of the benefits as well as the burdens.

1. How Scientific Uncertainties Inhibit Government Intervention

Much of this book is devoted to the discussion of alternative viewpoints for grounding the value assumptions needed to make policy decisions.

But the other half of the grounding that is also needed for policy decisions is an appropriate assessment of the *empirical* realities that must be known before any effective plan of action can be devised or implemented. It would be foolish to implement the death penalty in order to reduce crime if the empirical facts do not support the hypothesis that use of the death penalty *does* lead to reduced crime.

It is precisely in this area of *overlap* between value assumptions and factual assumptions that the most thorny (but also the most interesting) issues in policy analysis arise. To a greater or lesser extent, our interpretation of scientific findings are inescapably influenced by our value assumptions. Because scientific research involves a type of reasoning that always leaves room for uncertainty, our decision whether to interpret the results as demonstrating a given conclusion often will be influenced by *the value we place on implementing the findings in a practical context.* This happens essentially in two ways. In the first place, since scientific conclusions involve uncertainty, there is the tendency to let a conscious or unconscious prejudice in favor of our preferred political agenda affect our interpretation of the findings. And second, our decision as to whether the level of certainty of the scientific findings is great enough to warrant accepting the conclusion depends to a large extent on the perceived value or disvalue to be achieved by acting on the given findings. For example, the consequences of trying a criminal rehabilitation program that fails to have the expected results may not be too severe, whereas the consequences of allowing the use of a new drug whose safety is in question could be devastating. Moreover, there is a great deal more room for varying interpretations of empirical research results than most people realize. A realistic assessment of the ways in which empirical uncertainties inhibit government action, especially in a strictly rights-based political theory, hinges crucially on this problem.

For example, we know that poverty correlates very strongly with crime rates (Short 1980; Freeman 1983; Ellis 1987a), but we are less sure how much of this correlation results from a causal relationship between poverty and crime, and how much of it results from the fact that poverty and crime tend to occur in the same geographical areas for other reasons—for instance, because crime is aggravated by crowded living conditions, while at the same time poverty happens to be concentrated in inner cities, where population density is high (Sutherland and Cressey 1972, 95ff; McCaghy 1980, 97–99). Thus poverty and crime could be concentrated in the same areas even if one does not cause the other (as Vold, 1967, 159–82, suggests). It is therefore necessary to carry out more extensive research before concluding that poverty is a cause of crime. How such a conclusion *can* be adequately supported will be discussed later in this section.

Perhaps an even worse problem is that the probabilistic nature of scientific reasoning lends itself to the possibility that people who are strongly motivated to deceive either themselves or others about an issue may use forms of reasoning that have all the apparent trappings of scientific precision yet contain hidden fallacies of reasoning. These fallacies may be so well disguised that only someone who is fairly sophisticated in the interpretation of scientific reasoning can detect them. We seem to have reached a time in human history when the results of scientific reasoning are so often crucial to the process of social decision making that it is now necessary for everyone to become sophisticated with regard to these interpretive issues in scientific reasoning.

There seem to be four main areas of malleability and uncertainty in scientific reasoning, corresponding to the four most important requirements for good scientific reasoning accepted by most scientists and philosophers who have thought extensively about these matters. These same four requirements are emphasized not only by traditional philosophers of science (Popper 1957; Hempel 1963), but also by more radical thinkers who stress the social and historical relativity of scientific theory and research (Kuhn 1962; Laudan 1990). The differences between these approaches do not involve any fundamental disagreement over what good scientific reasoning should ideally consist of; the controversy hinges on how feasible it is for researchers to actually *achieve* the ideal, given the difficulty of overcoming theoretical prejudices, tacit presuppositions of which we are unaware that distort our conceptual categories, and selective biases in the gathering and interpreting of data. But, to the extent that reliable empirical knowledge is achievable, there are four essential requirements regarding the ways this knowledge is to be verified: (a) the need for *prediction* in order to verify a hypothesis; (b) the need for quantification in an adequately precise way to determine whether the relationship in question is *statistically significant*, that is, a stronger mathematical relationship than would have been expected by chance or coincidence; (c) appropriate *operational definitions* that define items under investigation in such a way that they can be empirically observed and measured, and that is not misleading as to *what* is being observed and measured; and (d) elimination of plausible alternative explanations for the observed statistical relationship (for example, through experimental controls). Each of these areas create uncertainties that lend themselves to competing interpretations.

(a) It is usually expected that a hypothesis should predict *previously unknown* information or statistical relationships. It is not good enough that the hypothesis agrees with or explains information and relationships about which we *already* know. Given any collection of facts, one can think up a number of different explanations that, *if true,* would explain the known facts, but there still would be no way to decide which of these possible explanations is the *true* explanation. On the other hand, if a hypothesis predicts some previously unknown fact or relationship, and *then* the prediction *comes true,* we are warranted in concluding that this predictive power increases the probability that the hypothesis is true (Popper 1957). For example, Einstein's theory of relativity not only predicted that light from a distant star would be bent as it passed through the gravitational field of the sun, but also predicted (based on its mathematical equations) the exact *extent* to which the light would be bent (Calder 1980; Bridgman 1962; Salmon 1980). But if an astrologist predicts that I am going to receive some money in the future, and indeed it turns out that I do receive some money later, this prediction does not convince anyone that astrology is a true scientific theory because it was already obvious that I would probably receive some money sooner or later. The astrologist's prediction, therefore, is not a genuine prediction at all; in scientific terms, it is not a "falsifiable" prediction.

A common reason for remaining somewhat skeptical about a causal theory even when it can make accurate predictions is that, in many instances, a theory may be *close enough* to the truth *in certain respects* to generate some very accurate predictions, yet still may not get at the exact truth in some crucial respects. For example, in spite of the remarkable accuracy of many predictions from Einstein's theory of relativity, a few of its predictions do not seem to pan out. Einstein's theory predicts that nothing can travel faster than light, but recent experiments in quantum theory show that the transmission of energy between subatomic particles in some instances is faster than light (Aspect 1982).

There is a similar problem with the poverty–crime hypothesis. Many of the most impoverished areas (i.e., rural areas) have the *lowest* crime rates. But, in urban areas, the prediction that crime rates would correlate with poverty is a very reliable one—and it becomes more reliable still when adjusted for the effects of welfare programs in the impoverished areas (DeFronzo 1983; Ellis 1987a, 1989).

In general, then, prediction alone is not an adequate test of a theory unless the other requirements for scientific verification are met.

(b) A second main requirement for good scientific reasoning is that observed relationships must be quantitatively measurable and statistically significant (Lordahl 1967; Helmstadter 1970). For some purposes, a modest level of certainty may be considered sufficient evidence to warrant accepting a theory or explanation. For example, if we have confirmed that there is a 95-percent probability that increasing welfare benefits would dramatically reduce crime rates, then we would probably want to go ahead and increase the welfare benefits, since there will then be only a 5-percent chance that the desired effect will fail to be achieved (Ellis 1987b, 1989). For other purposes, however, even a 1-percent probability of error may be considered too high. For example, we would not want to take a 1-percent risk that a nuclear power plant will melt down. The consequences of error would be much too severe. In either case, the choice as to the level of certainty required is value driven, since it depends on the value of the *consequences* of being right or wrong when the results are actually applied.

(c) The need for operational definitions is often a major source of confusion and misrepresentation of research results and their implications. Suppose a social scientist wants to study the relationship between the presence of multinational corporations in Third-World countries and economic growth in those countries. This means that "economic growth," "Third-World country," and "presence of multinational corporations" must be defined in such a way that they can be unambiguously observed and measured. Now suppose that a social scientist defines "Third-World countries" in such a way as to include countries like Saudi Arabia and Taiwan (countries with considerable economic growth in recent years) and economic growth as growth in the gross national product of a country (rather than defining it, say, as growth in average real *income* in the country). Then it may appear that there is a positive statistical correlation between economic growth and presence of multinational corporations (Brandt et. al. 1980, 73, 187–92; Ballmar-Cao 1979; Berweger and Hoby 1978). Someone may then interpret this to mean that the presence of multinational corporations in Third-World countries is economically beneficial to those countries (a thesis popularized by Willy Brandt, 1980, which has strongly influenced the foreign policies of the United States and many other developed nations). This interpretation, however, would be far from the truth. The problem is that, if we define economic growth as growth in the *average real income of the people* in a country and "Third-World countries" as countries whose average income in 1980 was under $400 per year, then we find that the correlation between economic growth and presence of multinational corporations not only is *not positive*, but in fact is *negative* (Bornschier 1980). That is, the presence of the multinational corporations actually seems to *retard* economic growth when measured in this way.

So it seems that "economic growth" can mean very different things, depending on whether we define it as growth in gross national product or growth in average real income of the people of the country. And what is true for one meaning of "economic growth" may not be true for the other. In fact, it may be that multinational corporations do improve the gross national product of Third-World countries, yet the benefit of this increased production ends up in the pockets of foreign investors and does not benefit the people in the host country at all. So to give out the results of a study that operationally defines "economic growth" as growth in gross national product, as if this indicated an economic benefit for the people of the countries involved, is a distortion of the meaning of the study's results.

The point is that we must guard against misleading presentations of research findings that do not spell out clearly how the concepts under investigation were operationally defined. When the Centers for Disease Control found no significant correlation between exposure of Vietnam veterans to Agent Orange and the veterans' subsequent cancer rates, almost every newspaper in the country printed this finding in large headlines but failed to point out that the operational definition of "Agent Orange exposure" was in terms of the amount of dioxin found in the veterans' blood twenty years later (Purvis 1990; "Rule Overturned on Agent Orange" 1989). But it is well known by dioxin specialists that Agent Orange tends to be eliminated from the blood over a twenty-year period, so no correlation between blood dioxin levels and cancer rates should be expected even if the Agent Orange did cause elevated cancer rates (Weisskopf 1989). The operational definition in this case was simply inadequate to serve as a measure of what it was supposed to be measuring.

(d) In aggregate studies—often the ones most relevant to policy decisions—controlling for all relevant intervening variables is difficult. We saw that the mere fact that poverty and crime significantly correlate does not necessarily show that poverty is a cause of crime; there may be other possible explanations for the correlation between them. For instance, the increased opportunity to commit crimes in densely populated areas may account for the increased crime rates in poor (and crowded) inner-city neighborhoods (Sutherland and Cressey 1972, 95ff; McCaghy 1980, 97–99). There may be just as much crime in crowded conditions regardless of whether poverty is involved—for example, in the locker room of a well-to-do, suburban high school or in the cramped living spaces aboard a navy ship. How do we know whether it is the poverty that is causing the increased crime in inner-city neighborhoods, or whether it is the crowded conditions (and thus increased opportunities to commit crimes) that explains the elevated crime rates?

In order to find out, we must control for the effects of population density when we examine the relationship between poverty and crime, and then see what the correlation between poverty and crime is (in cities of all sizes) after the effect of population density has been compensated for by using statistical methods such as partial correlation or multiple regression. But no matter how much precision has been used in the design of scientific research and the interpretation of its conclusions, the fact will always remain that empirical research is inherently probabilistic and, in principle, can never attain complete certainty. This fact has very important implications as it relates to policy analysis and as it interrelates with the value judgments that also enter into policy decisions. In essence, the choice of design aspects of scientific studies and interpretations are in part *value driven*. The level of certainty we demand, the completeness of controls, operational definitions, and the amount of time and money spent trying to increase the accuracy of measurements—all these choices depend on the *purposes* for which the information is to be used. Similarly, a policy analyst's decision to accept a cause-and-effect conclusion even though it is supported with data at a fairly high level of uncertainty, or to reject conclusions even though based on a fairly low level of uncertainty, may depend on the results to be achieved, as well as the consequences of acting on a cause-and-effect interpretation that later turns out to be wrong. Also, as Kuhn and Laudan have emphasized, many of the background assumptions used in any scientific study are partly grounded in similar value judgments in the choice of operational definitions, control variables, levels of certainty, etc., that someone made at an earlier point in time when the studies verifying this background information were originally done, and for similar kinds of pragmatic reasons. This contributes still further to the need for a certain amount of skepticism about scientific conclusions, and about the political agendas of anyone who may have been involved in making any of the relevant value judgments just mentioned.

In political contexts, there is often an important distinction to be drawn between the types of cases in which it is appropriate to go ahead and act on a scientific assumption, even though it involves risk of error, and the types of cases in which this would be inappropriate. An obvious and extreme example is offered by murder trials. Prosecutors refrain from asking for the death penalty when there is much uncertainty in the evidence that "proves" the defendant's guilt, because they know that jurors will refuse to render a guilty verdict if the consequences of being wrong are too earthshaking. Similarly, in cases of protecting guaranteed rights, there is a tendency for courts and other political agencies to demand a stricter criterion of verification than in cases in which the only issue is to increase the general welfare without any infringement of anyone's rights. But, since every political action either directly or indirectly affects someone's freedom to act in some way or other, this distinction becomes much less clear-cut than one might initially suppose. All these consequences of the value-drivenness and inevitable uncertainties in scientific research become increasingly important as societies become more complex and technology dependent.

We can now see more clearly how the inherent uncertainty of the scientific method tends to straightjacket a strictly rights-based approach to policy making: To regulate someone's freedom (an important right) will always require fairly strict "proof" of a rights violation (see Mishan and Page 1992). The essential problem involved here follows straightforwardly from the nature of scientific verification as traditionally conceived, and would follow still more obviously from post-Kuhnian philosophies of science (for example, Laudan 1990). That science is a game of uncertainties is well known by scientists and intellectuals of whatever persuasion, though dimly understood by the general public. The hypothesis that A causes B predicts that A and B would be observed to correlate "significantly" in a well-controlled study, but only after we have decided what level of uncertainty we are willing to live with and what methods of measurement we are willing to accept. The margins for error thus chosen are value driven. A correlation strong enough to motivate legislators to adopt a social welfare policy may not be strong enough to support a physical theory on the basis of which nuclear plants will operate.

Because decisions about acceptable uncertainties are value driven, it is always possible to insist on a standard of proof so strict that nothing can be proven, or to insist on technical reasons for an operational definition that conveniently fails to yield the causal conclusions one would like to avoid. Since an operational definition must stipulate ways in which the phenomenon being studied can be precisely measured, someone who is predisposed (for political or other reasons) to want to reject a finding can simply say that the operational definition being used is unacceptable because it does not measure the phenomenon precisely enough.

These were essentially the strategies used by Vernon Houk of the Centers for Disease Control (CDC) in failing to find significant correlations between Agent Orange exposure and colon cancer (and other health problems) among Vietnam veterans. Some scientists, such as Steven and Jeanne Stellman at Columbia University, had found that if troop movements were used as the criterion to determine Agent Orange exposure in Vietnam, then there was a significant correlation between such exposure and subsequent cancer (Weisskopf 1989; Leary 1990). But Houk, in organizing the CDC study, decided that records of troop movements were not accurate enough to satisfy his strict demands for what could be considered "scientific" (Purvis 1990). He therefore insisted on using the presence of elevated dioxin levels in the blood of veterans (twenty years after exposure) as the criterion for degree of exposure (Purvis 1990). Of course, dioxin is eliminated from the body at different rates by different individuals, so any correlation that might have existed between Agent Orange exposure and subsequent cancer would not show up using this criterion. As Peter Kahn, a Rutgers biochemist specializing in dioxin, has pointed out, dioxin levels are not likely to be significantly elevated after twenty years, and Houk must have known this before the CDC study was conducted (as Magnuson 1990 suggests). Nonetheless, the CDC study concluded that there was no observable connection between Agent Orange exposure and cancer. Houk then stated in a senate testimony that the Stellmans were "pretty lousy scientists" because they had not used blood dioxin levels as the criterion for Agent Orange exposure, since Houk considered this criterion to be more "scientific" than the less precisely measurable troop movements (Weisskopf 1989).

Whether or not there is ample evidence, then, depends on the level of uncertainty one is willing to settle for, along with the degree of imprecision in measurement required by the choice of an operational definition. Since the general public is not aware of the ins and outs of all these methodological debates (indeed, senate testimony even managed to confuse the senators present at the hearing just mentioned), enough scientific controversy can be generated to leave people free to believe whichever scientific conclusion they are politically or ideologically motivated to believe.

Accordingly, court cases involving the Agent Orange issue have been resolved in utterly contradictory ways and have tended to hinge on how strict a criterion of proof of harm the court should insist on for the litigative context in question (for example, "Rule Overturned on Agent Orange" 1989). Most litigation requires that at least the *existence* of harm be proven in a fairly strict way. Even those cases won by the veterans have ended up awarding only small disability pensions to the veterans. In most contexts, a court order either to compensate victims or to ban the use of a hazardous chemical will require strong evidence that someone's rights have been violated, which in turn requires strong evidence that they were harmed (Findley and Farber 1988; Georgia Bar Association 1991). This is because in the absence of highly specific legislation regulating the use of specific toxins, courts must operate from a rights-based perspective. And to penalize someone for a rights violation that has not been proven is, in turn, to violate that person's freedom, which is also an important right. This is essentially why a predominantly rights-based political philosophy, in which rights automatically "trump" consequentialist concerns, will generally tend to consider pollution innocent until proven guilty.

Even in the legislative arena the problem of scientific uncertainties often leads to environmentally disastrous policies, especially at the state and local levels, where districts are in economic competition with each other. The rights-based approach weakens the federal government's ability to protect the general health interest of the overall population against economically driven concerns of local governments. This is all the more true when the fortunes of politicians and the use of mass media depend on money that flows from corporate entities and business or labor groups with an interest in protecting environmentally harmful activities (Brown 1979). I add labor groups to this list because workers often fear that their jobs are threatened by costly pollution-control or environmental protection legislation (Baumol and Oates 1977).

As an example of the way this problem is confounded by scientific uncertainties in the legislative context, it is instructive to note that the central issue for political controversy regarding the spraying of malathion in California is whether the malathion, in fact, does or does not harm people—with scientific studies adduced on both sides. (See "Californians Will Pay for Not Spraying" 1989; "Controversy over Malathion Continues" 1989.) Not coincidentally, the state government opts to reject the evidence of harmfulness; the state's citrus crop depends on the spraying in order to remain competitive with the citrus industries of Florida, whose own state government therefore faces the same problem. In effect, because the fragmentation of local governments exacerbates the problem of "externalities" in such contexts, the local and state governments tend to be aligned with the local area's business interests against the general interest of the national population and the health of its own citizens. This aspect of the problem of externalities is explained very well by Peterson (1981). The main interest of local governments is to compete against other local governments to attract businesses and well-to-do citizens who will pay more in taxes, and to avoid policies that might drive away such taxpayers and economy boosters. If the federal government then operates according to a rights-based rather than a consequentialist philosophy, the relevant scientific uncertainties will force the federal government to respect the states' rights to promote their local industries' interests against those of other states, so that the externalities problem cannot be resolved.

Some people hastily assume that it is easy to define a clear criterion for whether and in what cases rights should be infringed, simply by saying that everyone has the right to do whatever we want as long as we refrain from harming others. This is often expressed in the formula, "Your freedom to move your fist ends where my face begins." But the problem with this simplistic view is that in a society where people are constantly affected by the actions of others (as all societies are), almost everything we do harms someone. If I apply for and obtain a job, the applicant who would have gotten it if I had not is harmed. If I buy a product, the maker of the competing product is harmed, as are all the employees and stockholders of the competing company. A genuinely rights-based approach must therefore qualify its criterion for limiting rights and liberties in some way—for example, by saying not that my freedom ends where its exercise harms someone, but rather where it harms someone *in a particular way* in which the person *has a right* not to be harmed. In this case, it could be argued that we have no right to expect competitors in the job market not to harm us by taking a job, whereas we do have a right to expect people's fists not to interfere with our health by punching us. It is then incumbent on the rights-based theorist to clarify the criterion by which we have a right not to be harmed in some ways but we do not have a right not to be harmed in other ways. One way to spell this out is to say that people violate our rights when they "purposely and knowingly" harm us. But this too is hard to make clear, because it can be argued that when I get a job, I *know* that others have applied, and I *purposely* prevent them from getting it.

Without getting into details that would be beyond our scope, the important point for our purposes is that even a rights-based approach must sometimes allow for rights infringements for the sake of preventing people from being harmed in certain ways. Also, rights infringements must still be allowed for the sake of the general welfare in some instances in order for the society even to survive, let alone prosper. Even if flagrant toxic polluters do not knowingly and purposely destroy the environment and cause cancer deaths, they still must be stopped from doing so. So a rights-based approach needs a complex and carefully-thought-out philosophical basis in some theory of justice if it is to have any hope of being coherent and defensible, and at the same time be concretely applicable.

Whereas a rights-based approach must make room for infringements of rights in certain cases, a consequentialist approach may often find itself championing rights. For example, if equal voting rights are not respected (as they were not in the southern United States prior to the 1960s, for example), the result is distributive injustice in a variety of social and economic contexts, and most people would agree that distributive injustice is an undesirable consequence. To deprive a person of the legal right to vote is to force that person to assume grave risks that grotesquely distributively unjust burdens will be imposed. In fact, we could summarize the consequentialist notion of rights by saying that each person has the right to live under the best possible governmental system, in which "best" might mean (in the thinking of many consequentialists) not only "beneficial," but also "most conducive to distributive justice."

The difference between rights-based and consequentialist political theories, then, is not as rigid as we might initially suppose. Rights-based theories must allow that vastly beneficial consequences (or the prevention of vastly harmful ones) do sometimes justify rights infringements, and consequentialist theories do allow for a concept of 'rights' derived from the value of distributive justice.

But the difference between the two approaches is not negligible either, because their ultimate criteria for resolving conflict between individual rights and the general welfare are different. In a purely rights-based approach, in which rights are considered intrinsic values not to be infringed except for the protection of other rights, the burden of proof is on those who advocate infringing liberty because (as such an advocate would assert) the activity in question is harmful. In a consequentialist approach, on the other hand, individual liberties do not necessarily enjoy any special priority over policies meant to prevent harm, so what is to be done in cases of conflict must be decided on the basis of some further criterion such as a notion of distributive justice. Yet, until now, very little philosophical attention has been paid to developing an adequately precise notion of distributive justice to allow for a concretely applicable decision formula for this type of conflict.

Rawls and his followers are the main exceptions to this generalization, but their work so far remains notoriously ambiguous in this regard, and part of our purpose here must be to improve on it. According to Rawls's "original-position" argument, a person who did not know her particular station in life would not be willing to risk the loss of extremely necessary interests for the less-advantaged station she might occupy, in exchange for a chance to enjoy frivolous luxuries in case she should end up in a more-advantaged position. A major problem with this argument is that there is no way of knowing how conservative or liberal the rational person in the original position would be in risk-taking behavior, and thus no reason for this rational person's preferring one decision principle over the others, as David Kaye (1980) and others have shown quite clearly. Moreover, Rawls's use of the "maximin" principle would imply that the least-advantaged position in a decision situation must always be improved regardless of the expense to the more-advantaged positions (see Wolff 1977, 77ff). But this reasoning ultimately would seem to imply zero-risk policies, since the least-advantaged person in a policy decision regarding automobile traffic safety, for example, is the one who will die in an accident; thus Rawls's position would seem to imply that we should forgo the economic benefits of auto transportation in order to avoid traffic fatalities altogether—an obvious reductio ad absurdum of the zero-risk option in public policy. The question is a quantitative one: *How much* risk of death, disease, or injury should be tolerated for the sake of *how much* economic benefit? Thus, although Rawls's concept of 'justice as fairness' may seem somewhat convincing in the abstract, its concrete political implications are interpreted in diametrically opposed ways. We have already seen that Sterba (1980) derives ultraconservative, *laissez-faire* policy implications from Rawls's theory, whereas Schweickart (1978) interprets the same theory as implying very socialistic, redistributive policies.

The essential dilemma can be posed as follows: Whether in the context of litigation, legislation, or the action of regulatory agencies, a purely rights-based political philosophy, in which freedom is not to be infringed except to protect others' rights, would be inadequate to enable government to take effective action against such problems as pollution and environmental destruction, because it requires a notion of strict "proof" of rights violations. A nonutilitarian consequentialism can avoid this problem by simply acting in ways that appear most probably to produce the best outcomes, recognizing distributive justice as *one of* the important outcomes to be produced. A "rights violation" could be claimed on this basis only if a distributively unjust burden has been imposed. At the same time, it must be admitted that a consequentialist political philosophy poses threats to individual liberty and to the ideal of 'inalienable rights'. If we are to advocate broadening federal power according to consequentialist rather than rights-based considerations, then we must show how a consequentialist approach could respect the rights of citizens and the principle of justice, rather than becoming a heavy-handed, dictatorial, "Big Brother." What is needed is a fairly precise determination as to what 'distributive injustice' consists of, especially as applied to "distributively unjust burdens."

2. Incorporating Justice into a Consequentialist Approach

I have argued that to make a consequentialist approach defensible requires that such an approach can avoid a crass utilitarianism that would ignore questions of justice. It is all too true that current consequentialist approaches show little success in this regard. The most advanced such approaches use occupational-risk studies to determine the value that workers (it is argued) place on their *own* health, safety, and life, by determining how much of a pay increase a worker would demand in exchange for a given increase in the risk of injury, illness, or death (for example, Viscusi 1983, 1993; Kniesner and Leeth 1991; Zeckhauser 1975). But, in the first place, to use the willingness-to-pay criterion seems to assume that such decisions are to be reached by means of a simple cost–benefit analysis, which in turn presupposes a straightforwardly utilitarian decision principle, thus exposing the consequentialist approach to most of the strongest traditional criticisms of utilitarianism, which are formidable (see Gillroy 1992a; Kelman 1992; Anderson 1988). Utilitarianism tries simply to maximize beneficial consequences, even if doing so sometimes causes injustice. A classic example would be the proposal on a recent California referendum to quarantine all AIDS victims. Such a policy, if enacted, would go a long way toward solving the AIDS problem (which, of course, would be very beneficial), but at the expense of grotesque injustice (and it is essentially for this reason that such legislation would be considered unconstitutional).

In the second place, we have already seen that the use of these occupational risk data neglects to consider that it is predominantly the *poorer* workers who are willing to incur greater risks in exchange for pay increases, primarily because they require the additional money to provide the *most essential needs* for their families. Wealthier workers are not willing to incur nearly as much increased risk in exchange for even relatively large pay increments, because they anticipate that this money would be spent on less-essential or even frivolous goods (Viscusi 1978b, 1993; Siebert and Wei 1994; Robinson 1986; Biddle and Zarkin 1989). Thus the use of occupational-risk studies to justify trading ill health or death risks to the population in exchange for "equivalent amounts" of economic benefits aggregately distributed is precisely to neglect the crucial issue: Should the value of frivolous economic benefits be equated with the value of human lives or health in a purely utilitarian cost–benefit analysis? The essential problem is that in traditional cost–benefit analysis, as Gillroy points out, "[w]ith the potential Pareto improvement, it does not matter to whom the benefit falls, only that the net welfare benefits exceed loss" (Gillroy 1992a, 201).

But we have seen that the solution to this problem is already contained in the way the problem is posed. The extent to which workers are less willing to take risks in exchange for less-necessary goods than in exchange for more-necessary ones can be used as a measure of the degree of necessity of goods. $100 contributes more to the well-being and happiness of a very poor person than to a very rich one, all else being equal, because the poor person is more likely to *use* the money for purposes that she perceives as more *important* to her overall well-being, whereas the very rich person will already have met her most important needs and desires and will tend to use the money for more frivolous and less-important purposes (Sinden and Worrell 1979,

470–84). The rate at which marginal utilities diminish in value can therefore be measured by the rate at which workers become less and less averse to risk the more well-to-do they become.

If we can measure the rate at which marginal utilities diminish (i.e., if we can determine *how much* more valuable $100 is to a poor person than to a rich one), we can then use this determination as a yardstick for identifying distributive justice or injustice. It is prima facie disvaluable to require someone to risk the loss of $100's worth of very basic or necessary goods so that someone else can enjoy $100's worth of much-less-necessary goods, because the $100's worth of very basic or necessary goods has more actual value (i.e., use value as opposed to exchange value) than the $100's worth of less-necessary goods. So, prima facie (i.e., unless there is some legitimate reason to the contrary), it is more valuable that the person for whom the goods are more necessary should have them than that the person for whom they are less necessary should have them. Otherwise, a prima facie distributively unjust burden has been imposed, and thus the one basic consequentialist 'right' has been violated—the right not to bear distributively unjust burdens. Ultimately, the reason is that very-necessary goods (or their loss in the form of burdens) have been inappropriately equated with an equal monetary amount of less-necessary goods. The crucial question, then, is *how much* more valuable the more-necessary goods are than the less-necessary ones.

Economists have established that very-low-paid workers are willing to assume at least *ten times* as much additional occupational risk for the same pay increase as are more well-to-do workers whose incomes are close to the average income in the economy (for example, Viscusi 1983, 1993). It follows that the goods for which the poorer workers are willing to assume these additional risks are ten times as *necessary* to them as are the goods that the average-income workers use their marginal income to buy. This is why the average-income worker is ten times less willing to assume the same risk that the poorest workers will assume in exchange for the *same monetary amount* of pay increment—because the goods that this pay increment will buy are *ten times less necessary* for the average-income worker and, therefore, ten times *less valuable* to him. That is, $100 to the lowest level of worker has at least ten times as much 'marginal utility', or true value, as does $100 to the average person in the economy.

Unjust distribution of benefits and burdens results when some people are deprived of very-necessary opportunities and benefits in order that others may enjoy a greater quantity of relatively frivolous opportunities and benefits—for example, when some must die of cancer in order that the many can enjoy cheaper plastic razors. This is essentially the problem that utilitarianism and cost–benefit analysis ignore, thus exposing themselves to the charge of injustice. But if the fact that health, life, and safety are much-more-necessary or important types of goods than plastic razors can be *taken into consideration* when determining the relative *importance* of such goods, then this problem can be solved. Thus Rawls (1971), for example, defines justice in terms of the risk-taking behavior of the person in the hypothetical "original position"—the position in which the person would have no knowledge about her own circumstances that might prejudice her judgment. A person judging from such an unbiased perspective would not be willing to risk very-necessary goods in exchange for a chance to obtain even large amounts of very-nonnecessary or frivolous goods. In effect, Rawls defines justice in terms of the principle of diminishing marginal utility. This means that, in a *fair or just* public-policy analysis, the most-necessary kinds of benefits should be counted as having much more true value compared with their monetary value, whereas less-necessary kinds of benefits should be counted as having correspondingly less true value compared with their monetary value. And the same would apply to the *negative* value of burdens borne by some to facilitate a productive economy for the many.

Justice thus requires that benefits and burdens be assessed not only according to their exchange value in an aggregate market, but also in terms of their degree of necessity or nonnecessity. Marginal goods for the lowest-level of workers in occupational-risk studies are ten times as valuable as their exchange value would lead one to believe, because the goods bought marginally at this income level are ten times as necessary. A just decision principle would therefore count a given exchange value, or monetary value, at this lowest income level as being ten times as valuable as that same exchange value at the average income level. Thus, for example, government funds spent on housing for the poor promote ten times as much true value, or use value, as the same amount spent on housing for middle-income people, because the poor are at a level of neediness such that a given amount of financial assistance is ten times as necessary for them as for the average person.

This is the essential reason for the inappropriateness of traditional cost–benefit analysis as a decision principle in instances in which people's health, safety, and lives are being compared in value with economic considerations. A clear example is the cost–benefit analysis conducted by the Ford Motor Company to justify the production of the "exploding Pinto gas tank" (McCaghy 1980, 296). The value of a human life was assessed at $200,000 (based on figures used by the New York Highway Traffic Safety Board), and then the total value of the lives that were expected to be lost was compared with the total economic cost to consumers and to the company if the gas tank had to be redesigned, which would raise the price of each car by $11. The cost of the redesign exceeded the value of the lives lost, therefore Ford went ahead with the production—and the lives were lost.

But if the degree of necessity of various kinds of goods can be measured, then such problems can be avoided, since the essential problem is that life is a much-more-necessary kind of good than those that a marginal $11 for the average consumer would be spent on. And the measurable effect of worker wealth on occupational risk averseness allows us to quantify the relative necessity of goods. It is thus possible to set up a consequentialist decision principle for environmental and other such problems that avoids imposing unjust burdens on a few in order to support frivolous benefits for the many, thereby avoiding the traditional criticisms of utilitarianism. Gillroy says that "[t]here is . . . no sense of 'right' or 'good' in the economic model that is capable of [a moral] distinction [between two preferences]" (Gillroy 1992a, 209). Kymlicka's suggested answer to this problem is that preferences that require others' being treated unfairly are not legitimate preferences, or, in quantitative terms, we might say that the use value of preferences is affected by the extent to which they block much greater use values (i.e., much-more-necessary opportunities and resources) for others (Kymlicka 1989). I have suggested a way to determine this "moral" reason for considering one preference as more important than another by using the principle of diminishing marginal utility.

What must be done, if such a decision principle is to operate in the real world, is to empower federal government agencies, such as the Environmental Protection Agency, with legislation enacted on a purely consequentialist basis, but a consequentialism that takes the importance of justice into consideration. Congress need only legislate that the value of such goods as life, health, and safety must be valued according to a criterion such as the one suggested here, which takes the degree of necessity into account rather than merely using their "willingness-to-pay" value when determining the amount of money that should be sacrificed by government, industry, workers, and taxpayers to protect these values. And similarly, Congress should, in general, require that government agencies, when assessing the cost–benefit ratio of government programs and regulations, should take into account the effect on justice of distribution exerted by this difference between more-necessary and less-necessary kinds of opportunities and resources. For example, suppose the willingness-to-pay value of a human life according to occupational-risk studies (such as Viscusi 1978a, 1983; Robinson 1986) is about $1.5 million (before adjusting for inflation). Factoring in the "degree of necessity" of the most important types of goods (such as life) yields a true value ten times this much, or $15 million. Thus, if it is estimated that even two lives could be saved (a value of $30 million) by means of an environmentally safer technology that would increase the total cost of plastic razors by $29 million, then the $29 million must be spent. Of course, all "hidden costs" of the new technology, such as job loss, etc., must be taken into account in such a calculation. And the burden of these costs, in turn, must be shared equitably by the society as a whole (for example, by investing in relocation of the displaced workers).

Congress must then give the EPA (in cooperation with other relevant agencies) the *power* to regulate on this basis. The EPA could then assess the probable harmfulness of any given practice by using the standard *probabilistic* methodology of scientific research, since it would then have the power to regulate practices that are shown to be harmful *with a strong degree of probability* (as opposed to the absolute "proof" of harmfulness required by a rights-based approach). The EPA's adherence to the decision principle just mentioned could then be guaranteed by its liability to lawsuits if it should fail to conform to the decision principle. In this way, citizens would be ensured substantial and effective protection from deterioration of health and safety, but would not be subjected to ruthless and unfair governmental power. Justice would be ensured, but without tying the hands of government by demanding that it "prove" beyond doubt that one citizen's inalienable rights (presumably spelled out on some very short list) have been violated before limiting another's "freedom" to pollute or destroy the environment. Also, ordinary citizens would not have to avail themselves of specific technical knowledge about every scientific issue in order to press for legislative action on that specific issue. The power given to the EPA by Congress would be a blanket power to regulate on the basis of the decision principle just outlined (and only on that basis). It would then be up to the EPA to determine the specific applications of the principle, and citizens would be free to bring suit against the EPA if it should fail to do so.

It might be objected against this nonutilitarian consequentialist approach to government decision making that it would lead to the absurd implication that any life that can possibly be saved even by means of exorbitantly expensive technologies *ought* to be saved, and that the government should take the responsibility to save every one of these lives, at such an astronomical cost to taxpayers that not enough funds would remain to administer other important government programs and allow the economy to function adequately. It is well known among environmental policy analysts that the saving of lives through changes in technology becomes less and less cost effective as more and more lives are saved; a point of diminishing returns is reached as we attempt to squeeze out the last few lives (Kneese and Schultze 1975, 21). Even if the government should require that the needed monies be spent by private industry, ultimately it is the general citizenry who will bear this burden in the form of higher prices and lower wages.

This objection raises two important issues. First, the value of a life may not be, as we have argued, ten times as great as its "willingness-to-pay" value would suggest. Occupational-risk studies and other empirical methods of assessing "unpriced values" are inexact and controversial, as discussed earlier. But to suggest that the value of life is perhaps less than we have estimated is not to object to the basic principle that more-necessary benefits and burdens should be assessed as more important than less-necessary ones, but merely to disagree quantitatively as to the exact numbers involved. And this is really an empirical question that is open to further empirical investigation. It must be admitted, however, that diminishing marginal utility figures into this assessment, and it cannot be made simply by using traditional cost–benefit analysis, which fails to consider distributive justice because it fails to count more-necessary benefits and burdens as being more important.

Second, it may not be legitimate to require taxpayers to support government expenditures (either directly or indirectly) for beneficial activities with respect to which the people collectively *do not have a duty or responsibility* to take action. What we are assessing in the present context is only what the government has a *right* to do, in the interest of promoting justice, and what it prima facie ought to do. This prima facie ought does not necessarily take absolute priority over competing prima facie oughts. But neither should the relative importance of these competing prima facie oughts be resolved by means of traditional cost–benefit analysis, since we have already shown that such formulas fail to account for distributive justice. Instead, conflicts between prima facie values should, in principle, be resolved in a distributively just way, which in turn can be determined by comparing more-necessary and less-necessary benefits and burdens in accordance with diminishing marginal utility. There is no danger, then, that one specific goal, such as saving lives in some specific context, will be accorded absolute priority over all other concerns (as often occurs in rights-based approaches). What is required is that competing values be weighed against each other in an appropriate way—that is, by using an appropriate decision method. As in all instances, the society should avoid imposing distributively unjust burdens on anyone, whether individually or collectively.

Of course, there is still another obstacle to the feasibility of such an approach. If the scientific method lends itself to uncertainty and therefore invites people with opposing political interests to *interpret* the same findings as either "certain enough to warrant action" or "too uncertain to warrant action," then who is to ensure that political power brokers do not control the government's interpretation of scientific findings by enlisting the presidency (and thus executive agencies like the EPA) "on their side?" Moreover, if financial power is aligned with industry, and if substantial financial support from these interests is needed by any viable political campaign, then is it not inevitable (as Quarles 1976, Chapter 7, effectively argues) that the president, who ultimately controls agencies like the EPA, will be indebted to these interests and therefore support *their* preferred interpretation of the scientific research on any given issue? This is why campaign finance legislation is absolutely essential to the effective implementation of the kind of policy analysis we have been discussing.

The ubiquity of scientific uncertainties makes it possible for business interests to prejudice the government's interpretation of the facts if government officials are politically beholden to such interests (Ellis and Ravita, forthcoming). In recent years, the role that the flow of money plays in the political process has become increasingly evident (Jackson 1988, 36; Lind 1995; Ellis and Ravita, forthcoming). To cope with the rising costs, candidates often turn to the support of political action committees (PACs) and to wealthy business interests. Although some deny any evidence of direct PAC influence on legislative votes, there is ample evidence for bias in interpretation of information in favor of contributors (Morrison 1986, v; Shipper and Jennings 1984). For example, Shipper and Jennings cite numerous instances of influence peddling by the American Sugar Cane League, General Motors, Exxon, U.S. Steel, Proctor & Gamble, and a number of specific PACs. With the *Buckley vs. Valeo* ruling, a candidate essentially has unlimited reign to spend money (see "NCPAC's Terry Dolan: He's Playing Key Role" 1981, 2; "NCPAC's Terry Dolan" 1980). If a candidate's supporters spend money campaigning against the opponent, this type of spending does not fall under the FECA laws, and thus enables PACs and other private interests to exceed, in effect, the $5,000 limit ("PAC Scope" 1987, 38).

Many studies show that financial resources in the United States are controlled predominantly by a small percentage of the people (for example, Lind 1995; Morrison 1986; Jackson 1988; Lampman 1962). Unless disproportionate control over the political process is curbed, a government whose representatives are financially dependent on such interests will inevitably reflect those interests in its policies and in the interpretations of scientific data on which the policies depend (Cloud and Traver 1992, 65). The implementation of a distributively just method of policy analysis such as the one suggested here is therefore dependent to a great extent on campaign finance legislation to ensure a fair electoral process.

Armed only with the insufficient tools of natural-rights theory and the uncertainty of science, courts all too often cannot determine whose rights have been violated. Industry is therefore given reign to exercise its natural freedom to further deteriorate the environment, using cost–benefit analysis to make its case palatable to the public, which lacks a viable alternative decision principle. The examples of the exploding Pinto, malathion spraying, and Agent Orange show that when cost–benefit analysis is used, monetary interests tend to outweigh concern for the small numbers of individuals who suffer disproportionate burdens. But in the absence of some other equally concrete decision principle, government lacks the moral authority to act decisively.

What is needed is that a clear decision principle be used to weigh economic benefits against more important kinds of considerations such as risks to public health and safety posed by pollution and environmental destruction—but a decision principle that takes the value of distributive justice into consideration in a clear and unambiguous way. This presupposes a predominantly consequentialist approach to political theory, but one that is not utilitarian in its basis. Such a consequentialist approach can enable government to take effective action in the context of scientific uncertainty, and only a clear decision principle can justify such action. Such a decision principle, in order to facilitate distributive justice, must mandate the maximization not of *exchange* value but of *use* value; it must recognize the importance of distributing benefits and burdens in such a way as to maximize use value by accounting for the necessity-versus-nonnecessity dimension (in accordance with diminishing marginal utility). Such a decision principle, incorporating the concept of distributive justice, would ensure that government could play a role that is both strong and fair (assuming that the electoral process itself is fair enough to make government agencies responsive to the people rather than to economically elite power brokers—hence the indispensability of appropriate campaign finance legislation). Only on this condition can government agencies be free to implement policies based on no other agenda than the public welfare within the constraints of justice.

References

Aiken, Henry. 1948. *Hume's Moral and Political Philosophy.* New York: Hafner.

Anderson, Elizabeth. 1988. Values, Risks, and Market Norms. *Philosophy and Public Affairs* 17:54–65.

Ansari, Mahfooz. 1977. Socio-Psychological Dynamics of Risk-Taking Behavior. *Journal of Social and Economic Studies* 5:125–29.

Aristotle. 1974. *Politics.* London: Oxford University Press.

Aspect, Alain, J. Dalibard, and G. Roger. 1982. *Physical Review Letters* 39 1804–08.

Ayer, A. J. 1936–1949. *Language, Truth, and Logic.* New York: Dover.

Baier, Annette. 1986. Poisoning the Wells. In Douglas MacLean, ed., *Values at Risk.* Totowa, N.J.: Rowman and Allanheld.

Ballmar-Cao, Thanh-Huyen. 1979. Système politique, répartition des revenus et pénétration des entreprises multinationales. *Annuaire Suisse de Science Politique.*

Baumol, William, and Wallace Oates. 1977. *Economics, Environmental Policy, and the Quality of Life.* Englewood Cliffs: Prentice-Hall.

Baynes, Kenneth. 1992. *The Normative Grounds of Social Criticism.* Albany: State University of New York Press.

Benedict, Ruth. 1934. *Patterns of Culture.* New York: Houghton Mifflin.

Bentham, Jeremy. 1789–1962. An Introduction to the Principles of Morals and Legislation. In John Bowring, ed., *The Works of Jeremy Bentham.* New York: Russell & Russell.

Beristain, Antonio. 1977. Capital Punishment and Catholicism. *International Journal of Criminology and Penology* 5:321–335.

Berweger, Gottfried, and Jean-Pierre Hoby. 1978. Wirtschaftspolitik gegenuber Auslandskapital. *Bulletin of the Sociological Institute of the University of Zurich* 35:1–136.

Biddle, Jeff, and Gary Zarkin. 1989. Worker Preferences and Market Compensation for Job Risks. *Review of Economics and Statistics* 70:660–67.

Bloom, Allan. 1987. *The Closing of the American Mind.* New York: Simon & Schuster.

Bornschier, Volker. 1980. Multinational Corporations, Economic Policy, and National Development in the World System. *International Social Science Journal* 32:158–72.

Bradie, Michael, and David Braybrooke, eds. 1982. *Social Justice.* Bowling Green: Philosophy Documentation Center.

Brandt, Richard. 1971. Some Merits of One Form of Rule-Utilitarianism. In Thomas Hearn, ed., *Studies in Utilitarianism*. New York: Appleton-Century-Croft.

Brandt, Willy, and the Independent Commission on International Development Issues. 1980. *North–South: A Program for Survival*. Cambridge: MIT Press.

Bridgman, P. 1962. *The Sophisticate's Primer of Relativity*. Middletown, Ct.: Wesleyan University Press.

Brightman, Edgar. 1945. *Nature and Values*. New York: Holt.

Brown, Michael S. 1984. *Workers at Risk*. Chicago: University of Chicago Press.

Brown, Michael. 1979. *Laying Waste*. New York: Washington Square Press.

Calder, Nigel. 1980. *Einstein's Universe*. Middlesex: Penguin.

Californians Will Pay for Not Spraying. 1989. *Los Angeles Times*, 17 February.

Campen, James. 1986. *Benefit, Cost, and Beyond*. Cambridge, Mass.: Ballinger Press.

Chateauneuf, Alain, and Michele Cohen. 1994. Risk Seeking with Diminishing Marginal Utility in a Non-Expected Utility Model. *Journal of Risk and Uncertainty* 9:77–91.

Cloud, Stanley, and Nancy Traver. 1992. Mr. Smith Leaves Washington. *Time*, 8 June, 64–68.

Controversy over Malathion Continues. 1989. *Los Angeles Times*, 23 May.

DeFronzo, James. 1983. Economic Assistance to Impoverished Americans. *Criminology* 21:119–36.

DePaul, Michael. 1986. Reflective Equilibrium and Foundationalism. *American Philosophical Quarterly* 23:59–69.

Dreyfus, Hubert, and Paul Rabinow. 1983. *Beyond Structuralism and Hermeneutics*. Chicago: University of Chicago Press.

Drysek, John. 1987. *Rational Ecology*. Oxford: Basil Blackwell.

Duncker, Karl. 1939. Ethical Relativity? An Enquiry into the Psychology of Ethics. *Mind* 48:39–57.

Durkheim, Emile. 1947. *The Division of Labor in Society*. Glencoe, Ill.: Free Press.

Dworkin, Ronald. 1986. *Law's Empire*. Cambridge: Harvard University Press.

———. 1987. What Is Equality? Part III: The Place of Liberty. *Iowa Law Review* 73:1–54.

Ellis, Ralph D. 1982. Existentialism and the Demonstrability of Ethical Theories. *Journal of Value Inquiry* 16:165–75.

———. 1986. *An Ontology of Consciousness*. Dordrecht: Martinus Nijhoff.

———. 1987a. General Assistance and Crime Rates in the U.S. *Policy Studies Review* 7:291–303.

———. 1987b. Fairness and the Etiology of Criminal Behavior. *Philosophy and Social Criticism* 13:175–94.

———. 1989. *Theories of Criminal Justice: A Critical Reappraisal*. Wolfeboro, N.H.: Longwood Academic.

———. 1990. The Moral Significance of Hard Toil: Critique of a Common Intuition. *Philosophical Forum* 11:343–58.

———. 1991. Toward a Reconciliation of Liberalism and Communitarianism. *Journal of Value Inquiry* 25:55–64.

———. 1992. *Coherence and Verification in Ethics*. Washington, D.C.: University Press of America.

Ellis, Ralph D., and Tracienne Ravita. Forthcoming. Scientific Uncertainties, Environmental Policy, and Political Theory. *Philosophical Forum.*

Ettenson, R., and R. Coughlin. 1982. Effects of Type of Payoff and Instructions on Individual Risk-Taking Behavior. *Psychological Reports* 51:855–60.

Etzioni, Amitai. 1991. Beyond Self-Interest. In Weimer, 65–84.

Fagothey, Austin. 1981. *Right and Reason.* St. Louis: C. V. Mosby.

Faludi, Andreas. 1987. *A Decision-Centered View of Environmental Planning.* Oxford: Pergamon.

Findley, Roger, and Daniel Farber. 1988. *Environmental Law.* St. Paul: West.

Fishbain, D., J. Fletcher, and T. Aldrich. 1987. Relationship between Russion Roulette Deaths and Risk Taking Behavior. *American Journal of Psychiatry* 144:563–67.

Foot, Philippa. 1978. Reasons for Action and Desires. In *Virtues and Vices.* Berkeley: University of California Press.

Foucault, Michel. 1978. *The History of Sexuality.* New York: Random House.

———. 1979. *Discipline and Punish.* New York: Random House.

Foucault, Michel. 1980. *Power/Knowledge: Selected Interviews and Other Writings by Michel Foucault.* Colin Gordon, ed. New York: Pantheon.

Frankena, William. 1963. *Ethics.* Englewood Cliffs: Prentice-Hall.

———. 1976. *Perspectives on Morality.* Notre Dame: University of Notre Dame Press.

Freeman, Richard. 1983. Crime and Unemployment. In James Q. Wilson, ed., *Crime and Public Policy.* San Francisco: Institute for Contemporary Studies, 89–106.

Fried, Charles. 1992. Difficulties in the Economic Analysis of Rights. In Gillroy and Wade, 217–33.

Garen, John. 1988. Compensating Wage Differentials and the Endogeneity of Job Riskiness. *Review of Economics and Statistics* 70:9–15.

Gendlin, Eugene. 1962. *Experiencing and the Creation of Meaning.* Toronto: Macmillan.

———. 1981. *Focusing.* Toronto: Bantam.

Gendlin, Eugene. 1992. Thinking Beyond Patterns: Body, Language, and Situations. In B. den Ouden and M. Moen, eds., *The Presence of Feeling in Thought.* New York: Peter Lang.

Georgia Bar Association. 1991. *Environmental Law.* Athens, Ga.: Institute of Continuing Legal Education.

Gewirth, Alan. 1978. *Reason and Morality.* Chicago: University of Chicago Press.

———. 1984. Replies to My Critics. In Edward Regis, ed., *Gewirth's Ethical Rationalism.* Chicago: University of Chicago Press.

Gibson, Mary, ed. 1985. *To Breathe Freely.* Totowa, N.J.: Rowman and Allenheld.

Gillroy, John Martin. 1992a. The Ethical Poverty of Cost–Benefit Methods: Autonomy, Efficiency, and Public Policy Choice. In Gillroy and Wade, 195–216.

———. 1992b. A Kantian Argument Supporting Public Policy Choice. In Gillroy and Wade, 491–515.

Gillroy, John Martin, and Maurice Wade. 1992. *The Moral Dimensions of Public Policy Choice: Beyond the Market Paradigm.* Pittsburgh: University of Pittsburgh Press.

Gold, Louis. 1961. A Psychiatric Review of Capital Punishment. *Journal of Forensic Science* 6:465–73.

Golec, Joseph, and Maurry Tamarkin. 1995. Do Bettors Prefer Long Shots Because They Are Risk-Lovers, or Are They Just Overconfident? *Journal of Risk and Uncertainty* 11:51–64.

Goodin, Robert. 1995. *Utilitarianism as a Public Philosophy.* Cambridge: Cambridge University Press.

Gregory, Nathaniel. 1980. Relative Wealth and Risk Taking: A Short Note on the Friedman-Savage Utility Function. *Journal of Political Economy* 88:1226–30.

Gutman, Amy. 1986. Communitarian Critics of Liberalism. *Philosophy and Public Affairs* 15:308–22.

Haigh, John, David Harrison Jr., and Albert L. Nichols. 1992. Benefit–Cost Analysis of Environmental Regulation: Case Studies of Hazardous Air Pollutants. In Gillroy and Wade, 15–57.

Hall, Everett. 1949. The Proof of Utility in Bentham and Mill. *Ethics* 60:1–18.

Hare, R. M. 1997. Justice and Equality. In Pojman and Westmoreland, 218–28.

Hearn, Thomas, ed. 1971. *Studies in Utilitarianism.* New York: Appleton-Century-Croft.

Heller, Agnes. 1987. *Beyond Justice.* Oxford: Basil Blackwell.

Helmstadter, G. C. 1970. *Research Concepts in Human Behavior.* Englewood Cliffs: Prentice-Hall.

Hempel, C. G. 1963. *Philosophy of Natural Science.* Englewood Cliffs: Prentice-Hall.

Hersch, Joni, and Todd Pickton. 1995. Risk-Taking Activities and Heterogeneity of Job-Risk Tradeoffs. *Journal of Risk and Uncertainty* 11:205–17.

Hobbes, Thomas. 1950. *Leviathan.* New York: E. P. Dutton.

Holtmann, Alphonse. 1991. Beyond Efficiency: Economics and Distributional Analysis. In Weimer, 45–64.

Hoyos, Carl. 1988. Mental Load and Risk in Traffic Behavior. *Economics* 31:571–84.

Hume, David. 1751–1948. *Hume's Moral and Political Philosophy.* Edited by Henry Aiken. New York: Hafner.

Jackson, Brooks. 1988. Growing Anti-PAC Sentiment Leads to Proposals to Overhaul Federal Campaign Finance System. *Wall Street Journal,* 20 January.

Jaffe, William. 1972. Pareto Translated: A Review Article. *Journal of Economic Literature,* December.

Josh. 7:21 Revised Standard Version.

Kant, Immanuel. 1956. *Critique of Practical Reason.* Translated by Lewis W. Beck. New York: Bobbs-Merrill.

———. 1789–1959. *Foundations of the Metaphysics of Morals.* Translated by Lewis W. Beck. New York: Bobbs-Merrill.

Kaye, David. 1980. Playing Games with Justice. *Social Theory and Practice* 6:33–51.

Kelman, Steven. 1992. Cost–Benefit Analysis: An Ethical Critique. In Gillroy and Wade, 153–64.

Kneese, Allen, and Charles Schultze. 1975. *Pollution, Prices, and Public Policy.* Washington, D.C.: The Brookings Institution.

Kniesner, Thomas, and John Leeth. 1991. Compensating Wage Differentials for Fatal Injury Risk. *Journal of Risk and Uncertainty* 4:75–90.

———. 1995. Numerical Simulation as a Complement to Econometric Research on Workplace Safety. *Journal of Risk and Uncertainty* 10:99–125.

Kohler, Heinz. 1979. *Welfare and Planning.* Huntington, N.Y.: Krieger.

Krishna, K. P. 1981. Risk Taking among Indian Adolescents. *Journal of Social Psychology* 114:293–94.

Kuhn, Thomas. 1962. *The Structure of Scientific Revolutions.* Chicago: University of Chicago Press.

Kydd, Rachel. 1946. *Reason and Conduct in Hume's Treatise.* Oxford: Oxford University Press.

Kymlicka, Will. 1989. *Liberalism, Community, and Culture.* Oxford: Clarendon Press.

———. 1990. *Contemporary Political Philosophy.* Oxford: Clarendon Press.

Ladouceur, P., Mayrand, M., and Y. Tourigny. 1987. Risk-Taking Behavior in Gamblers and Non-Gamblers during Prolonged Exposure. *Journal of Gambling Behavior* 3:115–22.

Lafferty, T. Realism and Risk-Taking. 1974. *Psychological Reports* 34:827–29.

Laird, John. 1932. *Hume's Philosophy of Human Nature.* London: Oxford University Press.

Lampman, Robert. 1962. *The Share of Top Wealth-Holders in National Wealth.* Princeton: Princeton University Press.

Lanoie, Paul, Carmen Pedro, and Robert Latour. 1995. The Value of a Statistical Life: A Comparison of Two Approaches. *Journal of Risk and Uncertainty* 10:235–57.

Laudan, Larry. 1990. *Science and Relativism.* Minneapolis: University of Minnesota Press.

Leary, Warren. 1990. Higher Risk of Cancer Found for Vietnam Vets. *New York Times*, 30 March.

Leigh, J. Paul. 1989. Compensating Wages for Job-Related Death: The Opposing Arguments. *Journal of Economic Issues* 23:823–39.

Lessnoff, Michael. 1986. *Social Contract.* Atlantic Highlands, N.J.: Humanities Press International.

Lind, Michael. 1995. *The Next American Nation.* New York: The Free Press.

Linton, Ralph. 1954. The Problem of Universal Values. In R. F. Spencer, ed., *Method and Perspective in Anthropology.* Minneapolis: University of Minnesota Press, 145–68.

Liu, Jin-Tan, and Chee-Ruey Hsieh. 1995. Risk Perception and Smoking Behavior. *Journal of Risk and Uncertainty* 11:139–57.

Lordahl, Daniel. 1967. *Modern Statistics for Behavioral Sciences.* New York: Ronald Press.

Machan, Tibor. 1989. *Individuals and Their Rights.* New York: Open Court.

MacIntyre, Alasdair. 1981. *After Virtue.* Notre Dame: University of Notre Dame Press.

———. 1992. Utilitarianism and Cost–Benefit Analysis: An Essay on the Relevance of Moral Philosophy to Bureaucratic Theory. In Gillroy and Wade, 179–94.

MacLean, Douglas, ed. 1986. *Values at Risk*. Totowa, N.J.: Rowman and Allanheld.

Madison, Gary B. 1990. *The Hermeneutics of Postmodernity*. Bloomington: Indiana University Press.

Madison, James, Alexander Hamilton, and John Jay. 1968. *The Federalist Papers*. New York: Washington Square Press.

Magnuson, Ed. 1990. A Cover-up on Agent Orange. *Time*, 23 July, 27–28.

Marx, Karl. 1964. Economic and Philosophical Manuscripts of 1848. In T. B. Bottomore, ed., *Karl Marx: Early Writings*. New York: McGraw-Hill.

Matson, Wallace, 1997. Justice: A Funeral Oration. In Pojman and Westmoreland, 191–203.

McCaghy, Charles. 1980. *Crime in American Society*. New York: Macmillan.

McCloskey, H. J. 1957. An Examination of Restricted Utilitarianism. *Philosophical Review* 66:466–85.

Mill, John Stuart. 1857–1931. *Utilitarianism*. New York: Dutton, 3–4.

———. 1859–1947. *On Liberty*. New York: Appleton-Century-Crofts.

Mishan, Ezra, and Talbot Page. 1992. The Methodology of Cost–Benefit Analysis, with Particular Reference to the Ozone. In Gillroy and Wade, 59–113.

Moore, G. E. 1903. *Principia Ethica*. Cambridge: Cambridge University Press.

Morris, Herbert. 1976. Persons and Punishment. In Herbert Morris, *Guilt and Innocence*. Berkeley: University of California Press.

Morrison, Catherine. 1986. *Managing Corporate Political Action Committees*. New York: The Conference Board.

Nagel, Thomas. 1991. *Equality and Partiality*. Oxford: Oxford University Press.

Nau, Robert. 1995. Coherent Decision Analysis with Inseparable Probabilities and Utilities. *Journal of Risk and Uncertainty* 10:71–91.

NCPAC's Terry Dolan. 1980. *U.S. News and World Report*. 17 November, 5.

NCPAC's Terry Dolan: He's Playing Key Role in New Right's Success. 1981. *Conservative Digest*, December, 2–5.

Nelkin, Dorothy, and Michael S. Brown. 1984. *Workers at Risk*. Chicago: University of Chicago Press.

Nielson, Kai. 1997. Radical Welfare Egalitarianism. In Pojman and Westmoreland.

Nozick, Robert. 1974. *Anarchy, State, and Utopia*. New York: Basic Books.

PAC Scope. 1987. *Congressional Digest*.

Paden, Roger. 1987. Post-Structuralism and Neo-Romanticism, or Is MacIntyre a Young Conservative? *Philosophy and Social Criticism* 13:135–36.

Pareto, Vilfredo. 1971. *Manual of Political Economy*. New York: Augustus Kelley.

Peskin, Henry, and Eugene Seskin, eds. 1975. *Cost Benefit Analysis and Water Pollution Policy*. Washington, D.C.: Urban Institute.

Peterson, Paul. 1981. *City Limits*. Chicago: University of Chicago Press.

Pojman, Louis. 1997. On Equal Human Worth: A Critique of Contemporary Egalitarianism. In Pojman and Westmoreland, 282–99.

Pojman, Louis, and Robert Westmoreland, eds. 1997. *Equality: Selected Readings*. New York: Oxford University Press.

Popper, Karl. 1957. Philosophy of Science. In G. Mace, ed., *British Philosophy in Mid-Century*. London: Mace.

Posner, Richard. 1983. *The Economics of Justice*. Cambridge: Harvard University Press.

Proposed Jimmy Carter Expressway. 1987. *Atlanta Journal and Constitution*. 12 November.

Purvis, Andrew. 1990. Clean Bill for Agent Orange. *Time*, 9 April.

Quarles, John. 1976. *Cleaning Up America: An Insider's View of the EPA*. Boston: Houghton Mifflin.

Railton, Peter. 1985. Locke, Stock, and Peril: Natural Property Rights, Pollution, and Risk. In Mary Gibson, ed., *To Breathe Freely*. Totowa, N.J.: Rowman and Allanheld.

Rakowski, Eric. 1991. *Equal Justice*. Oxford: Clarendon Press.

———. 1997. A Defense of Resource Equality. In Pojman and Westmoreland, 274–81.

Rawls, John. 1955. Two Concepts of Rules. *Philosophical Review* 64:3–32.

———. 1971. *A Theory of Justice*. Cambridge: Harvard University Press.

———. 1982. Social Unity and Primary Goods. In Amartyra Sen, ed. *Utilitarianism and Beyond*. London: Cambridge University Press.

———. 1985. Justice as Fairness: Political Not Metaphysical. *Philosophy and Public Affairs* 14:223–51.

———. 1993. *Political Liberalism*. New York: Columbia University Press.

Regis, Edward, ed. 1984. *Gewirth's Ethical Rationalism*. Chicago: University of Chicago Press.

Richards, David A. 1971. *A Theory of Reasons for Action*. Oxford: Oxford University Press.

Robinson, James. 1986. Job Hazards and Job Security. *Journal of Health Politics, Politics, Policy, and Law* 11:13–18.

———. 1988. Hazardous Occupations within the Job Hierarchy. *Industrial Relations* 27:247–50.

Rorty, Richard. 1979. *Philosophy and the Mirror of Nature*. Princeton: Princeton University Press.

Ross, W. D., 1930. *The Right and the Good*. Oxford: Clarendon Press.

———. 1942. *Human Nature and Utility in Hume's Social Philosophy*. Oxford: Oxford University Press.

Rule Overturned on Agent Orange. 1989. *New York Times*, 9 March.

Sagoff, Mark. 1984. Ethics and Economics in Environmental Law. In Tom Regan, ed., *Earthbound: New Introductory Essays in Environmental Ethics*. New York: Random House.

———. 1992. Efficiency and Utility. In Gillroy and Wade, 165–77.

Sahakian, William. 1974. *Ethics: An Introduction to Theories and Problems*. New York: Barnes & Noble.

Sahoo, Mihir. 1985. Predictors of Personality Dimensions and Risk-Taking Behavior. *Perspectives in Psychological Researches* 2:57–62.

Salmon, Wesley. 1980. *Space, Time, and Motion*. Minneapolis: University of Minnesota Press.

Sandel, Michael. 1982. *Liberalism and the Limits of Justice*. New York: Cambridge University Press.

———. 1984. *Liberalism and Its Critics*. New York: New York University Press.

Savage, Ian. 1993. An Empirical Investigation into the Effect of Psychological Perceptions on the Willingness-to-Pay to Reduce Risk. *Journal of Risk and Uncertainty* 6:75–90.

Scheler, Max. 1973. *Formalism in Ethics and Non-formal Ethics of Values.* Evanston: Northwestern University Press.

Schweickart, David. 1978. Should Rawls Be a Socialist? *Social Theory and Practice* 4:1–27.

Sen, Amartya. 1973. Behavior and the Concept of Preference. *Economica* 41:241–59.

Sheppard, Burton D. 1985. *Rethinking Congressional Reform.* Cambridge: Schenkman.

Sher, George. 1987. *Desert.* Princeton: Princeton University Press.

Shipper, Frank, and Marianne Jennings. 1984. *Business Strategy for the Political Arena.* Westport, Ct.: Quorum Books.

Short, James. 1980. *An Investigation of the Relation between Crime and Business Cycles.* New York: Arno.

Sidgwick, Henry. 1901. *The Methods of Ethics.* London: Macmillan.

Siebert, W. S., and X. Wei. 1994. Compensating Wage Differentials for Workplace Accidents: Evidence for Union and Nonunion Workers in the U.K. *Journal of Risk and Uncertainty* 9:61–76.

Simpson, Evan. 1982. The Priority of Needs over Wants. *Social Theory and Practice* 8:95–112.

Sinden, John, and Albert Worrell. 1979. *Unpriced Values.* New York: John Wiley & Sons.

Singer, Peter. 1979. *Practical Ethics.* Cambridge: Cambridge University Press.

Smart, J. J. C. 1956. Extreme and Restricted Utilitarianism. *Philosophical Quarterly* 6:244ff.

———. 1984. *Ethics, Persuasion, and Truth.* London: Routledge & Kegan Paul.

Smith, Adam. 1776–1950. *An Inquiry into the Causes of the Wealth of Nations.* London: Methuen.

Sterba, James. 1980. *The Demands of Justice.* Notre Dame: University of Notre Dame Press.

———. 1986. Recent Work on Alternative Conceptions of Justice. *American Philosophical Quarterly* 23:1–22.

Stout, A. K. 1954. But Suppose Everyone Did the Same. *Australasian Journal of Philosophy* 32:1–29.

Sutherland, Edwin, and Donald Cressey. 1972. *Criminology.* Philadelphia: J. B. Lippencott.

Taylor, Charles. 1985. *Philosophical Papers, Vol. 2: Philosophy and the Human Sciences.* Cambridge: Cambridge University Press.

Thaler, Richard, and Sherwin Rosen. 1976. The Value of Saving a Life. *Household Production and Consumption, NBER Studies in Income and Wealth No. 40.* New York: Columbia University Press, 265–98.

Toulmin, Stephen. 1950. *An Examination of the Place of Reason in Ethics.* London: Cambridge University Press.

Viscusi, W. Kip. 1978a. Labor Market Valuations of Life and Limb. *Public Policy* 26:359–83.

————. 1978b. Wealth Effects and Earnings Premiums for Job Hazards. *Review of Economics and Statistics* 60:408–18.

————. 1983. *Risk by Choice.* Cambridge: Harvard University Press.

————. 1991. Economic Theories of Decision Making under Uncertainty: Implications for Policy Analysis. In Weimer, 85–110.

————. 1993. The Value of Risks to Life and Health. *Journal of Economic Literature* 31:1912–46.

Vold, George. 1967. *Theoretical Criminology.* New York: Oxford University Press.

Warnock, G. J. 1980. Comments on Frankena's "Three Questions About Morality." *Monist* 63:86ff.

Weimer, David, ed. 1991. *Policy Analysis and Economics: Developments, Tensions, Prospects.* Boston: Kluwer.

Weisskopf, Michael. 1989. Scientists Say Vietnam Troops Heavily Exposed to Defoliant: Study Disputes CDC Finding. *Washington Post,* 25 January, A–2.

Westermarck, Edward. 1932. *Ethical Relativity.* New York: Harcourt-Brace.

Whitehead, Alfred N. 1959. *American Essays in Social Philosophy.* New York: Harper Brothers.

Wolff, Robert. 1977. *Understanding Rawls.* Princeton: Princeton University Press.

Wong, David. 1984. *Moral Relativity.* Berkeley: University of California Press.

Wynne, Brian. 1987. *Risk Management and Hazardous Waste.* Berlin, N.Y.: Springer-Verlag.

Zeckhauser, Richard. 1975. Procedures for Valuing Lives. *Public Policy* 23:427–63.

Index